THE
GOSPEL
~ OF THE ~
GARDEN

THE GOSPEL OF THE GARDEN

ANI YOSEF

TATE PUBLISHING & *Enterprises*

The Gospel of the Garden
Copyright © 2011 by Jerry Hegwood. All rights reserved.

No part of this publication may be reproduced, stored in a retrieval system or transmitted in any way by any means, electronic, mechanical, photocopy, recording or otherwise without the prior permission of the author except as provided by USA copyright law.

All scripture quotations, unless otherwise indicated, are taken from the *Complete Jewish Bible*, © 1998 by David H. Stern. Published by Jewish New Testament Publications, Inc. www.messianicjewish.net/jntp. Distributed by Messianic Jewish Resources. www.messianicjewish.net. All rights reserved. Used by permission.

Scripture quotations marked (ESV) are from *The Holy Bible, English Standard Version*, © 2001 by Crossway Bibles, a publishing ministry of Good News Publishers. Used by permission. All rights reserved.

Scripture quotations marked (KJV) are taken from the *Holy Bible, King James Version*, Cambridge, 1769. Used by permission. All rights reserved.

Scripture quotations marked (YLT) are from *Young's Literal Translation*, Robert Young, 1898. Public domain in the United States.

The opinions expressed by the author are not necessarily those of Tate Publishing, LLC.

Published by Tate Publishing & Enterprises, LLC
127 E. Trade Center Terrace | Mustang, Oklahoma 73064 USA
1.888.361.9473 | www.tatepublishing.com

Tate Publishing is committed to excellence in the publishing industry. The company reflects the philosophy established by the founders, based on Psalm 68:11,
"The Lord gave the word and great was the company of those who published it."

Book design copyright © 2011 by Tate Publishing, LLC. All rights reserved.
Cover design by Shawn Collins
Interior design by Stephanie Woloszyn

Published in the United States of America
ISBN: 978-1-61346-256-0
1. Religion / General 2. Religion / Biblical Studies / General
11.09.16

ACKNOWLEDGEMENT

I want to thank Yeshua for trusting me with His work and sending into my life the most incredible bride in the world. Anna you are the symbol of purity and faithfulness in my life. You have be a tremendous encouragement to me, many daughters have done well but you excel them all.

Rabbi Messer you have been a great mentor to me and instrumental in the change of direction in my life. Bradford Scott, Avi Ben Mordechai, MIA, Jeff Benner and all the great teachers of our day, you have been a blessing.

I want to thank the men of Fremont for allowing me to lead. To the set up crew for your great work, Nathan, Aaron, Ritchie, Steve, Mike, Mike, Eli, Jason and Nick, you are blessed men of God and righteous in our generation. To all the men at Fremont you are an amazing and set apart people.

To my community thank you for allowing me to grow in the gifting of God, Ronnie for your continued support. Thank you to all who helped in the process of this book. Tate Publishing you have been great. Natalie, thank you for all your work typing for me.

To all those who read this book, May Yeshua bless and prosper you!

TABLE *of* CONTENTS

INTRODUCTION	9
IN THE BEGINNING	11
B'REISHEET	17
IN THE FIRST FRUIT	31
WHAT IS MAN?	41
THE POWER OF TWO	57
NACHASH SERPENT	73
THE CURSE ASSOCIATED WITH WOMAN	93
SUMMARY ONE	109
THE ROMAN ROAD	119
THE TWO TREES	127
TWO HUSBANDS	141
REMARRIED	161
HELL	173
NAKEDNESS	189
TIME OF VISITATION	201
WHERE ARE YOU?	217
THE SPIRIT OF UNFORGIVENESS	225
GOSPEL OF THE GARDEN	235
KASHRU, KOSHER	243
FEAR	251
ALEF-TAV	259

INTRODUCTION

This book was written to bring renewed insight to an ancient topic. When studying the Torah, it is important to realize that there are many levels of understanding found in every verse. Tradition says that there are seventy levels in the Torah. Others have gone as far as to say that there were six hundred thousand men standing at Mount Sinai and they all heard and saw the words that were spoken. They all heard the words spoke and all had a unique revelation, just as each man has a unique fingerprint. The Torah is likened unto a diamond; when you turn a diamond, you will see a different facet of that same diamond.

    I will be looking at specific facets of the Torah in this book. I am by no means limiting the Torah to this revelation alone. I will be working hard to focus the reader toward these specific facets. Many times, our traditions, whether Christian or Jewish, cause our minds to immediately go in a specific direction when we hear certain topics and words. I will be looking at many topics including *HaSatan*. I will be focusing on how they relate to you specifically. Sometimes, our traditions have been so focused on the mystical that we miss the life application. As Christians, we focus on salvation (heaven). This book will focus a lot on redemption, our earthly walk.

    My goal is to bring the gospel out in a way that will dramatically change the way you look at the Word of God, life, and your relationships. This might challenge many of your beliefs. In many places in this book, I will challenge traditional thought, and it will appear as though I may be standing against some traditional thought; however, I am challenging you to think deeper about the Word. This is more challenging for someone from a Christian background simply because they are not as familiar with the Hebrew language, which is the most creative language in the world. Throughout this book, I will bring out Hebraic concepts or thought. This is how someone who grew up in the Hebrew culture that *Yeshua* (Jesus) grew up in would view the world and the Word.

I hope this book challenges your life and gives you a comfort in the reality that God chose you and you did not choose God. This book will give you an understanding that will cause you to be able to walk in a new level of authority in your life, with greater direction and purpose. Remember, when Adam ate of the fruit, he did not lose heaven; he lost his authority in the earth. If certain topics challenge you, put them on a shelf, continue on, and see if more comes to light as you read. These new understandings of the Scriptures will give new depth to what you already know. May *Yeshua* (Jesus) give you a greater revelation of your destiny.

IN THE BEGINNING

> I declare the *end from the beginning* and from long ago what is not yet done, saying: "My plan will take place and I will do all my will."
>
> Isaiah 46:10 (CBS)

God declares the end at the beginning. This reveals that if we want to know the end, we don't just go to the end of the Bible; we need to go back to the beginning, where He declared it. This is a Hebraic concept. You see, in Hebrew thought, everything moves in cycles. At the end, we are really just walking back into the beginning. God reveals these same patterns in creation. For example, our seasons move in cycles.

A cycle can begin with spring, move through summer and fall, and end in the winter as it rolls right back into spring. Our week moves in cycles, as do months and years. These same patterns are found in God's plan for man.

The beginning can be understood as a seed. Contained within the seed (beginning) is the fruit (end). In other words, contained in the seed are the tree, root, branches, leaves, bark, and the fruit.

The end result is already declared in the seed. The seed contains the plan. Nowhere along this plan does it change. For instance, if you plant an apple tree, will it somewhere along the way change into an orange tree? No, of course not. The apple seed will accomplish what it is sent forth to do: produce after its own kind. "I declared *the end* [fruit] *from the beginning* [seed] and from long ago what is not yet done, saying: 'My plan (seed) will take place, and I will do My will'" (Isaiah 46:10, CBS).

This teaches us that everything—every concept and pattern we find in our Bible—can find its origin in seed form in the beginning. There is much confusion surrounding the end because few people know the beginning.

This seven-thousand-year plan for man is like a beautiful tree that has been growing for six thousand years. Many people observe this tree from many different angles and perspectives. They guess what its end will be, what the tree will be in its fullness. But since the tree has not reached its fullness, no one is quite sure what it will be.

If we would trace this tree (plan) back to its origin and examine the seed, we would be able to identify its destiny. The destiny is contained within the seed. If we take the seven-thousand-year plan for man back to the beginning, we would find that our destiny is in the beginning. I hope for the duration of this book you can set aside some preconceived ideas of what the end holds. There are many theories out there these days, and I would like to take you on a journey in the beginning.

"The thing that *hath been, it is that which shall be*; and that which is done *is* that which shall be done: and *there is* no new *thing* under the sun" (Ecclesiastes 1:9). I'm not trying to teach some new idea of what will be but simply recovering an ancient idea. I'm sure this will be a challenge for many of us. It sure has been for me. We will be walking on some holy ground and around some sacred cows. It is not my goal to offend anyone, so please forgive me if I fall short in my wording. I just want to approach a modern concern from an ancient perspective. The way we see and understand the Word today is often different than the way the ancients would have understood it. "You favored those who were glad to do justice, those who remembered you in your ways. When you were angry, we kept sinning; *but if we keep your ancient ways, we will be saved*" (Isaiah 64:4(5)).

There is something about the sound of ancient things that excites me. I see it all around me. It is as if this generation has some kind of connection to the ancient ways. It sounds good, and I believe

I might have found a clue. If we are at the end, then according to Hebraic thought, we are simply walking back into the beginning. If so, then the last generation would have the closest connection to the beginning of any other generation.

"*From ancient times no one has heard,* no one has listened, no eye has seen any God except You, who acts on behalf of the one who waits for Him" (Isaiah 64:4, CBS). Could it be that our generation might be the one to hear what God has proclaimed from ancient times? Is it possible that we have been looking at the end when we should have been looking at the beginning?

Law of First Use or First Mention

In Hebrew, there is a law called the law of first mention. The first time a Hebrew word is used or mentioned in your Bible, it sets precedence for that word the rest of the way through the Bible. Hebrew words are like seeds. The root word holds a context that should be viewed in all words that stem from that root word. In other words, all words should be viewed in the context of their root. Hebrew is called *Lashon Ha Kodesh,* the holy tongue, and it contains within it deep truths.

Words are important to God. What His words meant in the beginning they mean in the end. God never changes, nor does He change the meaning of His words. It is man who changes the meaning of his words. This is an important foundation to lay down. We live in a culture that changes the meaning of words all the time. This is not how God's Word is. You can count on God that what He called evil in Genesis is still evil in the book of Revelation. What God called "good" in the beginning is what He calls good today.

This law of first use applies to words and also to concepts. God's will in the beginning is also His will in the end. In fact, most words and concepts can be traced right back to the first four or five chapters of Genesis. We will continue to expound upon this as we go.

What we are going to see is that what occurred in the beginning in seed form is being explained in more detail the rest of the way through the Bible, like a developing tree. The Torah is the *Brit Chadashah* (New Testament) concealed, and the *Brit Chadashah* is the Torah revealed. In other words, The *Brit Chadashah* is like looking at the fruit of a tree whose roots originated in the Torah. Everything in the *Brit Chadashah* is found or concealed in the Torah much the same way a tree is concealed inside of a seed.

A productive goal can be to trace concepts, thoughts, verses, and words back to their origin, especially if you have grown up in a Christian or Western environment, with a heavy focus on the *Brit Chadashah*. Keep in mind that nearly 85 percent of your *Brit Chadashah* is made up of the *Tanakh* (Old Testament). When we trace concepts and thoughts found in the *Brit Chadashah* to their origin in the *Tanakh*, we are able to make sure that they line up with the seed from which they originated . What started off as an apple tree in the Torah does not turn into an orange tree in the *Brit Chadashah*.

The author of the *Brit Chadashah* (the Holy Spirit) intended for you to understand it in the context of its origin, the *Tanakh*. The *Tanakh* is an acronym meaning Torah, *Nevi'im* (prophets), and *K'tuvim* (writings). The authors of the Brit Chadashah did not intend for it to be understood through the context of your current culture. God did not intend for the current cultural mindset to influence His Word or the culture of His Word. No, He intended for His Word and His culture to influence the one you live in. "Thus says the LORD: "Stand by the roads, and look, and ask for the ancient paths, where the good way is; and walk in it, and find rest for your souls. But they said, 'We will not walk in it'" (Jeremiah 6:16 ESV).

Let us be the ones who will take that ancient and good way. It has never changed. God never changes. His will never changes, but your life will. "I declared the end from the beginning and from long age what is not yet done, saying: 'My plan will take place, and I will do all *my will*'" (Isaiah 46:10 CBS).

God's will from the beginning is God's will in the end. "Doing *Your will*, my God, is my joy; *Your Torah* is in my innermost being" (Psalm 40:9(8)). David understood God's will to be His Torah.

ג

B'REISHEET

In the beginning God created the heavens and the earth.

Genesis 1:1 (KJV)

Here is what the verse looks like transliterated into Hebrew.

B'reisheet Bara Elohim Et HaShamayim V'et HaEretz.

Genesis 1:1

The first verse of our Bible is made up of seven words. These seven words hint at the seven-thousand-year plan for man. Example, the fourth word is *Et*, the alpha and omega. This alludes to the Messiah, who would come in the four thousandth year. Many Hebrew scholars believe that creation was complete in this first verse and that the creation fell into chaos in the next verse in Genesis.

I would like to take a deeper look into the first verse of Genesis. We will start with the word *B'reisheet*. Many Rabbis believe that if you can truly understand this word, you would understand the entire Torah because all of the Torah is contained in this Hebrew word.

The word *B'reisheet* is Strong's #7225/7218: "the first, in place, time, order, or rank (spec. first fruits)." *Reisheet* is translated as "beginning; first fruit, first, etc."

When we add the letter *Beit* (B) to the front of the word *Reisheet* it means: "in *Reisheet*" or "for *Reisheet*." This is how we get "in the beginning," but it can also read "in the first fruits." Let's take another look at *B'reisheet* in its Hebrew form. All of the following words can be found in the word *B'reisheet*.

B'reisheet : "In the beginning" or "In the first fruits"

Reisheet: "Beginning" or "First fruits"

Brit: "Covenant"

Bar: "Son"

Beit: "House"

All of these words can be found in the beginning. This alone begins to shed some light on Isaiah's verse, "I declare the end from the beginning, and from long ago what is not yet done, saying: My plan will take place, and I will do all my will" (Isaiah 46:10).

So let's see a little of what God declared in the beginning. When we look at the word *B'reisheet* in Hebrew, on an actual Torah scroll, you will see that the letter *Beit* is written larger than the other letters. This points out something. If the *Beit* is separated from the word, it can be read as, "for the beginning." If we put this all together in a sentence, it can read something like this: "For the sake of the beginning (*reisheet*), God made a covenant (*brit*), with a son (*bar*), in a house (*beit*)¹." Here is something else that I see here. It could be read, "In the first fruits, God made a covenant with son in a house."

This was declared in the beginning. The question could be asked, "Who are the first fruits?" Let's take a look at what the Scriptures say about that. "'*Israel* is aside for *Adonai*, the *first fruits* of His harvest; all who devour him will incur guilt; evil will befall them,' says *Adonai*" (Jeremiah 2:3).

We see here that Israel is called God's first fruits. This reveals that Israel was in the beginning. "But each in his own order; the *Messiah* is the first fruits, then those who belong to the Messiah, at the time of his coming" (1 Corinthians 15:23).

The Messiah, *Yeshua*, is called the first fruits. This teaches us that in the beginning, *Yeshua* and Israel were one (*echad*). This verse also teaches us that those who belong to the Messiah at His coming were also in the beginning. Might I suggest that they are Israel?

Remember, *Yeshua* is an Israelite. If you are joined to *Yeshua*, then you are joined to Israel. If you are one with the Messiah, then you are one with Israel.

The next question is: what is the covenant? The covenant is a marriage covenant also called a *ketubah* in Hebrew. The *ketubah* was given to Israel at Mount Sinai, called the Torah. It contains the wedding vows. This is when Israel said, "I do," three times in Exodus 19:8, 24:3, and 24:7 at Mount Sinai. The Torah is God's Word. "In the beginning was the word [Torah, covenant], and the Word was with God, and the Word was God" (John 1:1 KJV).

John confirms that the Torah was in the beginning. He also revealed that the Torah was one with God (*Yeshua*). If the Word was one with *Yeshua*, then it was one with Israel. In the beginning, *Yeshua*, Israel, and the Torah were one, *echad*.

The Torah is also called God's wisdom (*Chukmah*). Let's see what the book of Proverbs has to say about God's Torah or His wisdom: "*Adonai* made me [wisdom, Torah] as the beginning of his way, the first of his ancient works" (Proverbs 8:22).

The Torah was created at the beginning, the first of His works. Now we see the Torah as one with the first fruits (beginning). The first fruits were and are *Yeshua*, Israel, and the Torah as one, *echad*. That is how it was in the beginning, and that is how it will be in the end. This is how we will recognize the first fruits; they have both *Yeshua* and the Torah. They are Israel.

> But we have to keep thanking God for you always, brothers whom the Lord loves, because He chose you as first fruits for deliverance by giving you the holiness that has its origin in the Spirit (*Yeshua*) and faithfulness that has its origin in the truth (Torah).
>
> 2 Thessalonians 2:13

Paul says the first fruits have their origin in the Spirit (*Yeshua*) and the truth (Torah). Their origin is in the beginning. The first fruits have their origin in the beginning, and in the beginning, they were one with *Yeshua* (Spirit) and the Torah (truth). If God declared it that way in the beginning, then that is how it will be in the end. Let's take a quick look at the New Covenant. Actually, the *Brit Chadashah* in Hebrew means "Renewed Covenant." "For he finds fault with them when he says: 'Behold, the days are coming, declares the Lord, when I will establish a new covenant with the house of Israel and with the house of Judah'" (Hebrews 8:8 KJV).

Well this New Covenant is made with Israel and *Y'hudah*. If you are part of this New Covenant, you somehow fit into one of these two people groups. "For this is the covenant that I will make with the house of Israel after those days, declares the Lord: 'I will put my laws into their minds, and write them on their hearts, and I will be their God, and they shall be my people'" (Hebrews 8:10 KJV).

The Renewed Covenant reveals that God is taking Israel back to the beginning, where they were one with the Torah. Once again, He is now writing the Torah on their heart. This verse is a quote from Jeremiah chapter 31. This Torah is not being written on hearts of stone but of flesh. Ezekiel also wrote about this Covenant: "And I will give you a new heart, and a new spirit I will put within you. And I will remove the heart of stone from your flesh and give you a heart of flesh. And I will put my Spirit within you, and cause you to walk in my statutes and be careful to obey my rules" (Ezekiel 36:26-27 ESV).

Here, we see that Israel becomes one with *Yeshua* (Spirit). The Renewed Covenant is to have a new heart of flesh with the Torah written upon it and to have God's Spirit in you. The Renewed Covenant is to be Israel, *Yeshua*, and the Torah as one.

Yeshua is Israel (He is a Jew), Torah (He is the Living Word), and the Spirit as one, *echad*. *Yeshua* is called the Son of God. This leads me to my question. We looked at the first fruits and the covenant, but who is the son?

> Behold, I will bring them from the north country, and gather them from the coasts of the earth, *and* with them the blind and the lame, the woman with child and her that travaileth with child together: a great company shall return thither. They shall come with weeping, and with supplications will I lead them: I will cause them to walk by the rivers of waters in a straight way, wherein they shall not stumble: for I am a father to Israel, and Ephraim *is* my firstborn.
>
> Jeremiah 31:8-9 (KJV)

Israel is the son of God. *Efrayim* is called God's firstborn son. This was Israel's original image, the image of the son of God. *Yeshua* came in this very image to restore it back to His people, Israel, to renew their covenant and restore the image of the son of God. That image is *Yeshua*, Torah, and Israel as one. "For those He foreknew [first fruits] He also predestined to be conformed into the image of His son" (Romans 8:29, CBS).

Those He foreknew are the first fruits. He predestined them to be conformed to the image of sons. It was in the beginning that He declared end or destiny. In the beginning, it was Israel, *Yeshua*, and the Torah all *echad*, one; and they will all be one in the end, as this is their destiny and their purpose.

"For the creation waits with eager longing for the revealing of the sons of God" (Romans 8:19 ESV). When will these sons of God be revealed? When Israel, *Yeshua*, and the Torah come together as one. It will be life from the dead. I hope you are seeing the value of looking at the end from the beginning. We have looked at the first fruits, covenant, and the son also. *Yeshua* is the son, Israel is God's son, and all of creation is waiting for you to manifest as a son. Don't forget: "The Word [Torah] became a human being and lived with us, and we saw his *Sh'khinah*, the *Sh'khinah* of the father's only son, full of grace and truth" (John 1:14).

Now the Renewed Covenant is to have the Torah written on a heart of flesh and the Spirit of God dwelling in that heart. The

Word will become flesh in you, and we see the *Sh'khinah* of the only son, full of grace and truth, in you. This is the revelation of the sons of God.

The last question we will look at here is the house. We have looked at the first fruits, covenant, son, and now the house. Who or what is this house?

The first letter in the Torah is the letter *Beit*, which means "house," and the last word in the Torah is *Israel*. The entire Torah is teaching us that Israel is the house. Israel is the house that God dwells in since the beginning and will be in the end.

In the beginning, God made a *covenant* with a *son* to dwell in a *house*.

Every Hebrew letter carries a numerical value. The letter *Beit* carries the numerical value of two. This reveals to us that this house (Israel) is actually made up of two people groups. Could this possibly be God's two witnesses, the ones mentioned in Revelation 11:3? These two shall become one.

A true house starts with two people: a husband and a wife. When the two become one, life is produced, and that is a greater household. The very first letter of the Torah is teaching us about relationship. We will get into this more as we go along.

This letter, *Beit*, gives us a clue that God's house contains two people groups. There is a biblical law that is being fulfilled here, which is found in Deuteronomy and states, "Let everything be established by two or three witnesses" (Deuteronomy 19:15). One witness alone will not be sufficient to convict a person of any offence or sin of any kind; the matter will be established only if there are two or three witnesses testifying against him.

In the beginning, God is establishing His two witnesses. Adam was originally created male and female, and then God took Eve out of Adam's side. They became two witnesses. Realize that God only separated the two in order for them to come back together again as one.

Let's take a closer look at this house that God wants to dwell in.

And let them make me a sanctuary; that I may dwell among [in] them.
Deuteronomy 25:8 (KJV)

The word *among* used in this verse also means "in." God wants to dwell *in* His people.

And I will set my tabernacle among [in] you: and my soul shall not abhor you. And I will walk among [in] you, and will be your God, and ye shall be my people.
Leviticus 26:11-12 (KJV)

So God is telling Israel that He will put His tabernacle or dwelling in Israel. You will see this verse quoted by the Apostle Paul in Corinthians and also by John in the book of Revelation. The word *among* actually means "in." Just read how Paul quotes it: "And what agreement hath the temple of God with idols? for ye are the temple of the living God; as God hath said, I will dwell in them, and walk in *them;* and I will be their God, and they shall be my people" (2 Corinthians 6:16 KJV).

As you see, Paul quotes this word *among* as *in*. Many translators translate this word as either *among* or *in*. Let's look at the book of Revelation, and we will insert the word *in* into the verse, as John is also quoting the verse from Leviticus. "And I heard a loud voice from the throne saying, 'Behold, the dwelling place of God is with[in] man. He will dwell with [in] them, and they will be his people, and God himself will be with[in] them as their God'" (Revelation 21:3 ESV).

Now, just as in the beginning, God dwelt in Israel, and in the end, He again wants to dwell in Israel. *Israel* is the name of God's dwelling place. Contained within this name are two people groups.

Just like when God took Eve out of the side of Adam, God takes the house of Israel out of the side of the house of *Y'hudah* (Judah) or actually out of Israel. This established God's two witnesses.

> So *Adonai* said to Shlomo [Solomon], "Since this is what has been in your mind, and you haven't kept my covenant and my regulations which I ordered you to obey, I will tear the kingdom from you and give it to your servant. However for David your father's sake I won't do it while you are alive, but I will tear it away from your son. Even then, I won't tear all the kingdom; I will give one tribe to your son for the sake of Yerushalayim [Jerusalem], which I have chosen."
>
> 1 Kings 11:11-13 (CJB)

So God will tear away part of Israel from Solomon's son. He will leave one tribe with him plus the tribe he is from, which is the tribe of *Y'hudah* (Judah). This kingdom will be the tribes of *Y'hudah*, Benjamin, and half the tribe of Levi. *Y'hudah* will be the largest tribe, and their kingdom will be known as the house of *Y'hudah* or the Jews.

> Achiyah took hold of his new cloak that he was wearing and tore it into twelve pieces. Then he said to Yarov'am, "Take ten pieces for yourself! For here is what *Adonai* the God of Israel says: 'I am going to tear the kingdom out of Shlomo's hand, and I will give ten tribes to you.'"
>
> 1 Kings 11:30-31

The ten pieces represent ten tribes of Israel. These ten tribes are also called the northern kingdom or the house of Israel. They have as the largest tribe, *Efrayim*. As time goes along, they are also known as the lost ten tribes, *Efrayim*, and eventually are called the nations and today are often called Gentiles.

We have now seen the kingdom of Israel divided into two groups, the house of Israel and the house of *Y'hudah*. The house of

Y'hudah wanted to go to war and get the house of Israel back, but God said, "No, this dividing was His doing." God was establishing His two witnesses.

> But this word from God came to Sh'ma'yah the man of God: "Speak to Rechav'am the son of Shlomo, king of *Y'hudah*, to all the house of *Y'hudah* and Benyamin and to the rest of the people; tell them that this is what Adonai says, 'You are not to go up and fight your brother's the people of Israel! Every man is to go back home, because this is my doing.'" They paid attention to the word of *Adonai* and turned back, as *Adonai* had told them to do.
>
> 1 Kings 12:22-24 (CJB)

This separation that was taking place was actually a fulfillment of a prophecy given in Genesis 48, when Yaakov brought *Efrayim*, the youngest grandson, up to the place of the firstborn. This was an ancient eastern adoption custom. The firstborn receives the priestly anointing and a double portion of the land. Usually, they are the ruler of the family as well. However, Yaakov blesses *Y'hudah* with the kingly anointing and the right to rule.[3]

Together, the kingly and the priestly anointing are called the order of *Malchut-Tzedek* (Melchizedek). When Yaakov divided the right to rule from the firstborn, he was setting into motion what we would see manifest into the two kingdoms, but one day, these two would come back together as one.

Today, we most commonly know the house of *Y'hudah* as the Jewish people. When we look for the house of Israel, we will have to take a look at the Scriptures, and you might be a little surprised at what we find.

> But his father refused and said, "I know, my son, I know. He also shall become a people, and he also shall be great. Nevertheless,

his younger brother [*Efrayim*] shall be greater than he, and his offspring shall become a multitude of nations."

Genesis 48:19 (ESV)

The Hebrew word for growing into many nations is *Melo HaGoyim*. It means "his descendants will fill up the foreign nations" or "become the fullness of the Gentiles." We see the Apostle Paul word it in Romans 11:25. Yaakov prophesies that *Efrayim* will become the fullness of the Gentile nations. Later, when Israel divides into two kingdoms, the house of Israel (*Efrayim*) will be captured by the Assyrians and scattered into the nations. They will be driven to the ends of the earth. They eventually became lost, but the Messiah said He came for the lost sheep of the house of Israel (Matthew 15:24). He came to rebuild the fallen kingdom (tabernacle) of David (Amos 9:9-11, Acts 15:14-18).

The house of Israel was scattered into the Gentile nations so that Abraham's seed would intermingle into all the nations and fill the world. They, for all intents and purposes, became Gentiles (lost, pagan, confused, and without God). *Yeshua* came to bring these lost sheep back so that the two houses would become one.

The church knows these two people groups as the Jews and the Gentiles. If we trace these two people groups back to their origin, we discover the house of *Y'hudah* and the house of Israel. This is why the renewed covenant is made with these two people groups (Hebrews 8:8). Paul kept teaching that there was no longer Jew or Gentile but that the two had become one new man in the Messiah, *Yeshua*.

There is neither Jew nor Greek, there is neither bond nor free, there is neither male nor female: for ye are all one [just as in the beginning] in Christ Jesus. And if ye *be* Christ's, then are ye Abraham's seed, and heirs according to the promise.

Galatians 3:28-29 (KJV)

If you belong to the Messiah, it might be a clue that you are the seed of *Avraham*. You are Israel, and your origin was in the beginning. We see the two witnesses in the beginning, and we will see them in the end. These two witnesses are spoken of by many different names throughout the Scriptures.

> And I will give *power* unto my two witnesses, and they shall prophesy a thousand two hundred *and* threescore days, clothed in sackcloth. These are the two olive trees [one is wild named *Efrayim* and one is cultivated named Y'hudah; see Romans 11], and the two candlesticks [menorahs see Zechariah] standing before the God of the earth. And if any man will hurt them, fire proceedeth out of their mouth, and devoureth their enemies: and if any man will hurt them, he must in this manner be killed.
>
> Revelation 11:3-5 (KJV)

These two witnesses are God's first fruits. The *house* that God in the *beginning* made a *covenant* with a *son* to dwell in is Israel. Now we have taken a look at the fact that Israel is actually two people groups: the house of Y'hudah (or the Jews) and the house of Israel (the nations).

> So then, you are no longer foreigners and strangers [this is the house of Israel who became the Gentiles but no longer]. On the contrary, you are fellow-citizens with God's people and members of the family of God's family [Jeremiah 33:23-26 and Jeremiah 50:4-6]. You have been built on the foundation of the emissaries and the prophets, with the cornerstone being *Yeshua* the Messiah himself. In union with Him the *whole building* [house] is held together, and it is growing into a holy temple in union with the Lord. Yes in union with him, you yourselves are being built together into a spiritual dwelling-place for God!
>
> Ephesians 2:19-22 (CJB)

The letter *Beit* is called a house or tent. It is a picture of the holy of holies. In the holy of holies, there are two *k'ruvim* (cherubs) made out of one solid piece of gold. This is the house of Israel and the house of *Y'hudah* as one. The two *k'ruvim* are looking into the ark, which contains the two tablets (Torah), the jar filled with manna (*Yeshua*), and the rod of Aaron (the two houses of Israel together as one, as in Ezekiel 37:15-31).

The letter *Beit* revealed that the house (Israel) that God will dwell in is made up of two people groups who are one (i.e. two groups, one house). This is a picture of a husband and a wife. Adam and Eve originated from the same body. God is developing a pattern. Look at what Paul says:

> Who are you, a mere human being, to talk back to God? Will what is formed say to him who formed it, "Why did you make me this way?" Or has a potter no right to make from a given lump of clay [whole house of Israel] this pot for honorable use [House of *Y'hudah*] and that one for dishonorable use [house of Israel who became Gentiles].
>
> Romans 9:20-21 (CJB)

I hope you are able to see the picture. For more information on the two houses of Israel, see the following books: *Restoring the Kingdom of Israel* by Angus Wootten and *Israel Redeemed and Restored* by Batya Wootten.

One more topic on the house and the letter *Beit* in Hebrew. In its ancient paleo form, *Beit* looked like a tent. The ancient paleo or pictographic form of Hebrew is exactly that: a pictographic form of Hebrew. Throughout Scripture, a tent or house is an idiom for teachings. In other words, *tent* or *house* can be an idiom for *dwelling* in the Torah, God's teaching and instructions.

Within the first word of the Torah, *B'reisheet*, we see God's whole purpose within creation. For the sake of the beginning, God made a covenant with a son in a house. All of these words allude to Israel, *Yeshua*, and the Torah because they were all one, *echad*, in the beginning, and they will be *echad* in the end. "At the beginning I announced the end, proclaiming in advance things not yet done; and I say that my plan will hold, I will do everything I please to do" (Isaiah 46:10).

God's plan has never changed. His first fruits have never changed. If we will line up the end from the beginning, the picture becomes beautifully clear.

ז

IN THE FIRST FRUIT

In the beginning, God wanted to dwell in the earth, so He formed a house out of the dust of the earth. God wanted to dwell in the earth, so He made you from the dust of the earth. You are this house: "'Heaven is my throne,' says *Adonai*, 'and the earth is my footstool. What kind of house could you build for me? What sort of place could you devise for my rest?'" (Isaiah 66:1).

We have already begun to explore this. God intended to dwell in His first fruits. He declared from the beginning that He would dwell in His people, Israel. God does not intend on dwelling in a temple made of stone. Stephen spoke of this just before he was stoned.

> He (David) enjoyed God's favor and asked if he might provide a dwelling place for the God of Yaakov and Shlomo did build him a house. But *Ha'Elyon* does not live in places made by hand! As the prophet says, "Heaven is my throne," says *Adonai*, "and the earth is my footstool. What kind of house could you build for me? What kind of place could you devise for my rest? Didn't I myself make all these things?"
>
> Acts 7:46-50 (CJB)

The temple or house God wants to dwell in was announced in the beginning. *Yeshua* dwelt in Israel with the Torah in the beginning. Israel (you) is the tent or temple not made with man's hands. You were made by the Spirit of God, a heavenly temple: "The Spirit of God hath made me, and the breath of the Almighty hath given me life" (Job 33:4 KJV).

You are the temple not made with man's hands, but like Adam, you were created by the Spirit of God. "There he [*Yeshua*] serves in the Holy Place, that is in the true Tent of Meeting, the one erected not by human beings but by *Adonai*" (Hebrews 8:2). If you are the temple of God, the one not made by man's hands but the one erected by the Spirit of God, then are you the heavenly temple? "That is, God raised us up with the Messiah *Yeshua* and seated us with him in heaven" (Ephesians 2:6). If you are seated in heaven and you are the temple of God, then you are the heavenly temple.

> Here is the whole point of what we have been saying: We do have just such a *cohen gadol* [High Priest] as has been described. And he does sit at the right hand of *HaG'dulah* [the Majesty] in heaven [just as we are in heaven, Ephesians 2:6]. There he serves in the Holy Place that is the true Tent of Meeting, the one erected not by human beings but by *Adonai*.
> Hebrews 8:1-2 (CJB)

This might be a new approach for many. They stoned Stephen after he declared it, that you are the temple not built of stone. It is amazing that neither the Jews nor the Christians have fully grasped this understanding of the temple, but both Paul and Stephen understood it.

"Know ye not that ye are the temple of God, and *that* the Spirit of God dwelleth in you?" (1 Corinthians 3:16 KJV). God dwells in men. Let's look at this.

"'*Heaven is my throne,*' says *Adonai*, 'and the earth is my footstool ...'" (Isaiah 66:1). If God dwells in men and heaven is God's throne, then heaven is in the heart of men. God does not dwell in just any man but in the heart of His first fruits.

"He hath made everything beautiful in its time: also he hath set *eternity in their heart*, yet so that man cannot find out the work that God hath done from the beginning even to the end" (Ecclesiastes

3:11 ASV). And yet here we are, at the end of time, discovering what was declared in the beginning. God established the law of first use. That is why the end is found in the beginning. Let's take a look at the first verse of the Bible. Keep in mind that the word *beginning* is related to the word *first fruits* and heaven is also the place of God's throne and dwelling.

> B'reisheet Bara Elohim Et HaShamayim V'et HaEretz.
>
> Genesis 1:1 (Transliteration)

The word *Bara* means "to create something from nothing." There is a separate word in Hebrew that means "to make something from something that already exists." Man was both created and made—created from the Spirit of God and made from the dust of the earth.

The fourth word in the first verse of Genesis is the word *Et*. This word does not translate into our English translations. The word *Et* is made up of the first letter and the last letter of the Hebrew *Alef-Beit*, the *Alef* (E in *Et*) and the *Tav* (T in *et*). This is equivalent to the Alpha and Omega in Greek.

"I [*Yeshua*] am the Alpha and the Omega, the First and the Last, the beginning and the end" (Revelation 22:13 KJV). *Yeshua* is the *Et*, the *Alef* and the *Tav*. This fourth word alludes to the Messiah. *Et* also alludes to the Word of God. The *Alef* and the *Tav* is a way of summing up the Hebrew *Alef-Beit* and, thus, the Word of God. John alludes to this in his gospel: "In the beginning was the Word [Et], and the Word [Et] was with God, and the Word [Et] was God" (John 1:1 KJV).

Remember, John is also the author of the book of Revelation, where *Yeshua* refers to Himself as the Alpha and the Omega. John knew the Torah (Word of God) was in the beginning. He revealed that *Yeshua* was the Word of God, the living Torah scroll from *Alef* to *Tav*.

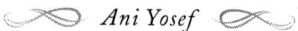

B'reisheet Bara Elohim Et HaShamayim V'et HaEretz.

Genesis 1:1 (Transliteration)

In the beginning God created the heavens and the Earth.

Genesis 1:1 (NIV)

Let's look at a few more of these seven Hebrew words and how they can be translated. Keep in mind, for every Hebrew word, there are about seven to eight English words. It takes multiple English words to describe a single concept, yet each Hebrew word is a concept. This means that a verse in Hebrew can have much more information than you see in an English translation. In fact, we lose a lot of this information in the translation.

The following are my own translations:

In the first fruits selected God, the place of His dwelling, [in] the earth.

Genesis 1:1

In the first fruits, created from nothing God, and sanctified by His Word [V'et], the place of His [Yeshua the Et] dwelling in the earth.

Genesis 1:1

From nothing created God first fruits, set apart by His Word [Et], [as] His [V'et] dwelling place in the earth.

Genesis 1:1

In the first fruits created from nothing God, by His Word His dwelling place in the Earth.

Genesis 1:1

I hope you are beginning to see the picture here. The beginning revolves around the first fruits, *Yeshua*, Israel, and the Torah. Remember the little word *et* does not translate in our English Bibles. Let me give you one more of my translations. This one contains a fuller meaning: "From the beginning, the foundation of the world, God chose you, His first fruits as the place of His dwelling, the place from which He would speak and manifest His name in the Earth" (Genesis 1:1).

Do you realize that if you are the first fruits, you contain the presence of *Yeshua*? His life and voice is in your blood. His Word is written in your heart. Your lungs are a picture of the two tablets. Your breath is a picture of the Spirit of God; His Spirit is in your breath. When you speak the words which are written on your heart and pictured in your lungs, are then carried by your breath (the Spirit of God). The breath moves across your lips; and contained in your saliva is blood (DNA), the voice of *Yeshua*. When you speak, He speaks and all other voices must submit. You see, in the beginning, God spoke.

> It is these who have not defiled themselves with women, for they are virgins. It is these who follow the Lamb wherever he goes. These have been redeemed from mankind as *first fruits* for God and the Lamb, and in their mouth *no lie* was found, for they are blameless.
>
> Revelation 14:4-5 (ESV)

These first fruits are the same ones Paul spoke about in 2 Thessalonians 2. These are the same first fruits that were in the beginning. There was no lie found on their lips. Why is this so important? It is called the law of first use. When God spoke, there was no lie found on His lips.

Man is the only one in creation who was given speech. Man was created in the image of God. Let's take a look at the first use of speech in the Bible, as it sets precedence for speech. The first use of speech teaches us a law of what speech was to be used for: "Then God said, 'Let there be light,' and there was light" (Genesis 1:3 KJV). God spoke, and it happened. Speech was given to take potential and make it actual. In Samoan Raphael Hirsch's *Dictionary of Biblical Hebrew*, we find that the root word for *beginning* means "to start motion or to set into motion."

In the beginning, God spoke to put creation into motion. The Torah is teaching us that speech was designed to set into motion our potential. God gave man speech to mobilize and set into motion his potential. Man was created in God's image. When God spoke, it took the potential in Him and caused it to come forth or actualize.

In Genesis chapter one, we see, "God said," ten times. God gave ten statements that brought into existence the physical order of creation. These ten statements allude to the Ten Commandments that God spoke to set in motion the moral order. The ten statements of creation and the Ten Commandments allude to the ten tribes of Israel. The tribes were scattered and lost because they rejected the Ten Commandments, which they were created to follow. These ten tribes, again, are known as the house of Israel, or *Efrayim*.

> When *Efrayim spoke*, there was trembling; he was a power in Israel. But he incurred guilt through Ba'al he died
>
> Hoshea 13:1

When was *Efrayim* a great power? When he spoke—our speech contains great power. There is power for life when there is no lie found on our lips and power for death when we lie. *Efrayim*, the ten tribes, died when they began to worship Ba'al and reject God's commandments and His covenant. Obviously, this death was a spiritual death, but it led to a great loss. "*Efrayim*'s guilt has been wrapped up, his sin is stored away. The *pain of being born* will come to him; but he is an unwise [no Torah] son. The time has come; and he shouldn't delay, there at the *mouth of the womb*" (Hoshea 13:12-13).

Do you see where the idea of birth pains and being born again point back to Hoshea and these lost ten tribes? It is connected to the spiritual death of the house of Israel, who was lost in the nations. God calls him an unwise son because he rejected God's Torah: "For *Efrayim* keeps building alters for sin; yes, alters are sinful for him. I write him so many things from my Torah, and yet he considers them foreign" (Hoshea 8:11-12).

Hoshea talks about the power *Efrayim* had when he spoke in chapter thirteen. This power is when the truth was on his lips. The Torah is God's truth. When *Efrayim* rejected the truth (Torah), he died, yet he will be born again one day. "Should I ransom them from the power of *sh'ol*? Should I redeem them from death? Where are your plagues deaths; where is your destruction, *sh'ol*? My eyes are closed to compassion" (Hoshea 13:14).

In Hoshea, we see that *Efrayim* will die, but he will also be born again. The birth pains will come to him, and he will be redeemed from the grave, or *sh'ol*. Interestingly, Paul keeps talking about these birth pains and this resurrection. In 1 Corinthians, Paul even quotes this verse from Hoshea, and this verse just happens to be in the chapter talking about the resurrection: "O death, where *is* thy sting? O grave, where *is* thy victory?" (1Corinthians 15:55 KJV). Paul's teachings about the resurrection allude back to *Efrayim*, the ten tribes who died and were lost in the nations. These are God's first fruits that had died. They died when a lie was found on their lips.

> We know that until now the whole creation has been groaning as with the *pains of childbirth*; and not only it, but we ourselves, who have *the first fruits of the Spirit*, groan inwardly as we continue waiting eagerly to *be made sons*—that is, to have our whole bodies *redeemed* and set free [from death].
>
> Romans 8:22-23

Paul mentions birth pains, which allude to *Efrayim* in the book of Hoshea. *Efrayim* was called God's firstborn sons in Jeremiah 31. When *Efrayim* died, he lost this image, the image of the son of God. Those who have the first fruits of the Spirit are waiting eagerly to be made a son, which is to be conformed back into the image of the son of God. Likewise, those who are in the image of God are first fruits. They have been raised from the dead or the image of death.

The ten statements of creation allude to the Ten Commandments and the ten tribes called *Efrayim* who would be raised from the dead and will be known as first fruits. They will have the Ten Commandments on their lips, and no lie will be found in them.

> It is these who have not defiled themselves with women, for they are virgins. It is these who follow the Lamb wherever he goes. These have been redeemed from mankind as firstfruits for God and the Lamb, and in their mouth *no lie was found*, for they are blameless.
>
> Revelation 14:4-5 (ESV)

When the first fruits speak the truth, there is great power. From the beginning, God chose the first fruits as the place of His dwelling, the place of His throne. God will speak from His first fruits. Speech is one of the activities of God. Speech is possibly one of the most powerful instruments given to men. Your confession (speech) was only designed to set into motion your conduct.

Notice that all ten times God said something, it happened: "God said, 'Let there be light,' and there was light" (Genesis 1:3 KJV). Not one time do you see something happen and then God say it. Speech mobilizes things, including our conduct. What you say comes toward you. Words should never leave our lips that we don't expect to walk into. This is a biblical law, the law of first mention.

What should be found on the lips of the first fruits? The Torah, the Word of God, they should be speaking the name (lifestyle) of *Yeshua*. When they speak the words of the Torah, which is the lifestyle of *Yeshua*, they are saying, "Let there be light!" Then the light of *Yeshua* will come forth out of the darkness of people's lives. They will rise from the dead.

Our words always lead to deeds: "One can be filled with good as a result of one's *words*, and one gets the reward one's deeds deserve" (Proverbs 12:14). When we speak a lie, we set into motion a false reality. Just ask Adam, who ate the fruit of a lie. The world became a place of illusions, and man became disconnected from his purpose.

One of the first principles God teaches His first fruit in the Torah is that what you say will come to pass. God said it, and it happened. Our speech mobilizes our potential and makes it actual. Our confession should lead to our conduct. God said, and there was. If you are a true prophet, then the truth will be on your lips: "A [good] man enjoys good as a result of what he says, but the essence of the treacherous is violence" (Proverbs 13:2).

We speak God's Word because His Word does not just say something; it accomplishes something. God's Word accomplishes what it was sent to do. This is why He sent His Torah into your heart; because it would accomplish what it was sent there to do.

God's Torah was written on your heart. His Torah was sent into you, and it will accomplish what it was sent to do. It was a seed planted in the earth (you).

The word for *speak* is Strong's #339 *Amar*. It means "to appoint, assign, or promise." Your words are your promise. *Amar* can also be translated as "answer." When you speak, it demands a response from creation. When God speaks, it affects the things that are spoken to. The name *Israel* contains in it *El* (God), the *El* of *Elohim*. Behind divine speaking is divine authority. When you (Israel) speak, God speaks. God speaks from His throne: "And I heard a loud voice from the throne saying, "Behold, the dwelling place of God is with

[in] man. He will dwell with [in] them, and they will be his people, and God himself will be with [in] them as their God" (Revelation 21:3 ESV).

Let's look at Genesis 1:1 this way. God's throne is where He speaks from and God's throne is in the heart of His first fruits. "In the first fruits God selected and sanctified by His word the place he would speak from [in] the earth" (Genesis 1:1). The first fruits are the place where God speaks from in the earth. No lie will be found on their lips.

ה

WHAT IS MAN?

> And there is a place where someone has given this solemn testimony; "What is mere man, that you concern yourself with him? Or the son of man, that you watch over him with such care?"
>
> Hebrews 2:6 (CJB)

In order to understand our purpose, we must look to the beginning: *Yeshua* is the beginning and the end; thus, *Yeshua* is Genesis. What was our purpose from the beginning? God says he knew you from before the foundations of the earth. This means our origin is from before creation. Wow. Our origin is not just the dust of the earth but our origin is the Spirit of God, that which existed before the creation.

God's Spirit is full of potential, and he wants to take potential and make it actual. God wants to manifest himself, and these manifestations are called names. This is why God has many names. Names in Hebrew mean lifestyle or activities. If you want to know what your name means, look it up in Hebrew.

Names are important in Hebrew because they tell you who you are. They describe your character. They describe your activities. God has many names that describe his many attributes. In Exodus 35:5-7, we find the thirteen attributes of mercy. However, without a creation to reveal these attributes to, they simply remain potential.

God is potentially longsuffering, potentially merciful until the opportunity arrives for Him to demonstrate or manifest these activities (names). It seems that the opportunity for God to manifest the names of the thirteen attributes of mercy arise in the midst of our weakness or our crisis. Crisis puts a demand on this potential.

In the Western mindset, we grow up in a culture where names don't mean anything. Bob just means Bob; it does not describe anything. They are abstract titles given to people. In Hebrew, they represent lifestyle, reputation, movements, activities, and attributes of the person. When you invoke or call on the name of God, you are calling on that specific attribute and reputation .

God's longest name is 304,805 letters long. It is the Torah, Genesis through Deuteronomy. This name contains the never-changing activities and movements of God. These are the activities and habits of *Yeshua*. *Yeshua* is a name of God that means "salvation." This teaches us that if Torah were the habits of *Yeshua*, then the Torah is the activities of salvation. Israel, *Yeshua,* and Torah are one.

The Hebrew understanding is that the world was created for Israel. Heaven and earth were created to serve Israel, the first fruits. Israel was created to manifest the names of God, to participate in His activities and movement called the kingdom of God. Israel was to be the dominant movement upon the earth.

"Then the King will say to those on his right, 'Come, you whom my Father has blessed, take your inheritance, the *kingdom prepared for you from the founding of the world*'" (Matthew 25:34 KJV). This is what Israel was created to do. I want to talk about just who Israel is. Israel is the first fruits, the seed, and the remnant. However, not all Israel is Israel. The first fruit Israel is made of both Jews and those from the nations called Hebrews.

> But the present condition of Israel does not mean that the Word of God [Torah] has failed. For not everyone from Israel is truly part of Israel; indeed, not all the descendants are seed of Abraham; rather, "What is to be called your 'seed' will be Yitzchak!" In other words, it is not the physical children who are children of God, but the children the promise refers to who are considered *seed*.
>
> Romans 9:6-8 (CJB)

The seed here is the remnant. It can be traced all the way back to the garden. It is the seed that crushes the serpent's head. The world was created for the seed, and the seed was chosen from the foundation of the earth, and you are that seed if you belong to the Messiah.

The name given to God's first fruits is Israel. Israel is also one of the names of God. It means to rule (as) God, to manifest God's name and activities in the world. Keep in mind that these first fruits are Israel, Torah, and *Yeshua* as one.

Here are a few verses that witness this:

> Who bore witness to the *word of God* [Torah] and to the testimony of Jesus Christ, even to all that he saw.
>
> Revelation 1:2 (ESV)

> And the dragon was wroth with the *woman*, and went to make war with the remnant of her seed [seed of woman, Israel], which keep the *commandments of God* [*Torah*], and have the testimony of Jesus Christ.
>
> Revelation 12:17 (KJV)

> Here is the patience of the saints: here *are* they that keep the commandments [*Torah*] of God, and the faith of Jesus.
>
> Revelation 14:12 (KJV)

Each of these verses is about the seed, the remnant, and the Israel Paul was speaking of in Romans 9. The Hebrews understand that heaven and earth were created to serve Israel, and Israel means to rule (as) God. They are God's movement on the earth, and they have dominion over the earth.

Now let's look at the creation of men: "And the LORD God *formed* man *of* the dust of the ground, and breathed into his nostrils the *breath* of life; and man became a living soul" (Genesis 2:7 KJV).

Other than just the literal reading of the Scriptures, we are going to look deeper to what God is revealing to us. In Hebrew thought, all wisdom is hidden, and we must search it out. In Hebrew, there are four levels of interpretation: *peshat*, the literal or surface; *remez*, to hint at a verse that is connected to another verse to reveal truth; *drash*, to dig below the surface, to discuss with people; and *sod*, the veiled or hidden meaning (this is the level of the secret or mystery).

The acronym for these four levels is *pardes*. This is an orchard or garden. We will be looking into the deeper levels and looking at patterns in verse that hint (*remez*) to other verse to unlock the secrets God has hidden for His first fruits, called hidden wisdom.

Adam was taken from the *dust* (matter) and *formed*. Formed alludes to the teaching and instruction of God called the Torah. The dust symbolizes the earthly realm as opposed to the heavenly realm. God *breathed* the breath of life (Spirit) into Adam. We also see this pattern repeated with *Yeshua* and His disciples.

Yeshua takes His disciples from the dust. They are common people of the land. The term is called *am-ha'aretz*.

"Has any of the authorities trusted him [*Yeshua*]? Or any of the *P'rushim*? No! True, these *am-ha'aretz* [people of the land, dust] do, but they know nothing about the Torah [no form], they are under a curse!" (John 7:48-49). *Yeshua* took His disciples from the dust: "When they saw how bold *Kefa* [Peter] and *Yochonan* [John] were, even though they were untrained [no form] *am-ha'aretz*, they were amazed; also they recognized them as having been with *Yeshua*" (Acts 4:13).

Yeshua took his disciples from the dust of the earth. He formed them as He taught them Torah. *Yeshua*'s ministry was three and one half years, the exact length of time it takes to make a Torah scroll. This is what *Yeshua* was doing: making His disciples into living Torah scrolls. *Yeshua* walked and taught Genesis through Deuteronomy for three and one half years to his disciples. He took them from the dust of the earth and then formed them in the Torah. Now watch what happens:

> In the evening that same day, the first day of the week, when the *talmidim* [disciples] were gathered together behind locked doors out of fear of the Judeans, *Yeshua* came, stood in the middle and said, "*Shalom aleikem!*" Having greeted them, he showed them his hands and his side. The *talmidim* were overjoyed to see the Lord. "*Shalom aleikhem!*" *Yeshua* repeated. "Just as the Father sent me, I myself am also sending you." Having said this, he *breathed on them* and said to them "Receive the *Ruach Hakodesh* [Holy Spirit]!"
>
> John 20:19-22 (CJB)

He breathed on them the breath of God, the Holy Spirit just like Adam. What *Yeshua* did with His *talmidim* was contained in seed form with the creation of Adam in the beginning. Now what took place with *Yeshua* and His disciples gives you deeper insight into what occurred with Adam. Let me show you one more picture of this pattern as it relates to the whole house of Israel. It is found in the story of the valley of dry bones.

> With the hand of *Adonai* upon me, *Adonai* carried me out by the Spirit and set me down in the middle of the valley, and it was full of bones. He had me pass by all around them—there were so many bones lying in the valley, and they were so dry! He asked me, "Human being, can these bones live?" I answered, "*Adonai Elohim*! Only you know that!" Then he said to me, "Prophesy over these bones! Say to them, 'Dry bones! Here what *Adonai* has to say!' To these bones *Adonai Elohim* says, 'I will make breath enter you, and you will live. I will attach ligaments to you, make flesh grow on you, cover you with skin and put breath in you. You will live, and you will know that I am *Adonai*.'"
>
> Ezekiel 37:1-6 (CJB)

A few things we need to know as we proceed into understanding this. First, the bones are in the dust. These bones have no breath in them, no Spirit. They have no muscles or ligaments. Now muscles and ligaments allude to the Torah. In most Jewish *Siddurs* (prayer book), you will quickly discover that they relate the 613 commandments to the 613 muscles and sinews in the human body. Two hundred and forty-eight muscles correspond to the 248 positive commands, and the 365 sinews correspond to the 365 negative commands. The muscles (flesh) and ligaments represent the Torah being formed.

Next, we are going to see that God tells Ezekiel to prophesy to the bones. Prophesy in Hebrew not only means to speak but to specifically speak the words of the Torah or to teach the difference between the clean and the unclean, the holy and the unholy, and about God's feast days. To prophesy to them is likened unto forming them.

> So I prophesied as ordered; and while I was prophesying, there was a noise, a rattling sound; it was the bones coming together, each bone in its proper place [order]. As I watched, ligaments grew on them, flesh appeared [form] and skin [identity] covered them; but there was no breath [Spirit] in them. Next he said to me, "Prophesy to the breath! Prophesy human being! Say to the breath that *Adonai Elohim* says, 'Come from the four winds, breath; and breathe on these slain, so that they can live.'"
>
> Ezekiel 37:7-9 (CJB)

Ezekiel, through prophecy, takes these bones from the dust of the earth and forms them and breathes on them just as God did with Adam. If you continue to read the story, you will see that the dust of the earth was called the grave. Dust symbolizes the grave, death, and curse. God took Adam from death and formed him and breathed into him life. Only then did God place him into the garden of Eden. *Garden* is "a place of protection," and *Eden* means "pleasure."

Amazingly, Adam was crated outside of the garden. Watch this next picture.

God takes Adam from the dust of the earth (nations). God formed Adam in the Torah and then breathed on him the breath of life. In other words, God filled him with the Spirit. Then God planted Adam, "In the place He prepared for him": the garden where the Tree of Life was. "And the LORD God planted a garden eastward in Eden; and there he put the man whom he had formed" (Genesis 2:8 KJV). So the garden was the place God had prepared for Adam.

> In my Father's house [garden] are many places to live. If there weren't, I would have told you; because I am going there to prepare a place for you. Since I am going and preparing a place for you, I will return to take you with me; so that where I am, you may be also.
>
> John 14:2-3

When *Yeshua* says this, He is alluding to Genesis, where he had prepared a place for Adam. Tradition has it that Adam was created on the Feast of Trumpets. Most every major event in the Bible occurs on one of the seven feast days of God. These feasts are called God's timing. Adam would have been created during the fall feasts, *Rosh Hashanah* (Feast of Trumpets), *Yom Kippur* (Day of Atonement), and *Sukkot* (Feast of Tabernacles). It would look something like this: God took Adam from the dust of the earth and formed him on *Rosh Hashanah*. He breathed into Adam the Spirit on *Yom Kippur* and placed him in the garden on *Sukkoth*.

Yeshua came and fulfilled the three spring feasts: Passover, Unleavened Bread, and Fruitfruits. In Acts chapter 2, we see the fulfillment of the summer feast of *Shavuot* or Pentecost. Now we are waiting for the fall feasts to be fulfilled. The church understands it as the rapture. In Hebrew, it is called the "ingathering." The fall feasts are called the feasts of the ingathering.

Tradition has it that the world was created at Passover, or the spring feasts, and Man was created during the fall feasts. I will be talking about the feast days more as we go. If you are not familiar with them, a great introductory book is *Israel's Feasts and Their Fullness* by Batya Wootten.

"And God said, Let us make man in our image, after our likeness: and let them have *dominion* [rule] *over* the fish of the sea, and over the fowl of the air, and over the cattle, and over all the earth, and over every creeping thing that creepeth upon the earth" (Genesis 1:26 KJV). God created Adam in His image or in His name to rule (as) God over all the earth. This name is Israel. Israel is a lifestyle, not just a title. One of the names of Adam would have been Israel. Israel is Strong's #3478 and means "to rule (as) God," and this is exactly what Adam was created to do.

The earth was created to serve Adam (Israel). The garden is the place where Adam would reach his full potential. This is the place where potential becomes actual. This is the place where the marriage of YHWH and His people will occur, where the love relation will be expressed. When Adam eats the forbidden fruit, he is driven out of the garden. I want to point out that the word *driven out* is Strong's #1644, and it means to divorce; so there is a time period where Man is exiled from the garden.

"So God created man in his *own* image, in the image of God created he him; male and female created he them" (Genesis 1:27 KJV). God is one, so He created Adam male and female as one. Adam was one, but contained within Adam was Eve. Adam is also a picture of the whole house of Israel. Contained within Israel are two people groups. God has two witnesses, as I mentioned earlier. Israel follows the same pattern that we see in seed form with Adam and Eve in the beginning.

Adam also is a type of the Messiah. *Yeshua* is the express image of the invisible God. Adam was created in the image of God. Just as Adam's bride, Eve, is taken out of the side of Adam, so the bride of the Messiah will be taken out of the side of the Messiah.

When Adam and Eve sinned, they were exiled out of the side of God. They were driven out of the garden. The garden is the realm of life. We always hear about the fall of man, but Adam did not actually fall out of the sky. He fell from the realm of heaven. The heavenly realm was a status that was manifest on the earth. In Hebrew thought, you're not trying to escape the earth to go to heaven. No! You are trying to bring heaven to the earth.

> Therefore the LORD God sent him forth from the garden of Eden, to till the ground from whence he was taken. So he drove out the man; and he placed at the east of the garden of Eden Cherubims, and a flaming sword which turned every way, to keep the way of the tree of life.
>
> Genesis 3:23-24 (KJV)

What exactly is taking place here? What is God trying to reveal? What are these to cherubim? The Hebrew reads, "With what looked like a flaming sword." These Cherubs are guarding the *way* to the Tree of Life. Did you know that *Yeshua*'s followers were a sect of Judaism called "the Way?" That is the very group of believers that Paul was persecuting.

> Meanwhile, Shaul, still breathing murderous threats against the Lord's *talmidim* [disciples], went to the *Cohen Hagadol* [High Priest] and asked him for letters to the synagogues in Dammesek, authorizing him to arrest any people he might find, whether men or women, who belong to *"the Way"* and bring them back to *Yerushalayim*.
>
> Acts 9:1-2 (CJB)

Here is Paul's latter statement: "I persecuted to death the followers of this *Way* arresting both men and women and throwing them in prison" (Acts 22:4).

Paul was persecuting those who kept or guarded "the Way." The Hebrew word for *guard* actually means "to keep." The two cherubs were to keep the way to the tree of life. God knew that even though Adam was being sent out of the garden, out into darkness, he would one day return. The two cherubs were to keep the way. They would have a flaming sword to light up the way. Even though man was going out into darkness described as the realm of death, the gnashing of teeth, and the way of destruction, they will return to the "Way to the tree of life."

God leaves us some brilliant clues along this seven-thousand-year journey. These two cherubs appear a little later on in man's journey. They appear on the ark of the covenant in the holy of holies. The tabernacle begins to lay out the path to the holy of holies, where the two cherubs are keeping the way to the tree of life. The flaming sword is revealed as the *sh'khinah* of God.

The holy of holies is the bridal chamber. It is symbolized in the seven-day feast of *Sukkoth*, where the husband and wife consummate their marriage in a bridal chamber. This is how the ancient biblical marriage was performed. See the story of Jacob and his marriage to both of his wives and the seven days of the marriage ceremony.

Yeshua makes an interesting statement right after he tells his disciples that He goes to prepare a place for them, a bridal chamber, if you will:

> Thomas said to him, "Lord, we do not know where you are going. How can we know the way?"
> Jesus said to him, "I am the way, and the truth, and the life. No one comes to the Father except through me.
>
> John 14:5-6 (ESV)

Thomas did not know where *Yeshua* was going, but when *Yeshua* said, "I AM the Way, the Truth, and the Life," I'm sure what came to mind was the tabernacle. The outer court symbolized the dust of the earth. *Yeshua* made a *way* for them to enter into the holy place that symbolizes the Torah, *truth*, being formed. Now they could enter the most holy place, the bridal chamber where they would experience the *life* (breath), the spirit life of the garden called eternal life.

The two cherubs made of one piece of gold are a picture of a husband and wife in intimate relations. The two have become one. A picture of Adam and Eve in the garden; the two were made of one body. This is also picture of the house of Israel and the house of Judah together as one and, of course, a picture of the Messiah with His bride in the bridal chamber, the place He prepared for her. They are face-to-face, which is an idiom for the feast of Yom Kippur, the Day of Atonement where we all dress in white like a bride on her wedding day.

Even though man was being sent out of the garden, out of the bridal chamber, God gave a promise in the beginning. This promise is the good news, the gospel. "I will put hostility between you [serpent] and the woman [bride] and between your seed and her seed. He will strike your head and you will strike his heel" (Genesis 3:15 CBS).

Before Adam's fall, he saw from God's perspective. He ruled like God over the earth, including the earth he was made from. When Adam fell, he fell from God's perspective. He no longer saw as God saw. The world became a place of illusions. Adam began to see the world from the limited human perspective that originated from the dust of the earth.

The human perspective can be described as a serpent because, by nature, it crawls through the dust of the earth. It sees from the limited view of its origin the dust of the earth. Again, the dust of the earth symbolizes death, the grave, and curse. "In the sweat of thy face shalt thou eat bread, till thou *return unto the ground* [grave]; for out of it wast thou taken: for dust thou *art*, and unto dust shalt thou return" (Genesis 3:19 KJV). Here, the dust speaks of the grave, both literally and also of the Spiritual grave—realm of death. "Here is what *Adonai* says: "A curse on the person who trusts in humans, who relies on merely human strength [human perspective], whose heart turns away from *Adonai*" (Jeremiah 17:5).

Those who trust in their human perspective will inevitably walk in curse. The human perspective can be understood as the realm of death. The analogy that the serpent's seed would bruise the heel of the seed of the woman and the woman's seed will bruise or crush the head of the serpent reveals that this is a process. The seed of the woman would not escape the serpent's seed but would overcome the serpent's seed. This process is alluded to in the book of Revelation.

> And he laid hold on the dragon, that old serpent, which is the Devil, and Satan, and bound him a thousand years, and cast him into the bottomless pit, and shut him up, and set a seal upon him, that he should deceive the nations no more, till the thousand years should be fulfilled: and after that he must be loosed a little season.
>
> Revelation 20:2-3 (KJV)

When I first started to study this, I thought, *Why in the world would he let him back out? Are you crazy? Don't ever let him out again.* Can you imagine being free from Satan for a thousand years and then he just shows up again? Have you ever thought about that? As I studied more from the Hebraic perspective and ancient Jewish wisdom, I began to read similar stories to this one found in Revelation. There is a verse about a day being like a thousand years: "But, beloved, be not ignorant of this one thing, that one day *is* with the Lord as a thousand years, and a thousand years as one day" (2 Peter 3:8 KJV).

I'm sure you are familiar with this verse. We picture the seven days of creation as alluding to the seven thousand years of man. When you read this verse and the verse from Revelation about the dragon being chained up for a thousand years, they are both written in the context of *Yom Kippur*, the Day of Atonement or Day of Judgment.

In ancient Jewish wisdom, it is written that on *Yom Kippur HaSatan* has no access to you. He is bound. The name *HaSatan* in Hebrew was a numerical value of 364 because one day out of 365 days of the year, Satan has no power. That Day is *Yom Kippur*, the Day of the Lord.

As Peter is teaching about *Yom Kippur*, he mentions that a day is like a thousand years. Very interestingly, *Yom Kippur* is the day that is like a thousand years. Satan is bound on that day (thousand years). This is a thought-provoking nugget.

The seed of the woman that will crush the head of the serpent is understood to be the Messiah who crushed the serpent at Calvary. However, this seed is also a reference to the remnant, Israel, who will overcome and defeat the serpent. The name *Israel* is made from two Hebrew words: *Sarah* and *El* (God). The seed was in Isaac, who came from an impossible conception. Now we see this pattern repeated in the story of Mary and *El* (God) another impossible conception.

Yeshua crushed the head of the serpent at Calvary, yet here we are two thousand years later, and it seems the serpent is alive and well. What are we missing? The seed, Israel, now, by the power of the Holy Spirit, will overcome the serpent. How do we know who the seed of the women are? "And the dragon [serpent] was wroth with the woman, and went to make war with the remnant of her *seed*, which keep the commandments [*Torah*] of God, and have the testimony of Jesus Christ [Spirit]" (Revelation 12:17 KJV).

The seed are the first fruits. They are Israel, Torah, and *Yeshua*, *echad* (one). This revolves around *Yom Kippur*. *Yom Kippur* is the wedding. *HaSatan* is bound on this day, and the seed is planted into the womb of your heart. Now, after *Yom Kippur*, *HaSatan* is let loose, but the seed is empowered to overcome the serpent. They will crush his head (authority). The remnant is the army of God. They will overcome the serpent and the world called Egypt and also the lake of fire.

We will explore the serpent much further, but for now, let's look at this. The seed of the woman is the Spirit of *Yeshua* called God's perspective. This perspective can be called the mind of Christ. He overcame the serpent, the serpent called the human perspective, Man's way or Man's mind. This process of overcoming or crushing is called salvation of the soul, salvation (*Yeshua*) of the soul (mind). Do you see it? Salvation of the soul is the mind of Christ, to see from God's perspective as Adam did in the garden.

"Obtaining the outcome of your faith, the salvation of your souls" (1 Peter 1:9 ESV). Wow. This is the goal of our faith to overcome the serpent with its evil desires, not just to go to heaven when you die. Paul talks about this as well. "Having one's mind controlled by the old nature [human perspective] is death, but having one's mind controlled by the Spirit [God's perspective] is life and Shalom" (Romans 8:6).

So Paul sets the seed of the serpent as the flesh or old nature and opposes this to the seed of the woman: the Spirit. He goes a little further to explain the difference between the two. We read early in Revelation that the seed of the woman has both Torah and *Yeshua* (Spirit). Now look at the seed of the serpent.

"For the mind controlled by the old nature is hostile to God *because* it does not submit itself to *God's Torah*—indeed it cannot" (Romans 8:7). So the seed of the woman is led of the Spirit and submits to God's Torah. However, the seed of the serpent cannot submit to God's Torah.

Here are some terms that describe the serpent: *HaSatan*; *Yetzer Hares*, which is the urge to do evil; the realm of death; the flesh;

carnal nature; old nature; and the human perspective. *HaSatan* is a huge topic, and, Hebraicly, it is understood a little bit differently than we may view it in the church world. I'm going to use the term *human perspective* to help see an aspect that is missed in the church world. Perspective also means desires. The human perspective is the earthly carnal nature with its desires to do evil. The Jews commonly refer to this as the *Yetzer Hara*, urge to do evil or evil inclination.

ו

THE POWER OF TWO

> I declare the end from the beginning, and from long ago what is not yet done, saying; my plan will take place, and I will do all my will.
>
> Isaiah 46:10 (CJB)

When we look back to the beginning, we realize that God is one, but relationships take two. God chose His creation as the place to express His love. The spirit of God is full of potential. God's many attributes, like love, mercy, etc., are only potential without His creation to express it to. God's creation presented the opportunity for God to manifest His attributes, His names, and character. "For the creation waits with eager longing for the revealing of the sons of God" (Romans 8:19 ESV). This was the intent in creating.

The Word revealed also means to manifest. The creation awaits the manifestation of the sons of God. A son is the express image of his father. Adam was the son of God. Israel is the son of God. *Yeshua* is the son of God, and all of creation awaits the manifestation of the sons of God. Adam was the express image of God. Adam was fully man and fully God.

"So God created man in his own image, in the image of God he created him; male and female he created them" (Genesis 1:27 KJV). If Adam is created in the image of God, then we can discover profound truths of God in the story of Adam. This is something we are going to dig deep into, as it holds profound truths about you and your image.

When Adam sinned, his image was shattered. When *Yeshua* came, He came to restore the image that Adam lost, He as the son of God. He was fully man and fully God. "He is the image of the invisible God, the firstborn of all creation" (Colossians 1:15 ESV). *Yeshua* came in the exact image Adam was created in, the express image of God.

Yeshua came to restore the shattered image of man back to the image of God. He is restoring His image to the first fruits. "For whom he did foreknow, he also did predestinate *to be* conformed to the image of his Son, that he might be the firstborn among many brethren" (Romans 8:29 KJV). If all of creation is waiting for the sons of God to manifest, then they are here somewhere. They have just remained potential. This means there are people who contain within them the potential of God. Remember, YHVH wanted to take His potential and make it actual, and God chose man as the vehicle to express Himself.

Here is one of my translations of Genesis 1:1: "In the first fruits, God created the place from which He would dwell and express Himself in the Earth." Earlier, we looked at Adam, as He was a picture of the first fruits. God *took* him from the *dust of the earth*. God wanted to dwell in the earth, so He created man from the dust of the earth. We also looked at this pattern as it was related to *Yeshua's* disciples. Now let's look at the first fruits in the last days. These are the ones who manifest as the sons of God.

> These are they which were not defiled with women; for they are virgins. These are they which follow the Lamb whithersoever he goeth. These were redeemed [took] from among men [dust of the earth], *being* the first fruits unto God and to the Lamb. And in their mouth was found no guile: for they are without fault before the throne of God.
>
> Revelation 14:4-5 (KJV)

By the way, first fruits are considered those who have resurrected. This is a spiritual death. "But the fact is that the Messiah has been raised from the dead, the first fruits of those who have died" (1 Corinthians 15:20).When Adam was taken from the dust of the earth (death), he was raised to life. Messiah is the first fruits of those who died not just physically but spiritually. A spiritual death will lead to a physical death. "Neither yield ye your members *as* instruments of unrighteousness unto sin: but yield yourselves unto God, as those that are alive from the dead, and your members *as* instruments of righteousness unto God" (Romans 6:13 KJV).

Paul also spoke about these same first fruits that are found in the book of Revelation. They are the ones who have Torah (form) and *Yeshua* (Spirit). They have been raised from the dead.

> But we have to keep thanking God for you always, brothers whom the Lord loves, because God chose you as first fruits [just as he chose Adam, Adam didn't chose God] for deliverance [from what? The dust of the earth, or realm of death.] by giving you the holiness that has its origin in the Spirit [breath of God] and faithfulness that has its origin in the truth [formed by Torah]. He called you to this through our good news so that you could have the glory [lifestyle] of our Lord *Yeshua* the Messiah.
>
> 2 Thessalonians 2:13-14 (CJB)

What is the Glory of the Lord, *Yeshua*? It is when the word becomes flesh, the manifest presence and character of God. God took His breath, potential, and put it into the earth, you. The seed, potential, is planted into the ground in order to produce fruit and a harvest made actual. This is called the manifestation of the sons of God. When Adam was placed in the garden, he ruled and reigned with the Messiah. He was one with Torah and *Yeshua*. This was called walking with God in the cool of the day, the Spirit life. In Revelation, it is called ruling and reigning. (See Revelation 11:17, 19:6, 20:6; resurrection equals first fruits.)

God placed His potential in Adam so it (He) could be manifest in the earth. We will discover the potential and pattern of God in Adam. In order for God to have a relationship, He needed a creation. Naturally, in order for Adam to have a love relationship, he would need a partner or someone to demonstrate this love to. We are about to see a big clue to our origin here.

"And the LORD God said, '*It is* not good that the man should be alone; I will make him an help meet for him'" (Genesis 2:18 KJV). God reveals that the purpose of His creation was so that God Himself would not be alone and also so that His creation would be a type of helpmate likened unto Eve. In other words, we were created as a companion to participate with God.

> And the LORD God caused a deep sleep to fall upon Adam, and he slept: and he took one of his ribs, and closed up the flesh instead thereof; and the rib, which the LORD God had taken from man, made he a woman, and brought her unto the man.
>
> Genesis 2:21-22 (KJV)

Why did God take Eve out of Adam and not just form her from the dust of the earth? This was to teach us that just as Adam's bride originated from Adam so God's bride originated from God. This was to teach us that our origin is from God. He knew us before the foundation of the earth. Wow. Paul alludes to this hidden truth:

> The husbands! love your own wives, as also the Christ did love the assembly, and did give himself for it, that he might sanctify it, having cleansed *it* with the bathing of the water in the saying, that he might present it to himself the assembly in glory, not having spot or wrinkle, or any of such things, but that it may be holy and unblemished; so ought the husbands to love their own wives as their own bodies: he who is loving his own wife—himself he doth love; for no one ever his own flesh did hate, but doth nourish and

cherish it, as also the Lord—the assembly, because members we are of his body, of his flesh, and of his bones; "for this cause shall a man leave his father and mother, and shall be joined to his wife, and they shall be—the two—for one flesh;" *this secret is great, and I speak in regard to Christ and to the assembly;* but ye also, every one in particular—let each his own wife so love as himself, and the wife--that she may reverence the husband.

Ephesians 5:25-33 (YLT)

The husband-wife relationship becomes our picture of our relationship with God. We originated from God. Relationship has been the Hebrew model from the beginning.

There are two main models that we see from the Scriptures: the corporate model and the individual model. There is our individual salvation and our corporate salvation. Both were contained in the beginning and throughout the Torah.

Israel, at the time of the Messiah, really only understood the corporate model, so Paul's teachings, many times, were to specifically reveal that the individual model was there all along. Now, Christians today, because of their primary focus on the New Testament, only see the individual model and don't understand the corporate model.

So the pattern we see is Adam was created male and female. God took Eve out of Adam. She is a reflection of Him, as her origin is Adam. We were taken from God and are a reflection of Him, as we originated from Him.

Eve was formed from a rib, which alludes to a *branch*. When Adam sees her, he says, "And Adam said, 'This *is* now bone of my bones, and flesh of my flesh: she shall be called Woman, because she was taken out of Man'" (Genesis 2:23 KJV). Eve originated from Adam's flesh and bone. Our origin is God's Spirit. We are Spirit of His Spirit.

Now, Adam became two separate people: Adam and Eve. We see the exact same pattern with Israel. The house of Israel is taken out of the side of the house of Judah; by the way, *Yeshua* represents the house of Judah, and the nations represent the house of Israel. They separated and become two separate nations. The house of Judah is the Jewish people, and the house of Israel becomes the wild branch (rib) as they intermingle with the nations.

"But I planted you as a choice vine of seed fully tested and true. How did you degenerate into a *wild vine* for me?" (Jeremiah 2:21). Adam and Eve were only separated for one reason: to be brought back together as one. "This is why a man is to leave his father and mother and stick with His wife, and they are to be one flesh" (Genesis 2:24 KJV).

The two shall be one. The only reason God took us out of Himself is to bring us back to Himself. "Don't you know that a man who joins himself to a prostitute becomes physically one with her? For the Tanakh says, 'The two will become one flesh'; but the person who is joined to the Lord is *one spirit*" (1 Corinthians 6:16-17).

This also means the house of Judah (Jews) and the house of Israel (nations/church) will come back together as one. This also reveals that those from the house of Israel who have lost their identity actually have their origin in Israel. They might be mixed in the nations, but their origin is Israel. This is why they are beginning to have a desire for Israel, the Torah and the Hebrew language; it's in their DNA (see Ezekiel 37 and Romans 11).

> And say unto them, "Thus saith the Lord GOD, 'Behold, I will take the children of Israel from among the heathen, whither they be gone, and will gather them on every side, and bring them into their own land: And I will make them one nation in the land upon the mountains of Israel; and one king shall be king to them

all: and they shall be no more two nations, neither shall they be divided into two kingdoms any more at all.'"

Ezekiel 37:21-22 (KJV)

In Romans 11, Paul talks about the wild branch, the house of Israel being brought back to the cultivated tree, the house of Judah. When the two become one, it is a picture of a marriage. The husband is the house of Judah, *Yeshua*; and the wife is the house of Israel, you or the church.

Adam is a picture of the Messiah. Eve was taken out of Adam's side. This is a type of exile. In a sense, Eve was exiled from Adam for a season until they came back together as one. This reveals that when the bride was taken out of God's side, she experienced a type of exile for a season; this was the exile from the garden, God's side. When they came back together as one, it is pictured in the two cherubs face-to-face and made of one solid piece of gold. It is only when the two become one that life is produced. God has emphatically embedded this understanding into the marriage covenant. This is where we become fruitful and multiply.

Eden, in Hebrew, means "place of pleasure." Pleasure alludes to intimacy, intimacy with the Messiah. *Garden*, in Hebrew, means "to protect, guard, and even cultivate." *Garden of Eden* means "to protect and cultivate intimacy." A husband should always protect and cultivate the intimacy he has with his wife, as it will be a river of life for them. This is exactly what *Yeshua* is doing with you today. *Yeshua* is drawing us back to Himself today for intimacy; He is returning His Torah to us as it is the book of cultivation. It takes two for a relationship, but in intimacy, they become one.

Let's take a look at the two in Israel.

- Two houses: Isaiah 8:14, Jeremiah 31:31-33, Hebrews 8:8-10

- Two nations: Ezekiel 35:10

- Two chosen families: Jeremiah 33:24

- Two sisters: Ezekiel 23:2-4
- Two olive branches: Jeremiah 11:10, 16-17, 2:18, 21; Zechariah 4:11-14
- Two sticks: Ezekiel 37:15-28
- Two witnesses: Deuteronomy 17:6; Revelation 11:3-4
- Two lamp stands: Revelation 11:3-4
- Two leavened loaves: Leviticus 23:17
- Two silver trumpets: Numbers 10:2-3
- Two cherubs: Exodus 25:18-20

God even calls heaven and earth as a witness or two witnesses that have become one; they are in agreement. "I call heaven and earth to witness against you today that I have presented you with life [tree of life] and death [tree of knowledge], the blessing and the curse, therefore choose life, so that you will live, you and your descendants" (Deuteronomy 30:19 KJV).

It is interesting that in Genesis 1:1, when we read about the heavens, they are plural. In Jewish tradition, there are seven levels of heaven, and we even see Paul refer to the third heaven in the *Brit Chadasha* (New Testament). Also, the Hebrew word for *heavens* is in the masculine form and the Hebrew word for *earth* is in the feminine form. The heavens and the earth require unity for the continuum of life, and we, as a people, male and female, only continue to reproduce if we become one. Think about what that says about *Yeshua* and his bride. The bride is the place where heaven (Spirit) and earth come together, the place where the two become one. This is where the Spirit dwells in the earth. Man is both heaven and earth.

Remember when we looked at the word *B'reisheet*, "in the beginning"? The letter *Beit* (the first letter in *B'reisheet*) carried a numerical value of two. This alluded to the fact that there would be two beginnings. Man is spirit (heaven) and body (earth). He is a creation. When he receives a new heart (earth) and a new spirit (heaven), he is a new creation. "I will give you a new heart [earth] and put a new spirit [heaven] inside you; I will take the stony heart [old earth] out of your flesh and give you a heart of flesh [new earth]" (Ezekiel 36:26).

Man has his first beginning, and then he has a new beginning. He was a first creation and a second creation. He is the new heaven and new earth. This might help you to take a more Hebraic approach to Revelation 21, where it refers to a new heaven and a new earth. What was John really talking about? The first fruits, they are the new heaven and the new earth. They are the ones who have resurrected. Keep in mind that as we look at the fall of man, we will see the same pattern manifesting in Israel.

So he *drove the man out [divorced]*...

Genesis 3:24 (KJV)

I saw that even though backsliding Israel had committed adultery, so that I had sent her away and given her a *divorce document*...

Jeremiah 3:8 (CJB)

Adonai says: "Where is your mother's *divorce document* which I gave her when I divorced her? Or: to which of my creditors did I sell you? You were sold because of your sins; because of your crimes was your mother *divorced*."

Isaiah 50:1 (CJB)

Both Adam and Israel were exiled. When Adam was exiled from the garden, he was sent out into darkness, the place of the gnashing of teeth, also called death, fiery furnace, lake of fire, and the way of destruction. This exile, or way of destruction, is opposite of the Way the two cherubs were to keep or guard. "And he placed at the east of the garden of Eden the *k'ruvim* and a flaming sword which turned in every direction to guard the Way to the tree of life" (Genesis 3:24 KJV).

These two cherubs show up later in the holy of holies. They kept the presence of God between them in the holy of holies. This temple was in the center of Israel. In the Torah, there are certain things, activities, or particular sins that if a person does and won't repent, they are stoned or cut off from the community of Israel. To be cut off from Israel meant you were sent out into the pagan nations, out into the darkness, into curse, poverty, and an unproductive lifestyle. You were considered as dead. Realize this meant you no longer had access to the temple or the presence of God that the two cherubs were guarding. This is a type of exile Adam suffered from the garden.

There are certain sins that will render a person unclean for one day and some that would render them unclean for a week. Being unclean meant you were unable to produce life. "When a person with a discharge has become free of it, he is to count seven days for his purification. Then he is to wash his clothes and bathe his body in running water; after that, he will be clean" (Leviticus 15:13).

This discharge can be associated with slander. We see this in the story of Miriam, where she slandered Moshe and became leprous and was sent out of the camp for seven days in order to examine her ways.

Adam's sin was connected to slander as well. The evil tongue in Hebrew is called *Lashon Harah*, the hiss of the serpent. Adams is exiled from the garden seven days or seven thousand years. On the seven thousandth year, he is purified and becomes clean. We see the same pattern in Leviticus 15 regarding the laws of Niddah (separation). When a woman is in her flow for seven days, she is unclean or in a status where she can't produce life. Look at what God says: "All of us are like someone unclean, all our righteous deeds like menstrual rags; we wither, all of us, like leaves; and our miss deeds blow us away like the wind" (Isaiah 64:5-6).

So Adam was cut off from the garden or presence of God. Keep in mind that Adam is a picture of Israel. Now Adam is driven out. God placed the two cherubs at the east of the garden to keep the Way. Here is how the Hebrew reads as my translation: "God lodged a place to dwell at the front [east] of the garden [place of protection that is hedged in and watched over] of Eden [pleasure]..." (Genesis 3:24).

Here is a little more of what we find in these Hebrew words. The cherubs placed at the east (front) speaks of an anticipation of a meeting with a connection to time or ancient time. Time also alludes to the feast days of God. They are appointments in time for God to meet with us for deliverance, and they lead us to a wedding. This meeting speaks of a time when Adam/Israel will return back to the ancient way, the Way the two cherubs are guarding. "You favored those who were glad to do justice, those who remembered you in your ways. When you were angry, we kept sinning; but if we keep your ancient ways, we will be saved" (Isaiah 64:4-5).

"Here is what *Adonai* says: 'Stand at the crossroads and look; ask about the ancient paths, which one is the good way?' Take it, and you will find rest for your souls. But they said, 'We will not take it'" (Jeremiah 6:16). *Yeshua* did not come to bring a new way but to return us to the ancient way where we will find rest for our souls. This is the way to the tree of life. Cherubs were imaginary figures that were connected with a message to herald the good news or the gospel of the garden and the bridal chamber where life can be conceived.

"I appointed sentinels to direct them: 'Listen for the sound of the shofar.' But they said, 'We will not listen'" (Jeremiah 6:17). This message is the good news. The cherubs guarded the gospel of the garden. These are the two witnesses of the God of creation. The Hebrew word for *guard* is *shamar*. It means "to guard, watch, protect, attend, preserve, and keep the Way." It was not just to keep man out, as it might seem in English, but to keep and preserve the way back to the tree of life. Therefore, it will never be lost. So what is this Way, this gospel of the garden? *Yeshua* said, "I am the way!" What did he mean by that?

The Hebrew word for *way* is *derek*. It means "a road, coarse of life, mode of action, a journey, pathway, custom, destiny, walk, and guide." All of these allude to the Torah, with its customs and pathways to the garden, the presence of God. Moses (Torah) prepares and leads the bride to her wedding.

When *Yeshua* said, "I Am the Way," He was declaring that He was the living Torah. If we look at the ark, what we see is two cherubs facing each other and looking down into the ark. What they are looking at is what is contained in the ark: the two tablets (Torah), the manna (*Yeshua*), and the rod that budded (two houses of Israel as one).

One cherub represents the Torah (truth), and one represents the Spirit. The cherub that represents the Torah is likened to Moshe, and the one that represents the Spirit is likened to Elijah. When Moshe and Elijah come together as one, it is *Yeshua*. The Torah and Spirit together are the manifest presence of God, *Yeshua, HaMashiach*.

> Then they looked and saw Moshe and Elijah speaking with Him [*Yeshua*]. Kefer said to *Yeshua*, "It's good that we're here, Lord. I'll put up three shelters [*sukkots* or tent of Meeting or Holy of Holies] if you want—one for you, one for Moshe, and one for Elijah." While he was still speaking, a bright cloud enveloped them [they were caught up into the cloud.]; and a voice from the cloud said, "This is my Son [when Moshe and Elijah came together, when Spirit and Torah came together it is the image of a son], whom I love, with whom I am well pleased. Listen to him."
>
> Matthew 17:3-5 (CJB)

They saw Moshe, one cherub, and Elijah, the other cherub. *Yeshua* was between them, and He transfigured and began to shine like a flaming sword between them.

The two cherubs are a picture of two people bent over, looking into, attending to, and preserving the customs of the Torah (Word of God). This is called a *midrash*. Remember, when *Yeshua* sent the seventy out in twos, He also said, "Where two are gathered in my name (lifestyle) there I am in their midst." The Torah is simply the habits or lifestyle of *Yeshua*. We study the Torah to do, we do the Torah to obey, and we obey the Torah to cling to God; for this is the purpose of our life: to love God.

> Loving *Adonai* your God, paying attention to what he says and clinging to him—for this is the purpose of your life! On this depends the length of time you will live in the land [garden], *Adonai* swore he would give to your ancestors Abraham, *Yitz'chak* and *Ya'akov*.
>
> Deuteronomy 30:20

To cling is to become one Spirit with *Yeshua*. "If you love me, you will keep my commands" (John 14:15) just as a man leaves his father and mother and clings to his wife. This involves a marriage. The Way is the way into a heavenly realm. This realm can be found in the heart of men, holy men. The two cherubs are a picture of a husband and wife face-to-face in intimate relations. This is to point us to the intimate relationship that Yeshua wants to have with His wife, He desires to come face-to-face with her in intimate relations.

> You are to make two *k'ruvim* of gold. Make them of hammered work for the two ends of the ark-cover. Make one *keruv* for one end and one *keruv* for the other end. *Make* the *k'ruvim of one piece* with the ark-cover at its two ends. The *k'ruvim* will have their wings [*tallit* or prayer shawls] spread out above, so that their wings cover the ark [like a *huppah* wedding canopy], and their

faces are towards each other and towards the ark-cover. You are to put the ark-cover on top of the ark. Inside the ark you will put the testimony that I am about to give you. There I will meet with you. I will speak with you from above the ark-cover, from between the two *k'ruvim* which are on the ark for the testimony, about the orders [way] I am giving you for the people of Israel [two houses].

Exodus 25:18-22

It is from between the two cherubs that He speaks. It is when we come together in Spirit and Truth with our brothers (house of Israel and house of Judah) that He speaks to us. This is the power of two. "For whenever two or more are gathered in my name (lifestyle, the way) I am in their midst" (Matthew 18:20).

Yeshua is the flaming sword that appears between them. The way to the tree of life (voice of God) opens up. Between the two cherubs appeared what looked like a flaming sword. The Hebrew word for *flaming* is *lahat*. *Lahat* means "to blaze, idea of being enwrapped, flaming enchantment, flaming, and to burn up." Therefore, it carries the idea of burning up and destroying enemies.

This is related to the two witnesses in Revelation 11, where the two witnesses consume their enemies with fire. This flaming sword is the sword of the Spirit. Thus comes the idea of the Word carried by the Spirit, the revelation of God. The revelation of God destroys our enemies. Revelation always precedes deliverance. The enemy is our earthly nature with its evil desires. "Then, so far as your *former way* of life is concerned, you must strip off your old nature [with the sword of the Spirit], because your old nature is thoroughly rotten by its deceptive desires" (Ephesians 4:22).

The house of Israel has the testimony of *Yeshua*. The church knows who *Yeshua* is. The house of Judah was the testimony of the Torah. The Jews know the Torah. Apart from each other, there is no spark of life.

Then there are those who have the testimony of *Yeshua* and the Torah. They are like a flaming sword; wherever they go, they destroy strongholds of paganism. They are like a beam of light sent out to destroy darkness. When we come together with our brothers, *Yeshua*, the flaming sword, is in our midst. He is like a laser beam of light that goes forth and destroys our enemies, which are sickness, disease, curse, lack, and decrease. *Yeshua* is the magnetic force that keeps us together.

God created us to come back together and to speak into each other, to stir up the life of God and His presence within each other. It is not good for man to be alone. When we come together, it is here that he speaks to us. It is here that we eat from the tree of life. When God sent Adam out of the garden, it was only to bring him back. The two cherubs represent when we will return face-to-face with our groom, *Yeshua, HaMashiach*.

*For more information on the tabernacle and two cherubs, see *Tabernacle Technologies* by Rabbi Ralph Messer, STBM, at www.TORAH.TV.

ז

NACHASH SERPENT

This, to me, is a fascinating topic to unravel. There is very little truly understood by people in our generation. I'm sure this will challenge many people's traditional thoughts on this topic. I want you to think about this. This serpent appeared in the garden, in paradise.

I will be following a specific train of thought, and it is not my goal to dismiss any other understanding that people have on this topic; however, in my attempt to make my argument and to help the reader to see a different perspective, it might appear as though I am. My goal is to reveal how this applies to us today. Before we can look at the mystical levels in the unseen realm, let's look at a level of understanding that applies to us in our lives.

The truth is that *Yeshua* is taking us back to the garden. The gospel of the garden holds many powerful truths, and these truths are to be found on the lips of the first fruits in the last days.

I will be dealing with these topics in layers. I grew up in a nondenominational Christian background, so if that is your background, I'm writing especially for you. I truly believe that when you begin to see this from a Hebraic perspective, you will begin to have such direction and encouragement that the things you have struggled with, the illusions that oppressed our lives, will begin to fade away. I believe what you discover here will change your life.

I want to mention that the Torah uses animals as a way to refer to people. Animals have different characteristics, and when people are referred to as animals, it is because of their characteristics. "Now the serpent was more crafty than any wild animal which *Adonai*, God, had made. He said to the woman, 'Did God really say, "You are not to eat from any tree in the garden?"'" (Genesis 3:1) The Hebrew language and world paints a picture to the heart and imagination, and using animals to describe people is one of the ways it does so. If we have not grown up in this world, many times, we miss this aspect of God's Word.

The Bible refers to false prophets as wolves and lions. The house of Israel was called the lost sheep. *Efrayim* is likened unto a wild donkey. Each time, it paints a picture in your mind. *Yeshua* told Peter to feed His sheep.

When God divorced the house of Israel, or *Efrayim*, He referred to them as wild animals because they were then outside of His Torah. They became wild or uncultivated because the Torah is the book of cultivation. Remember the wild branch that is grafted back in? I want to show you some examples of people being called animals. If we don't see how God uses animals to describe people, it can cause confusion and lead us to miss some of what God's Word is really telling us.

The animals are a reference to the house of Israel: people. "When that day comes, I will make a covenant for them with the wild animals, the birds in the air, and the creeping things of the earth. I will break bow and sword, sweep battle from the land, and make them lie down securely" (Hoshea 2:20(18)). You don't break the bow and sword of animals. In the next two verses, He goes on to say He will betroth them to Himself three times. This statement is made after He divorced them, the house of Israel. Betrothal is the first stage of a Hebrew wedding.

In the time of *Yeshua*, the house of Israel had been divorced from God and intermingled with the nations, becoming half-breeds. The house of Judah, or Jews, were living in the land of Israel and were, at times, referred to as Israel. These Jews would not have anything to do with the house of Israel. Some of these half-breeds were their neighbors known as the Samaritans. To the Jewish people, these Samaritans were an unclean people with whom they would not have any fellowship.

Now, I want you to see this. Remember the story where Peter denies *Yeshua three times* in front of the Jewish people? This reveals that Peter was intimidated by his Jewish brethren. Now, later, *Yeshua* asks Peter if he loves him *three times*; and each time, Peter responds, "Yes," and then *Yeshua* tells Peter to feed His sheep *three times*. The sheep *Yeshua* was talking about were the house of Israel; they were the half-breeds called the lost sheep, the Samaritans.

These were the very sheep the Jewish people would not have fellowship with. *Yeshua* knew that if Peter denied Him *three times* in front of the Jewish people, it would be difficult for Peter not to deny these sheep in front of the Jewish people because the Jews would not have any fellowship with the sheep that *Yeshua* was sending Peter to. The Jewish people would want to know what Peter was doing having fellowship with these people. "He [*Yeshua*] said, 'I was sent only to the lost sheep of the house of Israel (*Efrayim*)'" (Matthew 15:24).

Yeshua knew that this would be a challenge for Peter because it would go against Jewish tradition. He did not want Peter to deny them. Just as Peter denied *Yeshua three times*, He asks Peter if he loved *Yeshua three times*. The *three times* are used to connect, add emphasis, and also to remind Peter of the verses in the book of Hoshea, where He said He would betroth Himself to them *three times*. I will explain this further.

Now Peter has a vision:

> He fell into a trance in which he saw heaven open, and something that looked like a large sheet [*tallit*] being lowered to the ground by its four corners. In it were all kinds of four-footed animals, crawling creatures and wild birds [house of Israel as depicted in Hoshea].
>
> Acts 10:10-12

This *tallit* or prayer shawl was full of animals, and these animals are used to allude (*Remez*) to Hoshea. The *tallit* symbolizes the Word or covenant of God. These people (animals) are back in the covenant of God. "Then a voice came to him, 'Get up, Kefa, slaughter and eat!' But Kefa said, "No sir! Absolutely not! I have never eaten food that was unclean or *treif*" (Acts 10:13-14).

Obviously, *Yeshua* never taught Peter that all foods were clean or Peter would not have called these animals unclean. Seriously, if we don't pay attention, we will miss the whole point of this experience. We miss the revelation of God's plan in this verse. This is talking about the house of Israel—you if you come from the nations.

"The voice spoke to him a second time. 'Stop treating as unclean what God has made clean.' This happened *three times*, and then the sheet was immediately taken back up into heaven" (Acts 10:15-16). This occurred *three times,* and to Peter this would have brought back to mind when *Yeshua* asked him if he loved Him *three times* and told him to feed His sheep *three times*. Next, God sends *three people* to see Peter who are not Jews but rather from the house of Israel, which are people the Jews treated as unclean. These three people took Peter to meet a man named Cornelius.

> As he talked with him, Kefa went inside and found many people gathered. He said to them, "You are well aware that for a man who is a Jew to have close association with someone who belongs to another people [house of Israel], or to come and visit him, is something that just isn't done. But God has shown me [in a vision] not to call any person [this vision is not about food] common or unclean."
>
> Acts 10:27-28 (CJB)

Peter understood what *Yeshua* was doing, and he did not deny *Yeshua's* sheep but went and fed them. In this event, *Yeshua* was bringing the two cherubs, the house of Israel and the house of

Judah, face-to-face. Sometimes when we read the Word, we are more interested in finding what we want the Word to say and then miss what it is actually saying. Most Christians believe this vision was to declare all foods clean.

They are more concerned about the verses meaning that they can eat whatever they want that they can't even look into the truth of what is being said. Even when I say, "Let's put all food aside for the sake of this discussion. Let's not even worry about food. Let's just talk about what is happening here. What is taking place between Israel and Judah?" there is a block that won't let them get past the theme of food.

I have included the above to help us look at what God is really saying to us. After all, man does not live on bread alone but every word that comes out of the mouth of the Father. Let's take in the true food that *Yeshua* sustains his first fruits with. "Now the serpent was more crafty than any *wild* animal which *Adonai*, God, had made..." (Genesis 3:1a).

Have you ever come across a crafty snake when you were walking through a field? I have not. Then what is really being said? The serpent, also known as *HaSatan*, is craftier than any of the wild animals. Wild animals are a reference to those people who are outside of the Torah and covenant relationship with God. People who are living in their earthly nature don't stand a chance against *HaSatan*. The beasts of the field are those who are outside of the garden. Were Adam and Eve beasts of the field?

Let's look at this serpent. I hope to paint a good picture for you. I'm not saying there was not a physical snake in the garden, but let's look at the activities and characteristics associated with the word *snake*. These characteristics can be found in people as well.

The Hebrew word for serpent is *Nachash*. It means "serpent, to hiss, to whisper a magic spell, to learn by experience (i.e. to learn from omens), divine practice, divination, (i.e. those who practice divination), conjure, advance to the future through magic." Cognate meanings include, "scorn, *urge*, and penetrate." This is referenced from Strong's #5175, TWOT 1348a and also *The Etymological Dictionary of Biblical Hebrew* by Mattityahu Clark.

All of these are associated with evil. This can be understood as the urge to do evil. The Jewish people have understood the serpent as a reference to the *Yetzer Hara*, the urge to do evil, as opposed to the *Yetzer HaTov*, the urge to do good.

The serpent in this is the static in our mind, the whisper that would distract and seek to destroy our good conscience or desire to do good. We all have experienced the hiss, that whisper from our earthly nature that is almost like a magic spell that casts a desire to do evil over our mind. This whisper can come from inside us, like a voice in our blood that speaks to us, or this hiss can come from outside of us, from another person. This voice can flow from generation to generation in the blood, known as generational curses.

The word *Nachash* is also related to bronze. This gives us further clues that this serpent is connected to our earthly nature. Bronze is the metal associated with the outer court of the tabernacle. This is the common realm. This is the place we deal with the flesh, the serpent. The bronze altar is where we burn the flesh.

This *Nachash* is also related to the bronze laver. This is located in the outer court. This whole process is associated with dying to the old nature. This is the death, burial, and resurrection symbolized in a baptism. The laver is the place where we *Mikveh* (type of baptism) for a change of status from the common to the Holy. The laver is the place where we wash our hands and break off the spell the serpent has cast over our mind.

"Come close to God, and he will come close to you. *Clean your hands*, sinners; purify your hearts, you double-minded people" (James 4:8). James is referring back to the laver. When we sin or become defiled, we *ruachatz* (hand washing) to change status from the realm of death (*HaSatan*) to the realm of life. Water is the point of contact for the change of status. It is likened unto a rebirth. Even the world has stumbled upon this truth, this connection with water breaking the hiss. When someone has a spell of lust or anger cast over their minds, they tell them to go take a cold shower. It will break the spell, right?

This hiss tempts us to eat the forbidden fruit. Where does *HaSatan* dwell? Where we are forbidden to go. When we step outside of what we were created to do, we will meet this hiss. The *Yetzer Hara* can be likened unto the forbidden tree. Don't eat from this voice, or you will surely die.

The *Nachash* is also related to the bronze serpent that Moses fashioned in the wilderness. The *Yetzer Hara* is the urge to do evil. When it is given a voice, it is called *Lashon Hara*, the evil tongue. When we speak gossip, slander, and all forms of evil speech, it is called *Lashon Hara*. *HaSatan*, or the serpent, is called the slanderer. Paul goes further and refers to *HaSatan* as the ruler of the power of the air. Speech is carried in the air. The realm of death advances through our speech.

> You used to be dead because of your sins and acts of disobedience. You walked in the ways of the *'olam Hazeh* [present age, earthly nature] and obeyed the Ruler of the Power of the Air [Your earthly nature with its desires, *HaSatan*], who is still at work among the disobedient.
>
> Ephesians 2:1-2

Evil speech is associated with snake's venom. If we listen to slander and gossip, this is like being bitten by a poisonous snake. This is the venom of bitterness. It is also likened to the sting of a wasp or scorpion.

"The people spoke against God and against Moshe. 'Why did you bring us up out of Egypt? To die in the desert? There's no real food, there's no water, and we're sick of this miserable stuff we're eating [manna]'" (Numbers 21:5). We can see the serpent is already in their midst. They were bitten and full of bitterness. Watch what God does and look deep into what the Torah is revealing here: "In response, *Adonai* sent poisonous snakes among the people; they bit the people, and many of Israel's people died" (Numbers 21:6).

God sent something in the physical to teach them about what was happening in the spiritual. Was all this bitterness coming from a red-tailed creature with a pitchfork? No, it was coming from their bitter, wounded hearts. This was the result of a people who had been in Egypt, a pagan world full of evil. See, Egypt was still alive in the people. Egypt is the *'olam Hazeh* that Paul was referring to in Ephesians.

> Moshe prayed for the people, and *Adonai* answered Moshe. "Make a poisonous snake and put it on a pole. When anyone who has been bitten sees it, he will live." Moshe made a bonze snake and put it on the pole; if a snake had bitten someone, then, when he looked towards the bronze snake, he stayed alive.
>
> Numbers 21:7b-9

I don't know about you, but when I first read this, it seemed a little weird. Of course, many of my Christian brothers and teachers told me it pointed to Jesus on the cross: "Just as Moshe lifted up the serpent in the desert, so must the Son of Man be lifted up; so that everyone who trusts in him may have eternal life" (John 3:14-15).

"'As for me [*Yeshua*], when I am lifted up from the earth, I will draw everyone to myself.' He said this to indicate what kind of death he would die" (John 12:32-33). I could see that *Yeshua* would be lifted up on a pole, but I always thought the serpent referred to the one in the garden. How is looking at the devil on a pole supposed to heal people? When I discovered the serpent was actually a reference to our earthly nature, our flesh, it began to make more sense. I always wondered, *How can you compare Yeshua and Satan, this demonic being running around the earth?*

If the serpent is related to our earthly nature, as we have seen several allusions to in the tabernacle, the bronze, the hiss, and now the serpent on the pole. When *Yeshua* came to the earth, He took on an earthly nature just like ours: Satan.

> For what the Torah could not do by itself, because it lacked the power to make the old nature [serpent] cooperate, God did by sending his own Son as a human being with a nature like our own sinful one [*Yetzer Hara*—urge to do evil but without sin]. God did this in order to deal with sin, and in so doing he executed punishment against sin in the human nature [*HaSatan*].
>
> Romans 8:3 (CJB)

"We know that our old self [the serpent] was put to death on the execution stake with him, so that the entire body of our sinful propensities [*Yetzer Hara*, urge to do evil] might be destroyed and we might no longer be enslaved to sin" (Romans 6:6). I hope you caught that when *Yeshua* went to the stake, the serpent went to the stake. The *Yetzer Hara* was put to death. If you kill the urge to do evil, then you won't be a slave to sin anymore. That is for certain.

So *Yeshua* came in a body like ours. He dealt with *HaSatan*, the urge to do evil. God executed punishment against the serpent, our earthly nature. So what was nailed to the cross?

Now, if you were to step back a distance and look at the flesh of *Yeshua*'s body nailed to a pole and lifted into the air, you would see a serpent on a pole. Bronze is associated with judgment. You would see the judgment (bronze) against the flesh (serpent). You would see the bronze serpent.

The *Yetzer Hara* is the urge to do evil. There is a law associated with this serpent. It is the law of sin (urge) and death (to do evil). *Yeshua* came to free us from the law of sin and death. Unfortunately, many believers have misunderstood this and mistaken the law of sin and death for God's Torah, but *Yeshua* is bringing us back to His Torah.

The Torah will make you wiser than the serpent when you have the Messiah. The Torah, in union with the Messiah (Spirit), will set you free from the law of sin and death (the serpent).

I hope you are seeing the picture of how God uses animals to teach us about people or characteristics of people. I'm sure you are familiar with the beast nature. This might give you more to think about in regard to this beast nature. You believe *Yeshua* is God, the same God who wrote Genesis chapter 3, right? "Pay attention! I am sending you out like sheep among wolves, so be as prudent [wise] as snakes [serpent] and as harmless as doves" (Matthew 10:16).

Wolves were always associated with false prophets. Here, *Yeshua* compares the wolf to the serpent. A false prophet carries a message from the earthly realm, not the heavenly realm. He compares the sheep with the dove, which flies in the heavens. *Yeshua* tells us to be as wise as the false prophets but to be gentle; don't tear people's lives up with your wisdom like a wolf would.

> Likewise, you appear to people from the outside to be good and honest [like sheep], but inwardly you are full of hypocrisy and far from Torah [like wolves]. Woe to you hypocritical Torah-teachers, and *P'rushim*! You build tombs for the prophets and decorate the graves of the *tzaddikim* [righteous], and you say, "Had we lived when our fathers did, we would never have taken part in killing the prophets." In this you testify against yourselves that you are worthy descendants [seed] of those [serpent] who murdered the prophets. Go ahead finish what you started. You snakes! You sons of snakes! How can you escape being condemned to *Geihnnom* [to eat the dust of the earth].
>
> Matthew 23:28-33 (CJB)

Geihnnom was a reference to being cut off and exiled from Israel, from God's temple and his presence. It was a valley outside of Jerusalem where they burned trash and rubbish. It was a place where, in the time of the *Tanakh*, Israel got involved in paganism and passed their children through fire. This was a way of saying, "You will be cut off from Israel and sent out into darkness, where the pagans are, where the gnashing of the teeth and curse, lack, and decrease occur."

"Remember, I have given you authority; so you can trample down [crush the head of] snakes and scorpions, indeed, all the enemy's forces and you will remain completely unharmed" (Luke 10:19). This is a reference to people who are led by the earthly nature (enemy). Think about it. Who is your real enemy? Your enemy is your earthly nature with its desire for evil and the man who is operating in the earthly nature, doing evil against you. Your enemy is not so much a little, red, pitchfork-carrying devil. Think about this. Who tempts you?

> No one being tempted should say, "I am being tempted by God." For God cannot be tempted by evil, and God himself tempts no one. Rather each person is being tempted whenever he is being dragged off and enticed by the bait of his own desire [the serpent and urge to do evil]. Then, having conceived, the desire gives birth to sin; and when sin is fully grown, it gives birth to death.
>
> James 1:13-15 (CJB)

Is James not describing exactly what happened to Eve and what happens to us? Do you think Eve dealt with a different serpent than we do, or have we found another seed principle from the garden and now we are seeing a fuller picture of what might have happened in the past and what happens to us today?

The serpent was tempting Eve to eat fruit from the forbidden tree. Eve saw that the fruit looked desirable (urge) for making one wise. Look at what James says about wisdom: "Now, if anyone lacks wisdom, let him ask God, who gives to all generously and without reproach; and it will be given to him" (James 1:5). Eve was about to eat forbidden fruit in order to gain wisdom. The word *wisdom* in Genesis is the Hebrew word *sakal* and is related to the words:

abortion, *miscarry*, and *childlessness*. Look at what James says: "Then, having conceived, the desire [for this wisdom] gives birth to sin; and when sin is fully grown, it *gives birth* to death [childlessness, miscarry]" (James 1:15).

It might look desirable to our fleshy nature, but it will bring death in the day we partake of it. When Adam (a picture of the house of Judah) and Eve (a picture of the house of Israel) ate of this fruit, they were driven out of the garden, sent out into *Gehiniom*. They were sent out into an unproductive life or place of fruitlessness and miscarriage.

"'*Adonai*,' God, said to the serpent, 'Because you have done this you are cursed more than all livestock and wild animals. You will crawl on your belly and eat dust as long as you live'" (Genesis 3:14). The serpent is cursed to crawl on its belly and to eat the dust of the earth (death). The word *belly* is associated with the Hebrew word *gichon*, which is also the name of one of the rivers that flows from the garden. (See *Galatians* by Avi Ben Mordicia, pg. 461).

"A river went out of Eden to water the garden, and from there it divided into four streams" (Genesis 2:10). The Hebrew word *Nahar* means "river, prosperity, and light." Let's look a little into what is being said here. Light is associated with Torah. This is interesting because the root of the word *Torah* is *Yarah* (#3384). It means "to throw (to shoot an arrow), to point out, to teach, and to flow as water." It is also associated with rain.

The four rivers allude to the four levels of interpretation that flow from the Torah. The four levels are the *Pashat*, *Ramez*, *D'rash* and the *Sod*. This all points to the Messiah as the Holy Spirit who opens up the living waters found in the Torah. Remember, the river flowed from Eden, which meant "pleasure" and alludes to intimacy with the Messiah.

The four rivers also allude to the nations that flowed out to the four corners of the earth, as they rejected God's Torah. One day, they will come streaming back to God's mountain and His Torah.

In the *achrit-hayamem* [last days] the mountain of *Adonai*'s house will be established as the most important mountain. It will be regarded more highly than the other hills, and *all the Goyim [nation] will stream there*. Many peoples will go and say, "Come, let's go up to the mountain of *Adonai*, to the house of the God of *Yaákov*! He will teach us about *his ways*, and we will walk in his *path*." For out of *Tzion* will go forth *Torah*, the word of *Adonai* from *Yerushaliym*.

Isaiah 2:2-3, Micah 4:1-2 (CJB)

People are a body of living and moving water. "The name of the second river is Gichon; it winds throughout the land of Kush" (Genesis 2:13). This river is the one related to the belly. This is very interesting, as *Yeshua* speaks about this river as well. "Whoever puts his trust in me, as the Scripture says, rivers of living water will flow from his inmost being [belly]" (John 7:38).

Yeshua was alluding to the rivers that flowed out of Eden, the waters of salvation. However, outside of intimacy with the Messiah, called the Spirit life of Torah, this becomes a river of bitterness that flows. Bitterness is a poisonous serpent in the garden of greatness. This river of bitterness is spoken of in Revelation. "The name of the star was Bitterness and a third of the water became bitter, and many people died from the water that turned bitter" (Revelation 8:11).

The serpent, the urge to do evil, is a river flowing with bitterness. No one wants to drink the poison of these waters. Adultery is also connected to this bitterness. In fact, the fall of man was connected to idolatry and led to God divorcing Adam (Israel). There is a law in Numbers 5 about a woman suspected of adultery and it involves drinking a cup (lifestyle) of bitterness.

> When he has made her drink the water, then, if she is unclean and has been unfaithful to her husband, the water that causes the curse will enter her and *become bitter* so that her *abdomen* swells

and her private parts shrivel up; and the woman will become an object of cursing among her people.

Numbers 5:27

When *Yeshua* was about to go to the cross and He was in the garden, He said, "Let this cup pass before me, but not My will be done but your will be done." He was referring to the cup of bitterness that He drank for His bride.

It is from our belly that the serpent of bitterness and lies devours the dust of the earth (those living in the realm of death, the human perspective). When we break covenant with God, we stop the flow of living waters and we become the dust of the earth. This was the fruit of the forbidden tree.

When Adam fell, he fell from God's perspective, the living waters to man's perspective, the dust of the earth. The living waters are associated with Torah. The word for *water* is *mayim* and is related to *shamayim*, which is the Hebrew word for *heavens*. God's teachings fall like rain from heaven. These upper waters are alluded to in here. "God said, 'Let there be a dome in the middle of the water; let it divide the water from the water.' God made a dome and divided the water under the dome from the water above the dome, that is how it was" (Genesis 1:6-7).

So God's teachings fall like rain upon His people and then flow through them like a river. "May my teachings fall like rain, may my speech condense like dew, like rain on blades of grass, or showers on growing plants" (Deuteronomy 32:2).

Adam fell from God's perspective (living waters) to man's perspective (serpent, the dust of the earth). God now put enmity between these two perspectives. "I will put animosity between you and the woman, and between your seed and her seed; he will bruise your head, and you will bruise his heel" (Genesis 3:15). *Enmity* means "direct opposite, hatred or hostile." Paul speaks of the hostility between God's perspective and man's perspective. "For the mind controlled by the old nature [serpent] is *hostile* to God, because it does not submit itself to God's Torah—indeed it cannot" (Romans 8:7).

It cannot submit because of the enmity that was placed there, the curse of eating the fruit. This is the enmity between the *Yetzer HaTov* (desire to do good) and the *Yetzer Hara* (the desire to do evil). The woman is the bride. The Word of God is the seed planted in the heart of the woman. The Torah is written on the heart of the bride. They are the ones who have the Torah and *Yeshua*. The serpent is the earthly nature and the law of sin, and death is planted in their hearts. They are the ones who reject the Torah and have a beastly nature (mark of the beast).

> By God's grace, you, who were once slaves of sin, obeyed from the heart the pattern of teaching to which you were exposed [law of sin and death], and after you had been set free from sin, you became enslaved to righteousness [the Torah written on your heart]"
>
> Romans 6:17-18

The seed of the woman is Israel. They will rule over the earth (earthly nature). The human perspective (Satan) wants to be God but never will. The word for *fruit* in Hebrew is *pri* and means "fruit, reward or earnings (wages)." The fruit or reward of the tree of knowledge was to be bound or joined to the earthly nature, the human perspective.

"Then the eyes of both of them were opened, and they realized that they were naked. So they sewed fig leaves together to make themselves loincloths" (Genesis 3:7). We no longer viewed or experienced the world from God's perspective. See, the garden clothed man in God's perspective and protection. Now Adam found himself naked. Naked is outside of the Torah, hiding from the face of God. The tree of knowledge of good and evil is a tree of mixture. This is mixing man's ways with God's ways. Look what God says about mixing:

> I know what you are doing: you are neither cold nor hot. How I wish you were either one or the other! So, because you are lukewarm, neither cold nor hot, I will vomit you out of my mouth [drive you out of garden]! For you keep saying, "I am rich, I have gotten rich, I don't need a thing [sewed on the fig leaves]!" You don't know that you are the one who is wretched, pitiable, poor, blind and naked! My advice to you is to buy from me gold refined by fire, so that you may be rich; and white clothing, so that you may be dressed and not have to be ashamed of your nakedness; and eye-salve to rub on your eyes, so that you may see [from God's perspective]
>
> Revelation 3:15-18 (CJB)

The serpent's seed will bruise the heel of the seed of the woman (*Yeshua* and Israel). The word for *heel* in Hebrew is *aqueb* and it means "heel, to attack the rear (of an army), trickery, or heel catcher." This is where the name Jacob, or *Ya'akov* in Hebrew, comes from.

In the story of Jacob's life, we see the seed of the woman, God's perspective (Israel), overcomes the seed of the serpent, man's perspective (Jacob). On the feast day Yom Kippur, Jacob comes face-to-face with the angel of the Lord. He changes Jacob's name to Israel. He was moving from a lifestyle (name) of flesh (human perspective) to a lifestyle (name) of the Spirit (God's perspective).

> Then the man said, "From now on, you will no longer be called *Ya'akov*, but Israel; because you have shown your strength to both God and men and have prevailed." *Ya'akov* asked him, "Please tell me your name." But he answered, "Why are you asking about my name?" And blessed him there. *Ya'akov* called the place *P'ni-El* [face of God], "Because I have seen God *face-to-face*, yet my life is spared."
>
> Genesis 32:29(28)-31(30) (CJB)

This occurred on Yom Kippur, the Day of Atonement, also called the wedding of the Lamb, where we come face-to-face with God. This is a picture of the two cherubs. We receive a name change and begin the process of overcoming the serpent. We are given a new name or lifestyle. These are the white linen garments called the righteous deeds of the saints.

The Amalikites were a picture of *HaSatan* as they attacked the rear (heel) of Israel's army when they came out of Egypt. This reveals that the serpent whether in us or outside of us will always go for the weakest point. This is revealed in nature as the weakest point is the path of least resistance.

The human nature looks for the easy way or what appears as the path of least resistance. The serpent, the hiss, whisper and gossip loves to come from the rear, not head on. Ultimately, Israel will crush the head or strength of the serpent.

The Messiah crucified the *Yetzer Hara* so that we would manifest as sons of God (Israel) and have dominion over the earth and our earthly nature. On Yom Kippur, we are married to *Yeshua*. We become one spirit with Him. Now, by the Power of the Holy Spirit, we overcome the earthly nature. Look at what Paul says about this:

> So then, brothers, we don't owe a thing to our old nature [serpent] that would require us to live according to our old nature. For if you live according to your old nature, you will certainly die; but if, by the Spirit you keep putting to death [crushing the head] the practices of the body, you will live.
> Romans 8:12-13

So we are given God's perspective, called the mind of *Yeshua* or the Spirit. We will look at Romans 8:1-4. Let's see how Paul describes this: "Therefore, there is no longer any condemnation awaiting those who are in union with the Messiah" (Romans 8:1).

When? On Yom Kippur, also called the day of judgment, there is no condemnation awaiting those in Messiah. Paul's whole gospel revolved around Yom Kippur. He taught that when we showed up on Yom Kippur, the day God passes judgment on man's inner most secrets, we would be judged through the Messiah. Keep in mind that *judgment* in Hebrew means "deliverance." "On a day when God passes judgment on people's inmost secrets. [According to the good news as I proclaim it, he does this through the Messiah *Yeshua*]" (Romans 2:16).

"Why? Because the Torah of the Spirit which produces this life [life of Garden] in union with Messiah *Yeshua* has set me free from the torah of sin and death [the serpent]" **(Romans 8:2).** What is the Torah of the Spirit or the law of the Spirit? It is the Torah. God is Spirit, and He gave us His Torah. Therefore, the Torah of the Spirit is the Torah of God: "For we know the Torah is of the Spirit..." (Romans 7:14).

This Torah that produces the life of the garden only does so in union with *Yeshua*. The garden of Eden was the celebration phase of a Hebrew wedding between *Yeshua* and Adam (Israel). Israel, *Yeshua*, and Torah were one. This is the place of great liberty and freedom from the law of sin and death, the confines of the limited human perspective and its evil desire. "But if a person looks closely into the perfect Torah, which gives freedom, and continues becoming not a forgetful hearer but a doer of the work it requires, then he will be blessed in what he does" (James 1:25).

The human perspective is confined to the view of the dust of the earth. This place of restriction is where most of our pain comes from, the way we see and experience life. When Adam sinned, his image shattered. The oneness of Israel, *Yeshua*, and the Torah was broken. Adam no longer understood the oneness of God, and the world became a place of illusions. Man no longer saw things as they really are. Everything became fragmented and unrelated.

In this world of illusion, division is the norm. Things appear as being completely unrelated. Man's greatest difficulty understands God's oneness and how all of creation came from Him, including the things that appear as bad or wrong from our limited perspective. We think everything bad comes from the devil, when *HaSatan* is really the way we see things. Satan is just the illusion of the human perspective. The reason things often appear as bad is because of the devil, of our limited human perspective.

HaSatan can be understood as the human perspective and its desires, seeing from the realm of death (dust of the earth). The Jews associate *HaSatan* to the *Yetzer Hara*. Even in Judaism, the topic of Satan is not always easy to grasp. The influencing spirit from this realm has many names. Each name represents the activities of the name.

The exile from the garden has many names as well; but the most profound is *Egypt*, translated from the Hebrew word *Mitzaryim*. *Mitzaryim* means a place of constriction, limitation, and the narrow straights. This term describes a lifestyle in Hebrew called the world. This is what we are to overcome. We are to overcome the law of sin and death that flowed out of our limited human perspective that was like a river of bitterness, tears, and heartache.

Let's look at Paul's words again with these ideas in mind:

> For what the Torah could not do by itself, because it lacked the power to make the old nature [human perspective] cooperate [with God's perspective], God did this by sending his own son [or YHVH became like you] as a human being with a nature like ours [a Satan, human perspective] own sinful one [but without sin]. God did this in order to deal with sin, and in so doing he executed the punishment against sin in the human nature.
>
> Romans 8:3 (CJB)

In destroying the power of the human perspective and giving us God's perspective, we are able to approach the Torah by the power of the Holy Spirit. We are to walk out the Torah and interpret the Torah in the Spirit it was intended to be, to fulfill the Torah (Matthew 5:17). "So that the just requirement of the Torah might be fulfilled in us who do not run our lives according to what our old nature wants but according to what the Spirit wants" (Romans 8:4).

Without a marriage to *Yeshua*, we can never experience the life of the Torah of the garden. Those who try to get eternal life by Torah alone don't know the beginning (Genesis/*Yeshua*). God only took us out of Himself to bring us back to Himself. The Torah is the *Ketubah*, wedding covenant, not the groom. How can you have a marriage without the groom? The Torah (*Ketubah*) was given to us by the groom. We must see it from His perspective. It is all about relationship. This is the Hebrew model from the beginning.

Adam was married to *Yeshua*. He was one with *Yeshua* in the beginning. He saw from God's perspective. When Adam sinned, it led to a divorce. Adam was then bound or married to the human perspective, called Satan. We will explore this more later, but I want you to consider this verse as *HaSatan* is the human perspective:

> He [*Yeshua*] spoke very plainly about it. *Kefa* took him aside and began rebuking him. But turning around and looking at his *talmidim* [disciples] he rebuked *Kefa*. "Get behind me Satan!" he said, "For your thinking is from a human perspective, not from God's perspective."
>
> Mark 8:32-33

ה

THE CURSE ASSOCIATED WITH WOMAN

Now that we have looked at the fruit and its rewards as it was related to the serpent, I would like to explore the curse on the woman, bride: "To the woman he said, 'I will greatly increase your *pain in childbirth*. You will bring forth *children in pain*. Your *desire* will be toward your husband but he will rule over you'" (Genesis 3:16).

The curse associated with the woman, pain in childbirth, actually in Hebrew reads, "She is to conceive in sorrow and bear children in sorrow." The idea behind the Hebrew word *atzab* is "to sorrow, to labor, toil, carve, i.e. fashion or fabricate (in a bed sense)." This word is also connected to worship, worshiping fabricated or carved idols. This is not the worship of YHVH but idolatry. The only thing you will conceive in idolatry is sorrow.

She sorrows in conception. Conception speaks of bearing children but also of a mental conception. We see some interesting thoughts here. We can look at the obvious. Today, women have pain in bearing children. In this narrative, Eve also represents the house of Israel. Today, most of this house is found in the Christian church. We will look at this as it is related to the house of Israel, and there is some good insight here.

The woman saw the fruit looked good for making one wise, but this word for wisdom was related to abortion, miscarriage, and childlessness. When she ate the fruit, it aborted the life she once had. This was the life of the garden.

Because of this curse, the house of Israel will toil in sorrow, trying to conceive life. She will be desperate to conceive the life she once had. This life can only be found in the Messiah. Studying wedding vows (Torah) does not produce this life. Only intimacy with the Messiah, the groom, will produce children (sons of God).

This intimacy was pictured in the two cherubim and the spark of life that passed between them. The woman was created to receive. The house of Israel has been so desperate to receive that they have taken in anything. They have created gods of their own imagination, and this has not produced life but heartache and sorrow.

When we see this sorrow connected with bearing children, we see that even when the house of Israel is able to produce life, it will be in pain. Paul talks about this pain: "My dear children I am suffering the pain of giving birth to you all over again—and this will go on until the Messiah takes shape in you" (Galatians 4:19).

Paul is talking to those from the nations, the house of Israel. The pain will be in the Messiah taking shape in them. This taking shape is also called the manifestation of the sons of God.

Let's back up to the tree of knowledge for a minute. Remember, the word *fruit* also means reward or earnings. The earnings or wages of this tree is death. On the day you eat of it, you will surely die. Paul speaks of this same fruit as well.

"For the wages of sin is death, but the gift of God is eternal life in Christ Jesus our Lord" (Romans 6:23). Once Adam (Judah) and Eve (Israel) ate of this fruit, the serpent was cursed to eat the dust of the earth. Adam was joined or bound to the earthly nature. Adam was married to the earthly nature (*HaSatan*). This nature has a constant desire for sin and will pursue death like buried treasure. Paul explains this in Romans 7: "For we know that the Torah is of the Spirit but as for me. I am bound (married) to the old nature, sold as a slave to sin" (Romans 7:14).

Let's talk about this verse for a moment. Paul is obviously talking about before he had the Messiah. Paul explicitly explains in Romans 6 and 7 that he has been freed from the old nature. This is where I see many well-intentioned believers miss what Paul is saying here. In Romans 7:1, Paul explains who he is writing this letter to: "Surely you know brothers—for I am speaking to *those who understand Torah*..." (Romans 7:1).

If you don't understand the Torah, you will possibly miss what Paul is saying here. I assure you that when you do know the Torah, you will understand Romans much differently than you did before you knew the Torah.

Paul teaches us that the Torah is from the Spirit. It flows from God's perspective and is His desire and will. Paul explains that at one time, he was carnal and that he had the human perspective with its desires and will, the torah of sin and death, not God's Torah. If the Torah originated from the Spirit, God's perspective, then it can only be truly understood from His perspective. The Torah by the Spirit is the life of the garden. In fact, the Spirit is the river that flowed out of Eden, which only flows from intimacy with the Messiah.

In Romans 7:15-23, Paul begins to describe what it is like to try to follow God's Torah and yet have another torah at work in him, the law of sin and death. The serpent will always twist the Torah into something it is not: a religion.

Remember when *Yeshua* fasted for forty days and Satan came to tempt Him? *Yeshua* was in a body just like ours with a nature like ours. He was tempted by the same evil desire you and I are tempted by. The serpent tried to twist the Word and use it against *Yeshua*. *Yeshua* turned around and quoted the Word back from God's perspective or accurately (he did not add to or subtract from the Word), and the serpent had no authority.

The *Yetzer Hara* is at enmity with God's Word. It can't submit to God's Torah because it has its own torah. It can't submit to God because it wants to be God. The further we are removed from understanding the oneness of God and our oneness with Him the more we begin to create a god of our own imagination. In essence, we worship ourselves. The human perspective will never rule and reign with God because it wants to be God.

Paul wanted to be saved from the human perspective with its desire for sin, called law of sin and death, or a body bound for death (see Romans 24:25). Surely you will die the day you eat of it, for the wages of sin is death. Paul knew that if he could not be free from this body, bound for death, he could not receive the life offered in the Torah. The garden was an intimate relationship where Adam, *Yeshua*, and Torah were one. Unless we become one spirit with *Yeshua*, we will not fully understand the Torah.

> Similarly, the Spirit helps us in our weakness; for we don't know how to pray the way we should, But the Spirit himself pleads on our behalf with groaning to deep for words, and the one who searches hearts knows exactly what the Spirit is thinking, because his pleadings for God's people accord with God's will.
>
> Romans 8:26-27

The Spirit knows the mind or perspective of God. In fact, the Spirit is God's perspective and desire. Paul wanted saved from the *Yetzer Hara*; and then, in Romans 9, he explains how God did this through the Messiah. Our old nature was crucified with *Yeshua*. When *Yeshua* was crucified, died, and resurrected, Satan was defeated. However, this seems to have remained potential up to today. We still see people struggling with the body bound for death as much today as ever.

Until you come to the wedding, where you become one spirit with the groom, the spirit of *Yeshua*, this potential will not come into actuality. It won't manifest. God only took us from Himself to bring us back to Himself.

God took Eve out of Adam. Then He formed (Torah) her and then He presented her to him as a pure, spotless bride. This is exactly what God has done with us. He took us out of Himself and sent us out of the garden. He formed us and gave us His Torah, and now He will present us to Himself as a pure, spotless bride.

> As for husbands, love your wives, just as the Messiah loved the Messianic Community (His bride), indeed, gave himself up on behalf, in order to set it apart for God, making it clean through immersion (in Torah) in the Mikveh, so to speak, in order to present the Messianic Community *to himself* as a bride without defect.
>
> Ephesians 5:25-27

Eve was bone of Adam's bone. We will be spirit of *Yeshua*'s Spirit. Then the two shall become one. This happens at a wedding. You don't have intimacy unless you are married. You don't produce children, a greater household, until you get married. The bridal chamber where this potential is made actual is the garden of Eden. The garden is when we rule and reign on the earth.

The church world today is waiting for this marriage. That is why all of what *Yeshua* has done has remained potential for the most part. You see, Passover was about potential. Yom Kippur is the wedding where this potential is made actual. We move from a lifestyle of the flesh to a lifestyle of the Spirit. On Passover, we die with *Yeshua*. On Yom Kippur, we are resurrected with *Yeshua*. This is the first fruits of the resurrection.

God's intention with his creation was to manifest His names or Himself in the earth. While the church has been waiting to escape the earth, the creation is waiting for the sons of God to manifest in the earth. One of God's names is Son of God or Israel.

> The creation waits eagerly for the sons of God to be revealed [manifest] for creation was made subject to frustration—not willingly, but because of the one that subjected it. But it was given a reliable hope that it too would be set free from its bondage to decay and would enjoy the freedom accompanying the glory that God's children will have.
>
> Romans 8:19-21 (CJB)

The church is waiting to escape the earth, and creation is waiting for the sons of God to manifest. How will they manifest? For them, manifestation will be to return to their true identity.

The house of Israel has been in pursuit of God, but that is futile because God pursued Adam. Adam did not pursue God. God chose Israel. Israel didn't choose God. God chooses His first fruits, His bride. Now God is in pursuit of a people. He is re-gathering and ingathering them from the four corners of the earth. This is the exile from the garden. He is bringing them back to the garden, back to the beginning, back to Himself.

Let's finish looking at the curse on the woman. The woman's desire will be for her husband. The word *desire* in Hebrew also means "to run after." We have seen the effects of this curse in the world as women are often exploited in the earth as they try to find the approval of men or run after a husband. Men have not been a covering for women. There are only two types of men: those who exploit women and those who are a covering for women.

Let's talk about this as it is related to the house of Israel, which is primarily found in the church. She has a desire to run after a husband, to conceive the life she once had in the garden. Because she is unfamiliar with the wedding vows (Torah), she is left pursuing a husband but does not understand the approach or how to fully discern the counterfeit from the real: "*You did not choose me, I chose you*; and I have commissioned you to go and bear fruit, fruit that will last; so that whatever you ask from the Father in my name he may give you" (John 15:16).

In all the verses of the first fruits, God chose them. If the bride knew the Torah, she would know when and where to be waiting. You see, Moshe (Torah) leads the bride to the wedding, and the Spirit of Elijah transfigures the bride to the wedding. Remember the Mount of Transfiguration? Moshe and Elijah were there, and when they are together, *Yeshua* manifests.

The last prophet before the coming of *Yeshua* said this, as is written to the bride, the first fruits of the last generation: "*Remember the Torah of Moshe* my servant, which I enjoined on him at Horev, laws and rulings for all Israel (both houses). Look, *I will send you Eliyahu* [Elijah] *the prophet* before the coming of the great and terrible Day of *Adonai*" (Malachi 3:22(4:5)-3:23(4:6)).

The Torah teaches the bride the correct approach to God. It is the beauty preparation. This chasing after God has skewed her perception and can be heavily seen in the Greek Hellenistic mindset.

While in this desperate pursuit of God or a husband, she has opened herself up to many false teachings, counterfeit gods, and even idols over the centuries. This has brought on sorrow in conception and only heartache and division. Divorce leads us from place to place. This has only brought pain and suffering, a river of bitterness because life can only be found in the Messiah, but his is his choice, not hers. This heartache and sorrow is why so many are seeking to escape the earth instead of ruling and reigning in the earth. The desire to escape the earth should only be on the people who are under God's judgment. The rest should be manifesting as sons of God in the earth.

Do you remember the story of the woman at the well found in John chapter 4? Wells are associated with finding a bride in the Bible. Eliazar found Isaac's wife at a well. Jacob met Rachel at a well. He, *Yeshua* (house of Judah), meets a Samaritan (house of Israel) woman at the same well that Jacob (house of Judah) met Rachel (house of Israel).

Yeshua tells the woman she has had five husbands (this alludes to the Torah, which is also called the five husbands), and the one she is with now is not hers. She was not in pursuit of Him. At the right time, *Yeshua* pursued her and found her.

Part of the pain in childbirth that Paul described in Galatians is that even in the process of birthing new life in the house of Israel, they have a tendency to still think they are doing it. This mentality or perspective will actually try to abort the life in her. The labor pain is the pain of the struggle from one mindset (Greek, Western) to a Hebrew mindset. Remember the Hebrew word for *conceive* also meant a mental conception. The Messiah is choosing his bride and giving her the mind of Christ.

Cursed Ground: Adam's Pain

> To Adam he said, "Because you listened to what your wife said and ate from the tree about which I gave you the order, 'You are not to eat from it' the ground is cursed on your account; you will work hard to eat from it as long as you live. It will produce thorns and thistles for you and you will eat field plants. You will eat bread by the sweat of your forehead till you return to the ground—for you were taken out of it: you are dust, and you will return to dust."
>
> Genesis 3:17-19

The ground was cursed. Remember, Adam was made from this same ground, so this also alludes to his earthly nature, as we have been looking at already. The thorns and thistles also allude to curses and death. Notice the image this paints, as curses in our life are like thorns in the earth. This is all description of the serpent eating the dust of the earth. This is the hiss that would try to devour our lives. Both the ground and Adam's nature would produce bad fruit, sin, death, thorns, and thistles no matter how hard he worked it.

We see that Adam worked the land by the sweat of his brow. This speaks of both a physical and spiritual work. We realize that the physical work of the earth became more difficult. Many people believe Adam did not work in the garden, that he just lay around and ate fruit. That is not the Hebraic understanding of paradise, nor is it the biblical view. Adam ruled over the garden, and he cultivated it as well, only it did not produce thorns and thistles: "*Adonai*, God, took the person and put him in the garden of Eden to cultivate and care for it" (Genesis 2:15).

God created man to be active and full of life. He was created as a king with a territory to rule over. Paradise is not about being unproductive but a place to be fruitful. Hebrew has no word for *retirement* because it is not a concept that originates from the Torah. Paradise is where we are fruitful and reach our full potential. We originate from an active God, and He created us to be like Him on the earth.

Adam worked the garden in union with *Yeshua*. When in the scripture it says that Adam worked the soil by the sweat of his brow it is referring to him working by his own efforts. When Israel, *Yeshua*, and Torah were one, heaven and earth worked for Adam, but after the fall they worked against him. Adam's *desire* became to work by his own efforts rather than enter God's rest.

Adam represents the house of Judah. Judah will work the Torah, the law of the land, by his own efforts. The land speaks of Torah and the soil of our lives. Because of the human perspective, this Torah will produce thorns and thistles. The earthly nature is hostile toward God's Torah. Inevitably, curse and lack will be found in their lives.

Paul explicitly talks about this conundrum. No matter how hard he works, this Torah, it is not producing the fruit it offers but instead thorns and thistles, sin and death. It was not the Torah's fault but the curse of the earthly nature. Paul talks about how the commandment that was intended to bring me life was found to bring me death: "And I died. The commandment that was intended to bring me life was found to be bringing me death" (Romans 7:10).

Romans 7:14-26 is really a reference to the house of Judah. Paul talks about what it is like to be a Jew. One who has the Torah and tries to work the Torah and produce life by obeying it and yet they experience thorns and thistles. Sin springs to life and leads to death. He describes himself as a miserable creature.

Many people read these verses and relate to them and say, "I'm another Paul." However what Paul is actually describing here is what it is like to be a Jew who has the Torah but does not have the Messiah. He is describing being a Torah observant Jew who needs to be saved.

I want to mention something else about *HaSatan*. Most of the Hebrew scholars and Jewish sages place the definite article *Ha* in front of Satan. *Ha* is *the*. The Satan because they don't so much see *HaSatan* as a creature out there trying to get God's people but a realm. All things associated with the realm of death they sum up as the adversary. Everything associated with man's fall and the death he would experience. Remember, they know that Hebrew is a verb-oriented language. English is a noun-oriented language and takes the focus of our thought away from the action and focuses it onto a person, place, or thing.

English language will force movements and names into nouns, people, etc. When I say the name anti-Christ, a Christian begins to immediately think of a person, an evil person. A Hebrew will picture a movement on the earth opposed to the anointing (*Christ*, *Messiah* means anointed). This can be in a person as well, but the focus is on the movement or activity. This is a movement other than the anointing. Let me give you an example.

If someone were to read a story about Katrina five hundred years from now and how she brought great devastation to Louisiana when she moved and how she destroyed homes, drove people out of the city, and ruined lives, even killing people, well, of course, if they did not know the history of how there was a storm that built up into a huge hurricane in the Gulf of Mexico and we named this movement (storm) Katrina, this storm would almost seem as though it had a personality when it did, by nature or design, what storms do. They would naturally think, *Who was this Katrina lady?*

Most storms in your life are caused by *HaSatan*, the realm of death, and this is often connected to the earthly human nature with its desire for sin. "Having one's mind controlled by the old nature [*HaSatan*] is death…" (Romans 8:6).

One more example here in Malachi: "Look I will send to you *Eliyahu* the prophet before the coming of the great and terrible day of *Adonai*" (Malachi 3:23(4:5)).

It says Elijah, the prophet, yet it is not the person Elijah that is coming. Remember, *Yeshua* referred to John the Baptist as Elijah the prophet. It is talking about the anointing. The Spirit and movement that was upon Elijah will be upon us in the last days. I'm looking for a people whose lifestyles (movement) resembles that of Elijah's life. In the same way, *HaSatan* is the movement that is opposite of the anointing. Names like Jezebel, Ba'al, pharoah, anti-Christ, night, darkness, adversary, slanderer, and enemy all reveal a movement or lifestyle all related to the realm of death.

Let's talk again about *Yeshua* when He was in the wilderness, fasting. Have you ever fasted for long? Believe me, your flesh, the *Yetzer Hara*, begins to speak to you. The *Yetzer Hara* in *Yeshua*'s human body spoke to Him and tried to twist the Word and use it against the Spirit of God. *Yeshua*, in turn, quoted the Word in the correct perspective back to His flesh and by the power of the Holy Spirit, the Spirit of God in Him ruled over His earth.

Often, people read the Word and twist it into something that it is not, and it sure does not produce life. *Yeshua* overcame *HaSatan* as it is related to His own *Yetzer Harah*, the serpent.

Next, we see Peter trying to rebuke *Yeshua*.

He began teaching them that the Son of Man had to endure much suffering and be rejected by the elders, the head *cohanim* and the Torah-teachers and that he had to be put to death; but after three days, he had to rise again. He spoke very plainly about it. *Kefa* took him aside and began rebuking him. But, turning around and looking at his *talmidim*, he rebuked *Kefa*, "Get behind me, Satan!" he said, "For your thinking is from a human perspective, not from God's perspective."

Mark 8:31-33 (CJB)

Now *Yeshua* has overcome *HaSatan,* the realm of death, as it is related to other people. Here, He rebukes or corrects *Kefa* and overcomes the voice. The seed of the serpent is related to the human perspective with its desires. This is found in our old nature and in those still living in the old nature.

It is the seed of the woman, the Messiah and His Torah, that is planted in our hearts. We became one Spirit with the Messiah on Yom Kippur. We will then begin to crush the power of the seed of the serpent in us, and then we are overcomers—not just potentially overcomers but actual overcomers. Each level you overcome, you are anointed to mentor someone else to overcome, for the weapons of our warfare are not carnal but mighty to the pulling down of strongholds.

Truly, our Greco Roman mindset has skewed and even somewhat twisted the way we see God's Word, His Torah of life. The way we view the world has been fragmented, and it has caused great pain and sorrow. This mindset has skewed our approach to God and also to sin. This Greek Hellenistic mindset has seeped into the house of Judah as well.

Back to Adam and this ground that produces thorns and thistles. The thorns speak of pricking in the flesh. This carries the idea of the desire to serve oneself, to be grieved, loath, to fear and to be anxious. This alludes to the grief that Judah will experience as they *desire* to work the Torah by their own self-seeking efforts; not that they always will, but the curse is the desire to. When we are self-seeking, we are our own owners, and this creates anxiety, as God is our real owner.

When *Yeshua* came to fulfill the Torah, which simply meant "to walk it out correctly and to teach it accurately," the house of Judah had a hard time receiving or resting in the Torah of the Messiah. Their desire was to continue in the torah of their perspective. It took a Damascus road experience to wake up Paul, to open his eyes. *Yeshua* was never against the Torah, but he challenged many of the Jewish sages' interpretation of the Torah.

The whole forty days in the wilderness, *Yeshua* was confronting the interpretation of God's Word from this same perspective. *Yeshua* had exactly the same *Yetzer Hara* that the rest of the house of Judah had. In fact, the forty-day incident was a mini picture of His challenging of the house of Judah's interpretation of the Word from this human perspective. Once, He even tells them that their father is the devil or Satan: "You belong to your father, Satan, and you want to carry out your father's desires..." (John 8:44).

This is the same as saying you are committed to the human nature and its view, not God's perspective. Remember, He rebukes Peter, calling him Satan. *Yeshua* was just addressing the origin of this viewpoint. It did not originate with God but man.

Paul didn't want saved from the Torah but from the human nature, the body bound for death or serpent cursed to eat the dust of the earth. Paul wanted the mind of *Yeshua*. Now, with the mind of Christ and the Spirit of God, we could now go back into the Torah and produce life. The Torah was never intended to be walked in outside of a marriage, being one Spirit with *Yeshua*. See, the curse on Adam and the house of Judah was to work the Torah apart from the Messiah. Eve (the house of Israel) wanted a husband outside of a covenant (the Torah).

From the beginning, God took us out of Himself only to bring us back to Himself. The two cherubs at the front (east) of the garden were a constant reminder that the relationship was the plan from the beginning. Today, somehow, in the church, Paul's writings have been skewed to teach that *Yeshua* came to save us from the Torah, but that was not Paul's intent. This leaves us bound to the law of sin and death and the earthly nature. Nowhere in the prophets or the Torah does it say that is what the Messiah was coming to do. In fact, they say the opposite and call any prophet that would teach against the Torah a false prophet and an antichrist.

When Paul said we are no longer under the law, he was talking about the law of sin and death. We have been saved from the old nature. We are freed from sin's torah, not God's Torah.

These types of teachings have left the work of the Messiah as potential and not fully manifesting in the earth. The feast of Passover deals with potential, and the feast of Yom Kippur deals with potential becoming actual. On Yom Kippur, *HaSatan* is bound up, no access in your life. As I mentioned before, *HaSatan* has a gematria (numerical value) of 364 because one day a year, he is bound. On Yom Kippur, you are likened unto angels.

> On the contrary, you have come to Mount *Tziyon*, that is, the city of the living God, heavenly *Yerushalayim*; *to myriads of angels in festive assembly*; to a community of the firstborn whose names have been recorded in heaven; to a judge who is God of everyone; to spirits of righteous people who have been brought to the goal [a wedding].
>
> Hebrews 12:22-23

After Yom Kippur, *HaSatan* is set free for a little while. Watch this *Yeshua* come in a body like ours with a nature like ours but without sin. Every step of *Yeshua*'s life, He overcame the human nature, never once sinning, giving in to its desires. Every time He overcame, the anointing grew. Now, when *Yeshua* was crucified, death could not hold Him, for He never sinned. He never gave death a foothold. What was really crucified was the *Yetzer Hara*, our old nature: "We know that our old self was put to death on the execution stake with him ..." (Romans 6:6a).

Now, on Yom Kippur, you become one Spirit with *Yeshua*. Here lies the power. The very spirit that overcame the realm of death in *Yeshua*'s life is now in you. This anointed, set-apart Spirit is the power to overcome *HaSatan*. Now, after Yom Kippur, you begin to walk out or manifest the potential of God, which is to subdue the earthly nature and rule and reign in the earth. The amazing part is that it is the Spirit of God that is doing this in you.

The old nature does not want to be in union with God; it wants to be God. This is to achieve or live by our own efforts called religion instead of relationship. The further we move away from the revelation of God's oneness and our oneness with Him the more we begin to worship ourselves.

HaSatan can be understood as the adversary. The adversary is anything that blocks or hinders your ability or limits you from perceiving God. When Adam sinned, the world became the world of illusions. No longer could Adam see God in everything. This illusion is the Satan.

In Hebrew mindset, each time you sin, you create an adversary, another hindrance that blocks the reality of God in your life. This is a blindness that prevents you from seeing God.

When we look at the tabernacle, each court had a veil. From the outside, there were three veils that prevented you from seeing God's *Sh'khinah* and the holy of holies. These veils represent the flesh and can also be likened to character flaws. These flaws can hinder our ability to perceive God in our circumstances and in each other. All we see is people's flaws instead of the presence of God inside of them.

Yeshua pierced the veil when he died. This veil was nailed to the cross, and its representative in the temple was torn from top to bottom. When God removes this veil (human perspective), from our eyes, we will see Him as He is. "Dear friends, we are god's children now; and it has not yet been made clear what we will become. We do know that when he appears, we will be like him; because we will see him as he really is" (1 John 3:2).

ט

SUMMARY ONE

> At the beginning I announced the end, proclaiming in advance things not yet done; and I say that my plan will hold. I will do everything I please to do.
>
> Isaiah 46:10 (CJB)

We have looked at the seed principles in the beginning. We have followed them through Scripture to see them grow. Let's recap on some of what we have seen so far.

The curse that fell upon Eve, which also represents the house of Israel, as a result of eating the forbidden fruit was a desire to run after a husband. Biblically, the bride is chosen and presented a *ketubah*, which is a wedding covenant and a picture of the Torah. Her desire for a husband has led her to run after many lovers. The book of Hosea describes this in great detail. He refers to the house of Israel as having a spirit of whoredom. When her pursuit for lovers is fruitless, she will want to return to her first husband, the Messiah. "She will pursue her lovers but not catch them. She will seek them but won't find them. Then she will say, 'I will go and return to my first husband; because things were better for me then [before she ate the fruit] than now'" (Hoshea 2:9(7)).

This saga has been played out over the centuries by the house of Israel, which can primarily be found in the church today. You can see from the church history how this has played out. The house of Israel has gone after many lovers, and as a result, she has grown a mile wide and an inch deep.

She has tried to birth children while stating that she is waiting for the Messiah to come to marry her. There is no greater household or children before the wedding. This would not be the proper order. What this has done is produce children after the flesh. They are simply walking out what their forefather, Abraham, did, which further reveals just who these people really are. They are the seed of Abraham.

Abraham tried to birth a child of promise before he had received a name change. This name change is pictured as Yom Kippur, the wedding, where God added the letter *Hey* (H) to Abraham's and Sarah's names. The letter *Hey* in Hebrew represents the breath or Spirit of God. It also has a numerical value of 5, which represents the five books of Moshe. God placed the Spirit and Torah into Abraham's life, and only then could he produce the true seed, the child of promise.

By trying to produce a greater household before the wedding or outside of the wedding produced a child of the flesh. Abraham produced a child of flesh named Ishmael. Likewise, The house of Israel has produced a lot of fleshy children over the centuries.

She has not understood that you do not pursue God. He is in pursuit of a people. She has missed her appointments, which lead her to a wedding called the feast days of God. She has inherited some counterfeit appointments from the cultures she has been in. She, for the most part, has not accepted her *Ketabah*, the wedding vows called the Torah, but she soon will, as it is her destiny. This was only a season.

Adam, who also represents the house of Judah, has worked the soil in sorrow. He has sought his own efforts to walk out the Torah. This has resulted in compounding the commandments into thousands of manmade commandments. This is simply adding to the Torah. He has tried to walk out the Torah apart from a relationship with the Messiah fulfilling the curse related to the earth and Adam. This has become a yoke that has been unbearable for the Jewish people as well as the returning nations (house of Israel).

All of this brings us back to the way. Both cherubs are looking into the same mercy seat, ark, tablets, etc. They are just coming from different sides (views). This is the power of two when in unity. They keep the way to the garden of Eden and the tree of life (Torah by the Spirit). God only took Eve out of Adam (two separate people) to bring them back together (become one flesh). Likewise, He only took the house of Israel out of the side of the house of Judah to bring them back together as one new man.

> For He himself is our shalom—he has made us both one and has broken down the *m'chitzah* (flesh, law of sin and death) which divided us by destroying in his own body (earthly nature) the enmity occasioned by the Torah (which was supposed to produce life), with its commandments set forth in the form of ordinances. He did this in order to create in union with himself from the two groups a single new humanity (the one new man), and thus make shalom.
>
> Ephesians 2:14-15 (CJB)

The nations (house of Israel, picture of a bride) are returning to the Torah (*Ketubah*), and the Jewish people (house of Judah, picture of a husband) are beginning to see the Messiah *Yeshua*. They both have to shake off some religious baggage associated with the curse and fall of man. These two cherubs (witnesses) are finding themselves face-to-face on Yom Kippur.

The Jews (house of Judah) are beginning to recognize the house of Israel as she is stripping off her Egyptian garments (Gentile garments). These two cherubs are finding themselves face-to-face. One of them is carrying the testimony of the Torah, and the other is carrying the testimony of the Messiah. When the two come back together, it is here that conception, life, is found. "For if their [house of Judah] casting *Yeshua* aside means reconciliation for the world [house of Israel] what will their acceptance mean? It will be life from the dead" (Romans 11:15).

Yeshua said, "Where two or more are gathered in my name (lifestyle) I am in their midst." These cherubs are a picture of Torah and Spirit coming together, and that is the Way. This brings conception and a greater household.

The flaming sword (voice of God) appears between these two cherubs and begins to turn as the two begin a dialogue. As the *Midrash* intensifies and the unity grows, the flaming sword begins to turn in all directions, and light (fire) goes forth and consumes their enemies. This unity is a magnetic field that holds these two together. This magnetic field is the Messiah. This is called the *Olam Haba*, the world to come, or the Messianic age.

Because we in the church have not fully understood the beginning, we have created an end of our own imagination. Here is something to think about. Evangelical dispensation theology teaches a theory. Part of that theory is the age of law and the age of grace. It is taught that before *Yeshua* came, we were under the age of law (Torah) and that *Yeshua* came to save us from the age of law and usher in the age of grace.

They believe that the age of law was the age of Torah, as if to say there was a time period (age of law) when people had to do the Torah in order to be saved. That is absolutely a misunderstanding. The Torah was never given to anybody in any age to get them to heaven by keeping it. Torah taught them how to live successfully while on the earth.

It was taught that now that *Yeshua* came, we are no longer under law but under grace, that now we go to heaven because we believe in *Yeshua* and we no longer have to walk out the Torah. "He [Abraham] believed in *Adonai* and he credited it to him as righteousness" (Genesis 15:6). We have in all ages been saved by believing in God (*Yeshua*). This is not a new concept but an old one:

This is why it was credited to his [Abraham's] account as righteousness. But the words, "It was credited to his account..." were not for him only. They were written also for us, who will certainly have our account credited too because we have trusted in him who raised *Yeshua* our Lord from the dead.

Romans 4:22-24

We are saved the same way today as they were in ancient times. What does this mean for the dispensational theory? It means their view might be skewed a little from the Hebraic view, and we might have to adjust a little if we want to understand things Hebraicly.

They teach that Paul teaches, that *Yeshua* saved us from the law (Torah). This presents a problem. Paul never wanted saved from the Torah. He knew the Torah was the instructions of God that governed the garden, that *Yeshua* was the personification of the Torah. He wanted saved from the earthly nature with its desires for evil called the law of sin and death.

When Adam ate the forbidden fruit and sin entered the world, the wages of sin is death. The gospel of the garden says, "The seed of the woman (*Yeshua*) would crush the head of the serpent (power of the earthly nature)," not come and free people from the Torah. God's everlasting Word is not the serpent.

There are only two laws: the law of life and righteousness called the Torah and the law of sin and death. If you're not in the Torah, you are in the law of sin and death, for sin is violation of the Torah: "Everyone who keeps sinning is violating Torah—indeed, sin is violation of Torah" (1 John 3:4).

If *Yeshua* freed us from the Torah, then we were freed from a life of righteousness and blessing and bound to a life of sin and death, sickness and disease. This would obviously leave a people with a huge desire to escape the earth. People want to escape the furnace, hell on earth. This leaves them with no vision of overcoming the world and ruling and reigning in the earth as Adam did and gives a totally different direction in life.

Paul talks about how all of creation is waiting for the sons of God to manifest, not escape the earth. He continues that creation is set free from bondage by the glory they have, their lifestyle. They are bringing heaven to earth.

> And not only it, but we ourselves, who have the first fruits of the Spirit, groan inwardly as we continue waiting eagerly *to be made sons*—that is, to have our whole bodies redeemed and set free [from the *Yetzer Hara*, or law of sin and death]. *It was in this hope we were saved...*
>
> Romans 8:23-24

Paul said it was in the hope of being freed from the *Yetzer Hara*, the law of sin and death, that we were saved. Think about that. Was that the hope we were saved in?

Most people I meet were saved in the hope that they won't die and spend forever in hell. This has become a fear-based message. Is that what Paul really taught, or was it a message of faith that the Messiah came to save you not only to go to heaven but He wants to take you back to the garden? He came to free you from the desire to do evil and the shame and guilt that goes with it, the shame and guilt that is like a fire that never quits.

He is writing His Torah upon your heart so you will once again have the desire to do good. The earthly nature is the realm of earth. This is the hell from which Paul wanted saved. This realm produces the desire to do evil and is likened unto a fire that will never go out; there is torment and pain that flows from the guilt and shame of our miss deeds. *Yeshua* came to give you peace here on earth.

Yeshua came to save you from the law, the law of sin and death, so you could eat the fruit of the tree of life and manifest God's will in the earth. He put His potential in you to make you sons of God and to set all of creation free through you, as you (Israel) will rule (as) God in union with the Messiah, not apart from Him or His Torah.

In the beginning, Israel, Torah, and *Yeshua* were one. Now, in the end, they will all be one again. This is not a message of fear. Fear is a false representation of your future. It's an illusion. "He will wipe away every tear from their eyes. There will no longer be any death [sin]; and there will no longer be any mourning, crying or pain; because the old order has passed away" (Revelation 21:4). *HaSatan* is an illusion, a lie, and a lie is something that is not real. This exists outside of the garden, and at its root are disease, discomfort, and pain. "No longer will there be any curses. The throne of God and of the lamb will be in the city, and his servants will worship Him" (Revelation 22:3).

Watch these next two verses, as their origin is in Isaiah and we will look at it: "For the lamb at the center of the throne (your heart) will shepherd them, will lead them to springs of living water, *and God will wipe away every tear from their eyes*" (Revelation 7:17).

"When what decays puts on imperishability and what is mortal puts on immortality, then the passage in the Tanakh will be fulfilled: 'Death is swallowed up in victory'" (1 Corinthians 15:54). The question is: when will this happen? When will death (earthly nature) be swallowed (overcome) by victory (heavenly nature, Spirit)? When will the tears be wiped away?

> On this mountain, he will destroy the *veil* that covers the faces of all the people the *veil* enshrouding the nations. He will *swallow up death forever*. *Adonai Elohim* will *wipe away the tears* from every face, and he will remove from all the earth the disgrace his people suffer. For *Adonai* has spoken.
>
> Isaiah 25:7-8

Ani Yosef

The veil is the earthly human perspective. *HaSatan* is the illusion. When is a veil removed? At a wedding, Yom Kippur, the veil is removed from the face of the bride. Now death (the old nature) is swallowed (overcome) up by life. This is the Spirit life accompanying the sons of God.

Not having a good strong Hebraic understanding of the Word, the Torah, and the gospel message from the beginning can begin to skew our picture from the original intent. The church wants to escape the earth, and God wants them to overcome the world and to rule and reign in the earth.

Age of law verses age of grace. *Yeshua* came to save us from an age or time when we were divorced from God and sold as slaves to sin, an age of lawlessness called law of sin and death. By His grace, He is bringing us back to His Torah of life, the way of Shalom.

The house of Israel has the potential of God. She has just not been taught the Torah. The Torah teaches how that potential is to manifest in a life of righteousness, where we overcome, not escape, the law of sin and death that originated from the tree of knowledge. The end of Revelation is the beginning of Genesis. We are walking back into the garden. Even as this is happening, there are those who are outside still bound to sin and death. Remember, this is a process.

> How blessed are those who wash their robes, so that they have the right to eat from the tree of Life and go through the gates into the city! Outside are the homosexuals, those involved with the occult and with drugs, the sexually immoral, murderers, idol-worshipers, and everyone who loves and practices falsehood.
>
> Revelation 22:14-15

"For just as the new heavens [new Spirit] and new earth [new heart] I am making will continue in my presence," says *Adonai*, "so will your descendants and your name continue. Every month on Rosh Hadesh [new moon] and every week on Shabbat, everyone living will come to worship in my presence," says *Adonai*, "As they leave, they will look on the corpses of the people who rebelled against me. For their worm [related to serpent as they both eat dust, also means to blurt out] will never die, and their fire [shame and desire for evil] will never be quenched; but they will be abhorrent to all humanity."

Isaiah 66:22-23 (CJB)

I saw no temple in the city, for *Adonai*, God of heaven's armies, is its temple, as is the lamb. The city has no need for the sun or the moon to shine on it, because God's *Sh'khinah* gives it light [flaming sword] and its lamp is the lamb. The nations will walk by its light, and the kings of the earth will bring their splendor into it. Its gates will never close, they stay open all day because night will not exist there, and the honor and splendor of the nations will be brought into it. *Nothing impure* may enter it nor *anyone who does shameful things or lies*; the only ones who may enter are those whose names are written in the Lamb's Book of Life.

Revelation 21:22-27 (CJB)

I hope this is shedding a little more light on the gospel of the garden from the beginning and on Yom Kippur. As Paul proclaimed his gospel, "On a day when God passes judgment on people's inmost secrets (Yom Kippur). [According to the good news as I (Paul) proclaim it, he does this through the Messiah *Yeshua*]" (Romans 2:16).

I hope you are also seeing *HaSatan*, the realm of death from the Hebraic perspective. The realm of death is hell, and we will look at this more as we go. The terms and ideas presented here are only scratching at the surface. These concepts are huge realms in and of themselves. In no way are they limited just to these short explanations. My attempt is to give some direction and spark the desire for further studies and to give you another perspective that I hope adds to your revelation of God's plan for your life.

ל

THE ROMAN ROAD

The book of Romans really talks about taking the potential of God and bringing it into existence. Something is only concealed so that it can be revealed. Our salvation is the potential of God. Redemption is related to manifesting the potential of God, but that can only be done in union with Salvation. When salvation and redemption come together, it is the glory of God. The book of Romans is set in the fall feast season and has Yom Kippur as a major theme.

When Adam sinned, he was divorced from the garden and sent out or exiled. As mentioned before, this exile has many descriptive names: darkness, lake of fire, the furnace, and one we will be looking at, God's wrath or anger.

Paul explains God's wrath or anger as a lifestyle of sinning, such things as lying, stealing, cheating, blasphemers, God haters, disobedience to parents, etc. This is called the law of sin and death. The garden is the Spirit life and is a lifestyle completely opposite of God's wrath. It is a lifestyle of righteous deeds of peace and blessing free from the bondage of sin. "What is revealed [made manifest] is God's anger from heaven against all the godlessness and wickedness of people who in their wickedness keep suppressing the truth [Torah]" (Romans 8:19).

Now watch how Paul describes this anger against those who suppress the truth:

> This is why God has given them up to the vileness of their heart's lusts [law of sin and death written on their hearts], to shameful misuse of each other's bodies. They have exchanged the truth [Torah] of God for falsehood, by worshipping and

> serving created things, rather than the Creator—praised be he for ever. Amen... In other words since they have not considered God worth knowing, God has given them up to worthless ways of thinking; so that they do improper things. They are filled with every kind of wickedness, vile, greed and vice; stuffed with jealousy, murder, quarrelling, dishonesty, and ill-willed; they are gossips, slanderers, haters of God; they are insolent, arrogant and boastful, they plan evil schemes. They disobey their parents; they are brainless, faithless, heartless and ruthless. They know well enough God's righteous decree that people who do such things deserve to die; yet not only do they keep doing them, but they applaud others who do the same.
>
> Romans 1:24-32 (CJB)

Paul is talking not about people who don't know who God is but people who do know who God is and yet they continue to practice sin. This is Paul's description of God's wrath or anger. So rather than seeing people manifesting the potential of God, we see the opposite manifesting. This is still the same today. God's anger is a lifestyle of sin and death. Now watch this next verse as opposed to God's wrath.

> The creation waits eagerly for the sons of God to be revealed [to manifest God's favor] for the creation was made subject to frustration [God's anger, the law of sin and death] not willingly, but because of the one who subjected it, but it was given a reliable hope [that the seed of the woman would crush the head of the serpent, Genesis 3:15] that it would be set free from bondage to decay [the *Yetzer Haran*] and would enjoy the freedom [torah of the Spirit] accompanying the glory [lifestyle, Torah becomes flesh; John 1:14, Hebrews 8:10] that God's children will have. We know that until now, the whole creation has been groaning as with pains of childbirth [pain alludes to the curse on the woman as well as to Hoshea 13:12-14 and Galatians 3:19, the Messiah taking shape] and not only it but we ourselves, who have the

first fruits of the Spirit groan inwardly [potential of God] as we continue waiting eagerly to be made sons [overcome the earthly nature and manifest the potential of God]. That is to have our whole bodies redeemed and set free [from law of sin and death]. It was in this hope that we were saved...

Romans 8:19-24a (CJB)

This is all about taking what is revealed in the earth: the wrath of God, the lifestyle of sin and death, and, now that we are saved, overcoming that lifestyle, manifesting as son so that what is revealed or manifesting in the earth is the glory of God. This is the lifestyle of the garden. This is the opposite of the lake of fire. The glory of God is the Spirit life, walking with God in the cool of the day, entering His rest.

Here is the interesting part: Paul is speaking in future tense when He says, "waiting to be made sons." What does this mean? Is this a future event?

Is Paul teaching that being led by God's spirit is a future event? Once again, this is the difference between potential and actual. Do you realize that Paul also talks about being considered righteous (salvation, Abrahamic covenant) and being made righteous (the walk of redemption). In the church, many of us missed this.

In Romans 7, Paul explained what it was like to be a Jew to have the Torah and want the life that was offered in the Torah, the life of the garden, but because of the *Yetzer Hara*, with its desires, he found it impossible to obtain the life the Torah offered. He referred to it as having the body bound for death.

Paul desperately wanted freed from this curse so that he could experience this life, eternal life that the Torah offered. Paul goes further to describe that what the Torah lacked the power to do, make the earthly nature cooperate, God did by sending his son *Yeshua*. Now that our old nature was put to death, we would fulfill the righteous requirement of the Torah. This lifestyle would become actual in us who don't live our lives according to what the old nature (God's wrath) wants but according to what the Spirit wants (manifest as sons).

The Torah is our future and our inheritance. When Paul says, "Waiting to be made sons," he is talking about the process of overcoming, taking the potential and what *Yeshua* did at Passover, crucifying our earthly nature, and now making it actual.

The house of Israel has been waiting to escape the earth because what has been revealed is God's wrath. The church, for the most part, wants to escape earth, yet creation is waiting for them to manifest and set creation free by the glory of God that will accompany them.

The book of Romans revolves around the topic of Yom Kippur, taking the potential of Passover and making it actual. This involves a wedding and a name change. With this name change, we see a lifestyle change from the life of the flesh to the life of the Spirit.

Paul teaches that we are reconciled to God through *Yeshua*'s death (Passover, salvation, potential). The church has stopped for a season right here. Even though the potential of God is there, what is revealed is God's wrath. Paul, however, continues with how much more we will be delivered by his life (walk of redemption) now that we are reconciled (saved).

> Therefore, since we have now come to be considered righteous by means of his bloody sacrificed death (Passover), how much more will we be delivered through him from the anger of God's judgment (Yom Kippur). For if we were reconciled with God through his son's death when we were enemies, how much more will we be delivered by his life, now that we are reconciled.
>
> Romans 5:9-10 (CJB)

Salvation deals with what we can't see, like heaven and our confession. Redemption deals with what we can see, like earth and our conduct. When our confession (heaven) matches our conduct (earth), it is called *Ma HaKavod*, manifest presence of God. Heaven has come to earth. God has given us a new confession (new heaven) and a new conduct (new earth), and we are a new creation.

What does this mean? The book of Hebrews will shed a little light on this subject. The author talks about how the Israelites heard God's Word (Torah) at Mount Sinai; however, God was disgusted with them because they disobeyed the message.

> Who were the people who, after they heard, quarreled so bitterly? All those whom Moshe brought out of Egypt. And with whom was God disgusted for forty years? Those who sinned—yes, they fell dead in the wilderness. And to whom was it that he swore that they would not enter his rest? Those who were *disobedient*. So we see that they were unable to enter because of lack of *trust*.
>
> Hebrews 3:16-19 (CJB)

Disobeying the message is synonymous with lack of faith or trust. Faith and obedience are united. Look at this warning to us:

> Therefore, let us be terrified of the possibility that, even though the promise [potential] of entering his rest remains, any of you might be judged to have fallen short of it [of manifesting it]; *for Good News* has also been proclaimed to us, just as it was to them. But the message they heard didn't do them any good, because those who heard it did not combine it with trust.
>
> Hebrews 4:1-2 (CJB)

He warns us that the same good news is proclaimed to us, but if we disobey the message as they did, we will not enter His rest, the fullness of the Spirit life. We must combine the message with faith and obedience.

Ani Yosef

Well, if we are taught the same gospel that was taught at Mount Sinai, then what was taught at Mount Sinai? We know they received the Torah, so Torah has to be part of the message. What good news are we taught today? One that tells us to disobey the Torah, the same Torah Israel disobeyed. Paul obviously considered the Torah as absolutely part of the good news of *Yeshua*, and so did *Yeshua* when He said, "For if you really believed Moshe, you would believe me: because it was about me that he wrote. But if you don't believe what he wrote, how are you going to believe what I say" (John 5:46-47).

What did we think was given at Mount Sinai, just some set of rules? Did we think it was not the gospel of *Yeshua*? It was the same gospel that originated in the garden, and it is about the seed.

What did Paul and *Yeshua* see in the Torah that the church has not? These are some powerful words. We might ask ourselves, *Are we taught the same gospel today as was taught at Mount Sinai, or is there more?*

If it is not merely the hearers of the Torah who are considered righteous but the doers of Torah that are made righteous, are we doers or even hearers? Do we even hear the words of the Torah? It seems for a season the house of Israel has not been able to hear the Torah (voice of God), let alone do what Torah says at least in part, but today, *Yeshua* is taking us further.

If we understand that manifesting or being made sons is the Spirit life, entering God's rest, then we can begin to understand what Paul is talking about in Romans. He is writing to a group of people who are preparing for the fall feasts. They already believe in *Yeshua*. They died with *Yeshua*, and now they are waiting to be made sons, that is, to manifest the resurrection life. The sons of God are the Revelation of the Messiah. According to Paul, you don't have to die in order to be resurrected. Look at what he says:

> Now since we died with the Messiah, we trust that we will also live with him. We know that the Messiah has been raised from

the dead, never to die again; death has no authority over him. For His death was a unique event that *need not be repeated*, but his life, he keeps on living for God.

Romans 6:8-10

His death need not be repeated in order to experience this resurrection life. Paul continues about how we are no longer slaves of sin. No. In fact, by the power of this resurrection life, we can fulfill the Torah. *Yeshua* fulfilled the Torah and now empowers us in union with Him.

Paul absolutely believed that a person who believed in the Messiah would walk in the Torah and this would cause his salvation to manifest in the earth. When this happens, they won't want to escape the earth because they will have dominion over the earth and *Yeshua* will have taken dominion over their earthly nature.

We can look at the church history and see that sin and death has continued to be what is revealed. We have not seen the full manifestation of the sons of God. This is, in part, because we have not seen our Hebrew roots or the Torah. Paul taught that on Yom Kippur, we would be judged (delivered) through the Messiah and that we would move from a life of the flesh to a life of the Spirit.

The only way we could be freed from the serpent's power was through *Yeshua*. He came to return God's perspective to us so that we could once again walk with Him in the garden in the cool of the day. The Spirit life does not happen outside of Torah, for Torah is the law or order of the Spirit. The Torah is the teachings of the Spirit. The spirit life is the cool of the day, the secret place of the Most High, abiding in the shadow of the Almighty, entering His rest and rivers of living waters.

Outside of Torah and the Spirit is the lake of fire—a fiery furnace; a hot, dry place where there is darkness and gnashing of the teeth. The Torah and the feast days of God will lead us out of darkness back into the garden, but this can only happen by the power of the Holy Spirit, and that is the power to overcome the limited human perspective. The garden is the bridal chamber where the two become one again. *Yeshua* only took us out of Himself in order to bring us back to Himself. In the process, He has manifested His attributes to the world.

ב

THE TWO TREES

> Then *Adonai* God formed a person [Hebrew Adam] from the dust of the ground [Hebrew *Adamah*] and breathed into his nostrils the breath of life, so that he became a living being. *Adonai*, God, planted a garden toward the east, in Eden, and there he put the person whom he had formed. Out of the ground *Adonai*, God, caused to grow every tree pleasing in appearance and good for food, including the tree of life in the middle of the garden and the tree of the knowledge of good and evil.
>
> Genesis 2:7-9 (CJB)

Here is a little food for thought: God took Adam from the dust, formed him, and then breathed into Him. After all this, He placed Adam into the garden (Genesis 2:15). Adam was created outside of the garden.

Adam is given purpose in this garden. The garden will put a demand on Adam to fulfill what he was created to do. The Torah is a book of cultivation; it teaches you how to cultivate the right things in life, how to cultivate relationships.

God tells Adam that he can eat from any tree in the garden except one: the tree of knowledge. The word *fruit* means "rewards or earnings." The rewards of this tree are to experience both good and evil, which will ultimately bring death. We can get a glimpse of what becomes of this fruit. Let's take a look into the future. We will look at Deuteronomy 30. This chapter is about the ingathering of the exiles. This is the origin of the verses that many uses for the understanding of the rapture.

> When the *time* arrives that all these things have come upon you both the blessing [good] and the curse [evil] which I have presented [the tree in the middle of the garden] to you; and you are there among the nations [dust of the earth] to which your God has driven [divorce, driven out of the garden] you; then at last, you will start thinking about what has happened to you [as a result from eating of the tree of knowledge].
>
> Deuteronomy 30:1 (CJB)

Let me set the stage. Israel is about to enter the land of Israel (picture of Adam about to be placed into the garden). It is as though God begins to recall in His mind what took place when He placed Adam in the garden. He recalls the trees He gave Adam for food and the one in the middle of the garden that was not to be food. He recalls Adam choosing to eat the fruit and the wages of death that would ensue. Now He had presented Israel with life and death and told them to choose life. He was looking into the future to the *time* when the full results of eating the fruit would come. He saw that he would have to exile Israel from the land and that they would fully experience both good and evil.

God knew there would be a *time* when this fruit would reach its fullness. When that time had come, here is what He said: "And you will return to *Adonai* your God and pay attention to what He has said, which will be exactly what I am ordering you to do today... At that point *Adonai* your God will *reverse your exile* and show you grace..." (Deuteronomy 30:2-3).

At the end of this fruit, we would return to God and what He said. He would take us once again from the dust of the earth (nations), and form us with His Word.

This brings me to my next thought: When did Adam first stop paying attention to God's command? Was it when he ate of the fruit, or was that just when the physical action took place?

If Adam ignored God's instruction, he was putting himself above God, in essence, making himself a god. Could it be that the human nature had the potential to sin, it just was not bound or cursed to sin (eat the dust of the earth) until the fruit was actually eaten? When the fruit was eaten, this potential became actual.

When God said, "The tree in the middle of the garden do not eat or you will die," the potential for death was present in the garden. Think about that. The potential for death existed in the garden of Eden. The potential for death was there, but it was not made actual until the fruit was eaten.

This gives us greater insight into the tree of life. When *Yeshua* fulfilled His mission, the potential for eternal life was present. Could it be until we eat of the fruit of the tree of life, it won't be made actual? Could it be until we eat of the fruit, we will continue to die and experience both good and evil?

I believe so. Adam would have continued to live even though the potential of death was present in the garden until he chose to eat of the fruit. Likewise, we will continue to die even though the potential of eternal life is there until we eat of the tree of life and experience its rewards. Look at what Paul says: "For He will pay back [rewards] each one according to his deeds [the fruit he eats]. To those who seek glory, honor and immortality by persevering in doing good, He will pay back [reward] eternal life" (Romans 2:5-6).

Is salvation something that you earn? If the answer is no, then what is eternal life? If we believe that salvation is a free gift, that when we die we will go to heaven, then what is eternal life?

Rewards for doing good is connected to our earthly walk called redemption. So eternal life (life from eternity, garden) is a reward we receive for obeying Torah while on the earth, yet this is actually accomplished in us by the Messiah. Salvation is our reconciliation back to God, and when we die, we will go to heaven. Salvation is the Abrahamic covenant. Redemption is the Mosaic covenant. Eternal life comes when you are walking in both covenants. This is the Davidic and renewed covenant, the covenant of the kingdom. You can't have eternal life by good deeds alone. We are saved, and then we move into a lifestyle of good actions.

> For by grace you are saved through faith and this is not from yourselves; it is God's gift—not from works, so no one can boast. For we are His creation—*created in Christ Jesus for good works*, which God prepared ahead of time *so that we should walk in them*.
>
> Ephesians 2:8-10

We reaped the results (rewards) of eating from the tree of knowledge while on earth. "But to those who are self-seeking [want to be God], who disobey the truth [Torah] and obey evil [*Yetzer Hara*], he will pay back wrath and anger [law of sin & death]" (Romans 2:8, CJB).

If you cannot earn or lose your salvation by obedience or disobedience, then Paul must be referring to our earthly walk. This is the walk of redemption in connection with our salvation.

In the Hebrew mindset, the Messiah is the Savior and Redeemer. He came to give us a new confession and conduct, not just to make a way for you to go to heaven. He wants heaven (confession) to come to earth (conduct).

So if this eternal life and anger/wrath are rewards for our conduct, then this is something we experience here on earth, not just where we go when we die. Therefore, God's wrath is a lifestyle you experience here; it is not going to hell when you die for disobeying. If you could go to hell for disobeying God when you die, then you could go to heaven for obeying God. This is a biblical law called a measure for measure. We know that salvation cannot be earned even if you kept God's commandments, all of them. Commandments are related to redemption and your earthly walk.

> When he had finished speaking all these words to all Israel, he said to them, "Take to heart all the words of my testimony against

you today, so that you can use them in charging your children to be careful to obey all the words of this Torah. For this is not a trivial matter for you; on the contrary, it is your life! Through it you will live long in the land [earth], you are crossing the Yarden to possess."

Deuteronomy 32:45-47 (CJB)

Abraham was saved. He believed God, and it was credited to him. Abraham's salvation manifested in His walk of redemption. He obeyed God and lived long on the earth.

When the evangelical dispensation theory talks about age of law and age of grace, they are pitting the Torah against grace. That is an error. No one ever earned salvation by works. Never! The Torah is given to an already-saved people. It teaches them how to walk out a redeemed lifestyle called eternal life while here on the earth.

Could it be that in these verses in Romans, Paul is simply describing that if we obey God, which is associated with eating from the tree of life, now that we are saved, we will reap eternal life? Could he be describing the blessing? If we obey, we will be blessed.

Could it be that even if we are saved but we choose to disobey, which is associated with eating from the tree of knowledge, we will reap God's anger? Could he be describing the curse? If we disobey God, we will walk in curse, lack, and decrease.

> I call heaven [salvation] and earth [redemption] to witness [two witnesses] against you today that I have presented you with Life [Tree of Life] and death [Tree of Knowledge] the blessing and the curse. Therefore choose life, so that you will live, you and your descendants.
>
> Deuteronomy 30:19 (CJB)

I think it is interesting to note that when God presented the two trees to Adam, he told him which tree not to eat from. Here, He tells you, "Choose life." "By your stubbornness, by your unrepentant heart, you are storing up anger for yourself on the *Day of Anger* when God's righteous judgment will be revealed" (Romans 2:5).

Now, Paul gives us another clue to when this reward is given out. He called the day the day of anger or day of judgment. This is a reference to the Feast of Trumpets and Yom Kippur.

Those who show up with a repentant heart and in union with the Messiah will enter a year of glory, honor, and immortality, a year of blessing. Those who don't will enter another year in the furnace of anguish and misery.

Here is the big question: If the potential for eternal life, the life of the garden, is here, how do we manifest it? If we must eat the fruit before it becomes actual, then how do we eat the fruit? I often wonder if we are the first generation in almost two thousand years to ask this question. We will have to go back to the garden to answer this question: "*Adonai*, God, gave the person this order: 'You may freely eat from every tree in the garden except the tree of knowledge of good and evil. You are not to eat from it, because on the day that you eat from it, it will become certain that you will die'" (Genesis 2:16-17).

I have found that if we discover what the fruit of the tree of knowledge is, it will help us uncover what the fruit of the tree of life is. The Torah is revealing to us that there is more here than just a physical fruit. We will talk more about that later, but keep in mind that God has given every seed bearing plant and tree to Adam for food: "Then God said, 'Here! Through the whole earth I am giving you as food every seed bearing plant and every tree with seed-bearing fruit'" (Genesis 1:29).

Now God places Adam in the garden and tells him of all the trees he can eat except for one. We have to ask ourselves, *What is God revealing here?* Look at this verse closely: "Except the tree of knowledge of good and evil. You are not to eat from it, because on the day that you eat from it, it will become certain that you will die" (Genesis 2:17).

The Gospel of the Garden

God tells only Adam not to eat of the tree of knowledge. God places Adam in the garden and then takes Eve out of Adam's side. Eve is to be a helpmate for Adam. As we move forward, the scene is set, the serpent and the woman. Pay close attention to details here.

> Now the serpent was more crafty than any wild animal which *Adonai*, God, had made. He said to the woman, "Did God really say, 'You are not to eat from any tree in the garden'?" The woman answered the serpent, "We may eat from the fruit of the trees of the garden, but about the fruit of the tree in the middle of the garden, God said, *'You are neither to eat from it nor touch it*, or you will die.'"
>
> Genesis 3:1-3 (CJB)

There is an interesting clue found in this verse. Remember, most every principle in your Bible can be found in seed form in the beginning. These principles never change.

Eve told the serpent that God said, "You are neither to eat from it nor touch it." God never told Adam not to touch the fruit, only not to eat it. This may not seem like a big deal, but it is a huge deal. Why did Eve say they were not to touch it?

This opens up a whole world of thought. You might even say a religion is formed from this incident. The rabbis say that Adam told Eve they were not to eat or touch the fruit because the original command was given to Adam. This is revealed by God's statement: "To Adam he said, 'Because you listened to what your wife said and ate from the tree about which *I gave you the order*, 'You are not to eat from it,' the ground is cursed on your account; you will work hard to eat from it as long as you live'" (Genesis 3:17).

God confirms that he gave the order to Adam. Adam was the one teaching his wife, as Adam was the head. The rabbis said that Adam built a fence around the commandment "Do not eat the fruit" to protect them from accidently eating the fruit. They would have to first break the fence (manmade commandment) "Don't touch" before they would break the commandment "Don't eat."

From this verse, many of the rabbis drew their authority to build fences around all of the Torah commandments. They said if Adam was building fences around them in the garden, so should we.

They say these fences (manmade commandments) are there to "protect the actual commandments." In Judaism, there are thousands of manmade commandments built around the Torah. You would have to cross these fences before you would actually break the Torah command. This might seem like wisdom at first, but it presents a huge problem. Let's see what God says about adding to His Word.

> Now, Israel, listen to the laws and rulings I am teaching you, in order to follow them, so that you will live; then you will go in and take possession of the land [garden] that *Adonai*, the God of your fathers, is giving you. In order to obey the *Mitzvot* [commandment] of *Adonai* your God which I am giving you, *do not add to what I am saying, and do not subtract from it.*
>
> Deuteronomy 4:1-2 (CJB)

Why do you suppose God is being very specific not to add to or subtract from His commandments?

It is as if God is recalling what happened back in the garden, as though He is remembering what preceded Adam's fall and exile from the garden. Here, He is lovingly warning His people once again as they are about to be placed back into the land of Israel (type of garden). "Every word of God is pure; he shields [same root as garden] those taking refuge in him. *Don't add anything to his words*; or he will rebuke you, and you be found a liar" (Proverbs 30:5-6).

This is a strong warning. We know God never changes, right? If He does not want us to add to or subtract from God's Word

(Torah) today, then He did not want Adam to do it in the garden. Proverbs says, "God will rebuke you and you will be found a liar."

So let's just talk for a minute. *HaSatan* is the father of lies, right? So where do we see the first lie originate? Could the first lie ever alluded to in the Torah find its origin in Adam telling Eve that God said not to touch that fruit? This is a lie.

We already see *Yeshua* rebuke Peter, calling him Satan, referring to the perspective he was seeing from. Could the origin of lie in the earthly realm be found in Adam?

Is it possible that the reason Eve was deceived by the serpent is because she was following a manmade commandment? Is this why the Torah mentioned that the serpent was wiser than the beasts of the field? Eve was not a beast of the field, those living outside of Torah—or was she?

With all of this in mind, we open up a whole world (no pun intended) of thought. Adam, the father of lies—that will shake up somebody's theology. Could sin find its origin in adding to and subtracting form God's commandments, His Torah? Is this maybe why John gives us a strong warning at the end of the book of Revelation?

> I warn everyone hearing the words of the prophecy in this book that if anyone adds to them, God will add to Him the plagues written in this book (death). And if anyone takes anything away from the words in the book of this prophecy, God will take away his share in the Tree of Life and the Holy City, as described in this book.
>
> Revelation 22:18-19 (CJB)

Is John revealing to us how Adam lost his share in the tree of life? Absolutely. Now he is warning us. We should take heed to this warning. Look at our lives and see if there are places where we add to or subtract from God's Torah.

When we add to and subtract from God's Torah, we are saying that it is not perfect, it's not sufficient. We raise ourselves above God's Word and even elevate ourselves above God. In fact, it is declaring ourselves to be god. It sounds just like the story of *HaSatan*. It is possible that *HaSatan* was a false reality that rose up in Adam?

Maybe God told Adam of all the trees in the garden he may eat. "Of all My commandments (trees) and instruction in My garden, the place of protection, you may eat, but of the tree of knowledge don't eat. Don't ever eat the fruit of making your own commandments. Don't ever eat the fruit of adding to or subtracting from My Torah, for in the day you do, you will surely die; the plagues will overtake you. You will lose your share in the tree of life."

Look what the serpent says to Eve: "It is not true that you will surely die; because God knows that on the day you eat from it, your eyes will be open, and *you will be like God*, knowing good and evil" (Genesis 3:46-5).

The thought of adding to God's Torah or subtracting from God's Word is rooted in the desire to be like God, in the sense of being God. When we do this, we are severing the relationship with God.

It could be understood that human nature had the potential to add to or subtract from God's Word, this being the free choice. Man's only real free choice is life or death. We read earlier that Adam's human nature had its origin in the dust of the earth. God might have been telling Adam not to eat the fruit or desire of this nature.

It was not until the fruit was eaten that the curse was instituted and man became a slave to this nature and its desires. Not only that, but this nature was cursed to eat the dust of the earth. It will feast on sin and death.

If this is the case, then God understood that Adam could not approach the commandments from a human perspective but by faith. Adam was to approach the commandments or the Torah by the Spirit.

Adam must approach the Torah by the part of him that originated from God. If Adam approached God's commandments by the Spirit (from God's perspective), he would live. In fact, they would be a tree of life. "Happy the person who finds wisdom [Torah], the person who acquires understanding; [Spirit]... She is a tree of life to those who grasp her; whoever holds fast to her will be made happy" (Proverbs 3:13-18).

The Torah is wisdom, and the Spirit of God, *Yeshua*, is understanding. When the two come together, it is knowledge.

The Torah scroll is called the *etz chim*, tree of life. In fact, both of the rods that the scroll is wrapped around are called trees. The scroll itself is made up of thirty-nine sheep skins, specifically the skin from the stomachs of sheep. The skins are stretched and dried, and they are called leaves. When these leaves are sewn together, they are called robes or garments of righteousness. Remember the skins given to Adam and Eve?

The words of the Torah are written on leaves. The two poles are likened to the two houses of Israel. When wrapped in the Torah, they are brought together in the garments of righteousness. "For the time has come for the wedding of the lamb, and the bride has prepared herself—fine linen bright and clean has been given her to wear" (Revelation 19:7b-8). "Fine linen" means the righteous deeds of God's people.

Righteous deeds are a reference to walking in the Torah. The bride is clothed in the robes or garments of righteousness, the Torah. The word *time* here takes us back to Deuteronomy 30:1 and back to the two cherubs: ancient time.

The book of Revelation also describes that the leaves of the tree will be healing for the nations. Remember, the nations were likened to the dust of the earth, and now the leaves (Torah) will be healing (form) for them. Let's look at these next verses closely.

Between the main street and the river was the Tree of Life producing twelve kinds of fruit [twelve tribes of Israel], and different kind every month [each tribe is associated with a different month in the Hebrew calendar], and the leaves of the tree [Torah scroll] were healing for the nations—no longer will there be any curses...

Revelation 22:2-3a (CJB)

There is a lot described in this verse. A picture says a thousand words. The leaves were the thirty-nine sheepskins that allude to the verse, "By His stripes we are healed." *Yeshua* took thirty-nine stripes.

The main street is *Derick*, the Way. This talks about our walk of redemption. The river alludes to the Spirit life. Let's look at one more verse: "Next the angel showed me the river of water of life, sparkling like crystal, flowing from the throne of God and the lamb" (Revelation 22:1).

Where is the throne of God? In the heart of the believer. It is absolutely crucial that we understand that. Paul was emphatic about you being the temple of God. This river is the very river that *Yeshua* said would flow out of your belly (*Gihon*). The word for belly is associated with the river that flowed out of the garden of Eden.

This is a river of life and no longer a river of bitterness, as John said, "There is no more curse." This means the river flowing from the Spirit of God and not from the human perspective, the serpent cursed to eat the dust and to crawl on its belly. This river flows from Eden, intimacy with the Messiah.

This river is the Spirit life that flows out of the Torah. The root of the word *Torah* means "to flow like water." Now, as we look at the verses on the tree here, we get a better understanding. This Torah (tree) and the leaves that bring healing for the nations and produce twelve kinds of fruit, the twelve tribes, can only do so by the power of the Spirit. It can only produce life when approached from God's perspective, which comes through intimacy with Him. When approached from man's perspective (a wounded heart and a river of bitterness) it becomes the tree of knowledge of good and evil. It is the same tree. The tree of life and the tree of knowledge; the difference is how you approach it. When approached by the flesh, it is the tree of knowledge. You can't produce life. When approached by the Spirit, it is the tree of life. You can produce life.

In Revelation 22:3, it says, "There will no longer be any curse." Well, curse flows from the tree of knowledge, adding to and subtracting from God's Word. If there is no more curse, it is because they are approaching the Torah by the Spirit or in union with *Yeshua*. The curses mentioned here are the ones that were related to the woman, serpent, and the ground, Adam.

This takes me back to the question I asked earlier. If the potential for eternal life, the life of the garden, is available, how do we get it to manifest? If all we have to do is eat the fruit, then how do we eat the fruit of the tree of life?

ל

TWO HUSBANDS

> How blessed are those who wash their robes, so that they have the right to eat from the tree of life...
>
> Revelation 22:14 (CJB)

Those who have washed their robes can eat fruit of the tree of life. The question is: how did they wash their robes?

> One of the elders asked me, "These people in white robes—who are they, and where are they from?" "Sir," I answered, "You know." Then he told me, "These are the people who have come out of the Great Persecution [exile, the dust of the earth or realm of death—the term Great Persecution might also allude to them having just came through the ten days of Awe and Yom Kippur]. They have washed their *robes and made them white with the blood of the lamb.*"
>
> Revelation 7:13-14 (CJB)

They washed their robes with the blood of the Messiah, so they have the right to eat from the tree of life. The question remains: how do they eat from this tree? Now that we believe in the Messiah and have the right to eat (potential), how does it become actual? Why have believers not been able to experience this eternal life that we all know is available to believers?

Let's see if this helps: even though the potential is there, the house of Israel has been unable to see the tree. She has been unable to see the Torah.

What is more, their minds were made stonelike; for to this day, the same veil remains over them when they read the Old Covenant. It has not been unveiled because only by the Messiah is the veil taken away. Yes, 'til today, whenever Moshe is read, a veil lies over their hearts.

2 Corinthians 3:14-15

This simply means for a season they would not see the Torah (tree). This has resulted in the house of Israel being unable to see the Torah, and for the last two thousand years, she has believed that *Yeshua* came to save her from the Torah. This is the veil that Isaiah 25:7-9 spoke about.

If *Yeshua* did away with the Torah, then there is no such thing as sin. Sin is the violation of the Torah. No Torah, then no sin. Until the full results of eating the forbidden fruit is meted out, the house of Israel won't see the tree, but today, all over the world, Christians are returning to the feast days and the Torah.

The house of Judah has not been able to eat from the tree either because they are approaching it from the human perspective. They have not seen the Messiah and washed their robes. However, all over the world, Jews are beginning to see the Messiah, and they are washing their robes in His blood.

For, brothers, I want you to understand this truth which God formerly concealed but has now revealed. So that you won't imagine you know more than you actually do. It is that *stoniness*, to a degree, has come upon Israel [house of Judah], until the Gentile [house of Israel] world enters in its fullness; and that it is in this way that all Israel [both houses] will be saved. As the *Tanakh* says, "Out of *Tziyon* will come the Redeemer; he will turn away ungodliness from *Ya'akov*."

Romans 11:25-26 (CJB)

This simply means that for a season, the house of Judah would not see the Messiah, not until the house of Israel returns to the Torah. However, the house of Judah absolutely knows that when the Messiah comes, He will bring the Torah to glory, He will heal His people, and they will overcome the urge to do evil, the *Yetzer Hara*, and inherit the earth forever. Why do they believe this? Because this is what the Torah and the prophets say the Messiah will do.

As I mentioned earlier, Adam would work the soil (Torah) by the sweat of His brow, and the ground will produce thorns and thistles. Here is what is being alluded to. No matter how hard the house of Judah works and toils in the Torah because they are doing so from the human perspective with its desire to twist the word into something that it is not, it is not the tree of life but simply the tree of knowledge of good and evil. It simply reveals what is good and what is evil. Remember, *Yeshua* dealt with this perspective in the forty days he fasted. The Torah that was meant to bring life would end up producing thorns and thistles.

Paul explains this very well in Romans 7, when he talked about what it is like to be a Jew and have the Torah but be married to the earthly nature, sold as a slave to sin. I'm going to explain this in detail because many translators and readers miss what Paul is saying because they don't really know the beginning.

When Adam was placed in the garden, He was married (joined) to God. He was one with the Messiah and the Torah. Messiah is the groom, and the Torah is the *ketubah*, the wedding vows. Adam was a picture of Israel, the bride.

When Adam was divorced from the spirit of God, he was also freed from the Torah. Adam was joined (married) to the earthly nature (*HaSatan*), and this groom's *ketubah* is the law of sin and death. When Adam was divorced, he was sold because brides were always purchased and he became a slave of sin and death.

This pattern is repeated with Israel. When God divorced her, she "married other gods." Well, what she actually married was the earthly nature. The earthly nature creates a god of its own imagination. This is where idols come from. In essence, they became gods unto themselves. It sometimes reads as though they married idols. Idols means created a god of their own imagination. Who made the idol? Man. Who made the religion around the idol? Man. They married their earthly nature: Satan.

It is important that we have a little insight into what Satan is. When *Yeshua* told the rabbis that their father was Satan, He was saying that they were still carnal, sold as slaves to sin, a little different than what would first go through your mind in the average church. My goal is not to challenge the way the church has seen this but to show you a side many have never looked at and one that will change the way you view life.

Biblically, if you said someone was married to Satan, you are saying they are carnal and still a slave of sin.

When Adam and Israel were divorced they were released from the *Ketubah*, the Torah of righteousness. Naturally, they were now a slave of the torah of sin. "For when you were slaves of sin [*HaSatan's ketubah*], you were free [divorced] in relationship to righteousness [God's *Ketubah*]" (Romans 6:20).

Adam was married to *Yeshua* and then divorced and married to *HaSatan*. *Yeshua* was the *first husband*. *HaSatan* was the *second husband*. *Yeshua* will be the *last husband*. Since our generation is born joined to the carnal nature (*HaSatan*) some will describe *HaSatan* as the first husband and *Yeshua* as the second husband. This is also accurate. I'm going to use the pattern from the beginning, Adam's pattern, as we go through the first part of Romans 7. Notice how Paul starts off here: "Surely you know, brothers—for I am speaking to those who understand Torah [this is Torah by the Spirit]—that the Torah has authority over a person only so long as he lives?" (Romans 7:1).

First off, Paul clarifies who he is writing to: those who understand the Torah. If you don't understand the Torah, you will miss what Paul is saying. Paul assumes the reader will be familiar with the topic he is about to discuss. Next, Paul poses the sentence as a statement/question: "The Torah has authority over a person only so long as he lives?"

Again, the Torah governs our earthly walk. The blessing for obedience is that heaven and earth will work for you, and the curse for disobedience is that heaven and earth will work against you. The blessing and curses are meted out to you and your descendants here on earth. Obeying and disobeying does not decide whether you go to heaven or hell when you die. There has been a very Hellenistic view point coursing through Christianity and even into the Hellenistic Jewish world.

You do not earn the right to go to heaven when you die by keeping the Torah. Most Christians believe this. Nor have you ever been able to—never. Not in some "Age of Law." Therefore, measure for measure, you can't earn the right to go to hell when you die by disobeying the Torah. The wages of sin is death. It does not say hell when you die. You might die early, but death is also a reference to curse, lack and decrease, and a spiritual death.

Keep this in mind. When Adam and Eve ate the forbidden fruit in the garden, the wages were that they were clothed in mortality and exiled out of the garden. They began to experience the realm of death. They weren't sent to hell when they died. Think about that. They went out into a fiery furnace called the exile from the garden. Today, when we eat this same fruit, we get the same results. They have not changed. The gospel is about bringing us back to eternal life, the life of the garden. Eternal life and eternal punishment just might be connected to your life in the earth, not so much about where you go when you die.

"For example, a married woman is bound by Torah to her husband while he is alive, but if the husband dies, she is released from the part of the Torah that deals with husbands" (Romans 7:2). This is a weighty topic. Paul is alluding to Deuteronomy, the instructions regarding husbands and divorce. Adam was married to God and then divorced. Adam married another god: his earthly nature. He was joined to the *HaSatan*. Watch how Torah deals with this issue.

> Suppose a man [*Yeshua*] marries a woman [Adam] and consummates the marriage but later finds her displeasing, because he has found her offensive in some respect. He writes her a divorce document, gives it to her and sends [exiles] her away from his house [garden]. She leaves his house [garden], goes and becomes another man's [*HaSatan*] wife, but the second husband dislikes her and writes her a get, gives it to her and sends her away from his house; or the second husband whom she married dies. In such a case her first husband [*Yeshua*], who sent her away, may not take her again as his wife, because she is now defiled. It would be detestable to *Adonai*, and you are not to bring about sin in the land your God is giving you as your inheritance.
>
> Deuteronomy 24:1-4 (CJB)

According to the Torah, even if the second husband (*HaSatan*) were to divorce Adam or was to die, the first husband (*Yeshua*) could not take back Adam as a bride again. We see this verse quoted to Israel as the divorce is given to them:

> *Adonai* says, "If a man divorces his wife, and she leaves him and marries another man, then the first one marries her again, that land will be completely defiled. But you prostitute yourselves to many lovers, yet you want to return to me?" says *Adonai*. "I saw that even though backsliding Israel had committed adultery, so that I had sent her away and given her a divorce document, unfaithful Judah her sister was not moved to fear—instead she too went and prostituted herself."
>
> Jeremiah 3:1, 8 (CJB)

Israel had followed the same pattern as Adam. They committed adultery. Eating the fruit of the tree of knowledge was adultery. God said it would result in death. Look at what the Torah says: "If a man commits adultery with another man's wife, that is, with the wife of a fellow countryman, both the adulterer and the adulteress must be put to death" (Leviticus 20:10).

According to biblical law, both Adam and the serpent (Earthly nature, second husband) were cursed and both would be required to die.

So neither Adam nor Israel would be permitted to marry God again. It would be an abomination. Even if the second husband were to divorce them or die, it would still be an abomination.

However, if the first husband was to die, she would be released from the part of Torah that deals with the first husband. I hope you see what Paul is getting at. If *Yeshua* were to die, then Adam and Israel would be released from the portion of the Torah that said she could never be married to *Yeshua* again. The problem here is the husband is dead. Now, if this husband just somehow raised from the dead, she would be able to marry Him again.

One more issue to deal with: "Therefore, while the husband is alive, she will be called an adulteress if she marries another man; but if the husband dies, she is free from that part of the Torah; so that if she marries another man, she is not an adulteress" (Romans 7:3). The second issue that Paul is covering is even if *Yeshua* died, releasing her from the portion of Torah dealing with the first husband, and now rose from the dead, she still can't marry him because she is joined to the second husband. Adam/Israel would be an adulteress to try to marry God still while married to another. How can this problem be solved?

When *Yeshua* took on a body like ours with an earthly nature like ours (the second husband) and was crucified, the second husband (*HaSatan*) was crucified with *Yeshua*, "the serpent on a pole." We were released not only from the portion of Torah dealing with the first husband but we were released from the torah (of sin and death) of the second husband. *Yeshua* dealt with both issues at once. "We know that our old self [*HaSatan*, second husband] was put to death on the execution stake [serpent on the pole] so that the entire body of our sinful propensities might be destroyed and we might no longer be enslaved to sin [the ketubah of *HaSatan*]" (Romans 6:6).

Yeshua executed punishment against *HaSatan*, our old nature, because, according to Torah, if a man commits adultery with another man's wife, they must both be put to death. *Yeshua* died in place of His bride, and He crucified the serpent on the cross. When *Yeshua* died, it released His bride from the portion of Torah that required her death for being an adulteress.

In the garden, Adam committed spiritual adultery, and, therefore, the death was a spiritual death. However, spiritual death leads to a physical death.

> Thus, my brothers, you have been made dead with regards to the Torah [the part of Torah that said you could not be married to *Yeshua*] through the Messiah's body so that you may belong to someone else, namely, the one who has been raised from the dead, in order for us to bear fruit for God.
> Romans 7:4

Paul figures this verse is self-explanatory. You have been made free in regard to the Torah, the part that deals with husbands, both the first and the second husband. This was accomplished through the Messiah's body because He was fully God and yet had a body like ours with a nature like ours. His death released us from the aspect that said you could never be married to God again and the aspect that said you were bound to sin and death (the second husband). Now you might belong to someone else: *Yeshua*.

If you are joined (married) to the resurrected one, then you are joined to the resurrection life, the life of the garden, where we are one Spirit with God. Naturally, we will bear fruit (produce a greater household) for God. You only walk in deliverance in the areas you have revelation. Revelation proceeds deliverance, and *Yeshua* is revealing the mysteries of His good news.

God took us out of Himself (exile from the garden) in order to demonstrate His powerful love and attributes, like mercy and long-suffering, and then to perform the ultimate act of love, to lay down His life for his bride in order to bring her back to Himself, to bring her back to the garden. This is the story from God's perspective.

Now it has been quite a different story from man's limited human perspective. The experience has been a painful one. It might even seem like foolishness from the human perspective; but God declared it in the beginning, and His Word will not return to Him void.

> For the Messiah did not send me to immerse but to proclaim the Good News—and to do it without relying on "wisdom" that consists of mere rhetoric, so as not to rob the Messiah's execution—stake of its power. For the message about the execution-stake is nonsense to those in the process of being destroyed [earthly nature], but to us in the process of being saved [spiritual nature] it is the power of God.
>
> 1 Corinthians 1:17(CJB)

Do we even really know the things that God has planned for us?

> But as the *Tanakh* say, "No eye has seen, no ear has heard and no one's heart has imagined all the things that God has prepared for those who love him."
>
> 1 Corinthians 2:9 (CJB)

> For when we were living according to our nature (second husband), the passions connected with sin worked through the Torah in our various parts, with the result that we bore fruit for death [thorns and thistles].
>
> Romans 7:5 (CJB)

This takes us back to Adam. For when we were living (working the soil) according to our old nature, the passion connected with sin worked through the Torah (soil) in our various parts (our body and the land) with the results that we (our lives) bore fruit for death: thorns and thistles.

Paul is going to explain life according to the second husband, old nature, and set it against life according to the first husband, *Yeshua*, the spirit life.

Paul explains that when we were joined to *HaSatan*, we worked the soil of our lives with bad results. Even working the Torah still produced curse, lack and decrease.

When we tried to live our lives according to the Torah, because of our old nature, which twists the Torah, we ended up producing bad fruit instead of the fruit that the Torah should have produced. This was no fault of the Torah's but a result of our earthly nature and its desires.

> But now we have been released from *this aspect of the Torah* [the part that deals with husbands, and the part that had us bound to the old nature] because we have died to that which had us in its clutches [*HaSatan*, sin and death], so that we are serving [working the soil of our lives] in a new way provided by the Spirit [working the Torah from God's perspective with His desires] and not in the old way [human perspective with its desires] of outwardly following the letter of the law [while inwardly having the desire for sin and death, what a miserable creature].
>
> Romans 7:6 (CJB)

Paul is stating that now we are released from the portion of Torah that deals with husbands so we can be joined one Spirit with the Messiah. The next time someone says, "You're not under the law," you can say, "You're right! I have been released from the portion of the law that deals with husbands. I'm no longer married to the carnal nature, a slave to the law of sin and death."

So now that we are joined to the Messiah (wedding, Yom Kippur), we are able to eat the fruit of the Torah. This is done, as we now read and participate in the lifestyle of the Torah by the power of the Holy Spirit. God causes us to see the Torah from His perspective. It is when we approach the Torah by the Spirit that we are able to see the tree and eat its fruit. "Therefore, what are we to say? That the Torah is sinful? Heaven forbid! Rather the function of the Torah was that without it, I would not have become conscious of what greed is if the Torah had not said, 'Thou shall not covet'" (Romans 7:7).

Paul is explaining that without the Torah, you would not know what sin is. The Torah teaches the difference between good and evil. It is because of the old nature that even when we try to live according to Torah, we bear the fruit of sin. It is not the Torah that is sinful.

> But sin [old nature], seizing the opportunity afforded by the commandment [don't eat of the Tree of Knowledge], worked in me all kinds of evil desires [like the desire to add to or subtract from God's command]. For apart from the Torah [the free choice to choose to violate it or obey it] sin is dead.
>
> Romans 7:8

We begin to realize that the opportunity or the potential for death was in the garden when God gave the commandment, "Do not eat." It was not the commandment but the earthly nature that wanted to rebel.

Follow me through these next verses. I will overlay Adam's story in Paul's writing. Once again, it is the same pattern. We will be interpreting Paul's words through the eyes of the Torah.

> I [Adam] was once alive outside the frame work of Torah. But when the commandment [do not eat from the Tree of Knowledge] really encountered me, sin [in the human perspective or nature] sprang to life [Adam added to God's command, do not touch], and I died [ate of the fruit]. The commandment [do not eat] that was intended to bring me life [the life of the garden] was found bringing me death! [Because the commandment afforded Adam and us the opportunity to disobey it, a choice] For sin [in the earthly nature] seizing the opportunity [to disobey] afforded by the commandment deceived me [the serpent nature wanted to be like god and made its own commandments by adding to God's. This proved to be a lie. Proverbs 30:6]; and through the commandment [free choice], sin killed me, so the Torah is holy that is, the commandment is holy, just and good.
>
> Romans 7:9-12 (CJB)

Paul just gave a brilliant explanation. The Torah is holy, just, and good, and when approached by the Spirit, it produces life. It's the *Yetzer Hara* that seizes the opportunity to rebel against the Torah that kills us. Our enemy (*HaSatan*) is the urge to do evil. As a result of sin, we have been bound to the old nature. Look at what Paul says: "For the mind controlled by the old nature [serpent] is hostile to God, because it does not submit itself to God's Torah—indeed it cannot [it wants to add to or subtract from]. Thus those who identify with their old nature [seed of the serpent] cannot please God" (Romans 8:7-8).

Has our old nature twisted the Word of God, causing us to believe that God's Torah does not matter? Has it caused us to read into the words of Paul and *Yeshua* and twist them into something that they are not, saying that we can do away with God's commandments and add our own commandments? The serpent tried to twist the Word of God to *Yeshua*. Is he not going to pull the same moves on us?

We need to be saved and redeemed from the urge to violate the Torah, the old nature. We don't need saved from the Torah.

The Jews see the tree, but they see it through the old nature, from a human's perspective that bends the Torah into something that it is not. They have added to God's Torah and turned it into a system of legalism. The Torah is our purpose, but when we add to it, we leave the kingdom and enter religion. This is the fall from purpose. They have not washed their robes (cleansed their consciences) with the blood of the Messiah, so they have not been given the right (God's perspective) to eat from the tree of life. This is the rights of the kingdom.

The Christians have the potential to eat the fruit of the tree, but they have not believed that the tree of life is really the tree of life. They have been taught that the Torah is the tree of death. They still are seeing it from the human perspective and subtract from God's Torah. Once again, this takes us out of the kingdom into religion, the fall of purpose.

> Then did something good [Torah] become for me the source of death? [Was the Torah the source of death? Absolutely not!] Heaven forbid! Rather, it was sin working death [old nature with its desires] in me through something good [approaching Torah by the human perspective] so that sin [human nature] might be clearly exposed as sin, so that sin through the commandment might come to be experienced [knowledge] as sinful beyond measure [so that approaching the Torah from a human perspective might be experienced as death beyond measure].
>
> Romans 7:13 (CJB)

This is the full reward of eating from the forbidden fruit. The wages of sin is death. "For we know that the Torah is of the Spirit [Torah originated from the Spirit, the mind of God therefore it can only be understood by the Spirit], but as for me, I am bound [married] to the old nature, sold to sin as a slave" (Romans 7:14).

I hope by now this is becoming self-explanatory, as we have thoroughly looked at the origin of what Paul is saying. Paul is obviously talking about being a slave before he had the Messiah. This is Adam's exile from the garden, exile from the Spirit life.

The ground Adam was working was the soil of his life, which is governed by the Torah. Trying to work out his life from the human perspective or his own torah produces thorns (curse) and thistles (death).

Paul is now going to explain the life experience of trying to walk out Torah as a carnal man:

> I don't understand my own behavior—I don't do what I want to do; instead, I do the very thing I hate! Now if I am doing what I don't want to do, I am *agreeing that the Torah is good* [Paul is trying to obey the Torah. As Christians when we say we are experiencing the same struggle as Paul are we trying to obey the Torah?] But now it is no longer "the real me" [the part that originated from God not the earth] doing it, but the sin housed inside me [the earthly nature]. For I know that there is nothing good [desire to obey God] housed inside me—that is inside my old nature. I can want to do good, but I can't do it! For I don't do the good I want; instead, the evil that I don't want is what I do!
>
> Romans 7:15-19 (CJB)

In another place, Paul refers to the earthly nature as mortal or mortality, which means it was made from the earth. Its origin is from something created, not from the Creator. It was made from something that already existed, and it will return to its origin.

Immortal or immortality is that which originates from outside of creation. It is that which originated from the immortal God. Man is both created and made. His origin is both from God and the earth. When man is joined to the earthly nature, he is mortal. When he is joined to the Spirit of God, he is clothed in immortality.

> For this material which can decay must be clothed with imperishability, this which is mortal must be clothed with immortality. When what decays puts on imperishability and what is mortal puts on immortality, then the passage in the *Tanakh* will be fulfilled; Death [old nature] is swallowed [overcome] up in victory [new nature].
>
> 1 Corinthians 15:53-54 (CJB)

Mortal man, much like the secondary law of thermal dynamics, is in the process of decaying. He is serving or obeying creation not the Creator. The curse was for the serpent to eat the dust of the earth. We would eat the teachings and instructions that flowed from creation instead of the Creator. Therefore, we would be controlled by that which was created (mortal) rather than being controlled by the Creator, the Spirit of God. This results in decay and death. "But if I am doing what 'the real me' [the part that originated from God] doesn't want, it is no longer 'the real me' doing it, but the sin housed inside of me [the *HaSatan*]" (Romans 7:20).

Adam is being controlled by an illusion. This was Adam's tragedy after the fall. Adam became disconnected from his real image, the part of him that originated from God, the source of life. The life that Adam would now live flowed from the dust of the earth.

> So I find it to be the rule, a kind of perverse "torah" that although I want to do what is good, evil is right there with me [He is the tree of good and evil]! For in my inner most self, I completely

agree with God's Torah, but in my various parts, I see a different "torah," one that battles with the Torah in my mind and makes me a prisoner [cursed to eat the dust of the earth] of sins "torah," which is operating in my various parts.

Romans 7:21-23 (CJB)

No matter how hard Adam worked the land (his life), because his mind was controlled by the serpent, he would sin, eat the dust of the earth. "What a miserable creature I am! Who will rescue [redeem] me from this body [serpent] bound for death [curse to eat the dust of the earth]?" (Romans 7:24). Do you see Paul's desire, what he wanted saved from? Now here is the solution: "Thanks be to God [he will]—through *Yeshua* the Messiah, our Lord" (Romans 7:25).

This brings us back to the start of Romans 7. Adam was originally joined (married) to the Messiah. After the fall, he was joined (married) to the serpent. Without the death of the Messiah and His resurrection, which dealt with both husbands, man would never be able to enter back into the garden or be married to God.

This can be a stumbling block for many people because they might not fully understand the Messiah's full mission. God only took us from Himself to bring us back to Himself so the two would become one. This is not your doing but His doing.

In the same way, He took the house of Israel out of the house of Judah to bring them back together as one. This is not their doing but His.

Yeshua is YHVH (first husband) in a body like ours, bound to the earthly nature, the second husband. He did this so that in His death, we would be released from the aspect of the Torah that dealt with husbands. YHVH is our Savior (*Yeshua*). This is the plan from the beginning. This was so He might demonstrate His love.

The Torah is the *Ketubah*, the wedding vows. You can't eat the fruit of the wedding vows without the groom. You can't birth children by studying wedding vows. The wedding vows lead you into intimacy with the groom. This is where life is conceived.

Yom Kippur is crucial in our understanding. On the Day of Atonement, the blood of bulls and goats could not cleanse us from the urge to do evil. No, from the beginning, the seed of the woman would crush the head of the serpent. The curse of this nature would have to be overcome. The blood of bulls and goats did not have the power to cause you to see from God's perspective.

The Messiah *Yeshua* would have to overcome the seed of the serpent. *Yeshua* would overcome the human perspective with its evil desires. This is understanding. Now *Yeshua* would apply or give His life to us. This is knowledge. Knowledge is the place of conception. Yom Kippur is the wedding, where we become one Spirit with Messiah (knowledge). "On a day [Yom Kippur] when God passes judgment [deliverance] on people's inmost secrets [secret sins/vows and oaths]. [According to the good news as I proclaim it, he does this [delivers us] through the Messiah *Yeshua* [by giving us His life]" (Romans 2:16).

On Yom Kippur, we are delivered from the urge to do evil, the body bound for death, through the Messiah. Now we have the power to overcome.

> But when the Messiah appeared as *Cohen gadol* [high priest] of the good things [people] that are happening already, then, through the greater and more perfect tent [you] which is not manmade [that is, not of this created world], he entered the Holiest Place [your conscience] once and for all. And he entered not by means of the blood of goats and claves, but by means of his own blood, thus setting people free [from *Yetzer Hara*] forever.
>
> Hebrews 9:11-12 (CJB)

To be free of the Yetzer Hara is to be free from the human perspective with it's desire to do evil. *Yeshua* was not a sacrifice but offered up

His life. This is the fullness of the Torah. His life is in His blood. "For the life of a creature is in the blood" (Leviticus 17:11a).

> For if sprinkling ceremonially unclean persons with the blood of goats and bulls and ashes of a heifer restores their outward purity, then how much more the blood of the Messiah, who through the eternal spirit, offered himself to God as a sacrifice [offering] without blemish [came in a body like ours but without sinning] *will purify our conscience from works that lead to death* [urge to do evil], so that we can serve the living God! [Have dominion over the earth!]
>
> Hebrews 9:13-14 (CJB)

When it says to sprinkle us with the blood of Messiah, it means to apply or give us His life and his desires. This is what Adam had in the garden. *Yeshua* had to free us from the *Yetzer Hara* and unite us with Himself. In order to free us from the curse of the fall, he had to become a curse: "The Messiah redeemed us from the curse pronounced in the Torah by becoming cursed on our behalf; for the *Tanakh* says, 'Everyone who hangs from a stake [tree] comes under a curse!'" (Galatians 3:13).

What does this really mean? YHVH became like you, *Yeshua*. "Therefore, since the children share a common physical nature as human beings, he became like them and shared that same human nature; so that by his death he might render ineffective the one who had power over death [that is, the adversary]" (Hebrews 2:14).

In order to become like you, he took on a body like ours with its desires. He took on a body with its curse. Hanging on a tree not only referenced the execution stake but alludes back to the garden of Eden. Adam ate from the tree of knowledge. Our lives have hung on a tree (cursed) ever since.

Yeshua became a curse by taking on our body with its desire in order to save us. This is the ultimate laying down of one's life. We see this level of laying one's life down in Paul, and it should be our goal as well. "That I could wish myself actually under God's curse and separated from the Messiah, if it would help my brothers, my own flesh and blood" (Romans 9:3).

Paul was becoming like the Messiah and manifesting the same attributes as the Messiah. "Try to imitate me (Paul), even as I myself try to imitate the Messiah" (1 Corinthians 11:1).

When *Yeshua* took the *Yetzer Hara* to the execution stake for the first time since Adam, this nature was taken out of the world without bearing any fruit. *Yeshua* slayed its desire the whole time He was alive, and then it was executed on the stake. Death was swallowed up by the life of the Messiah. This is Israel's potential.

Now, on Yom Kippur, the blood (life) of the Messiah cleanses our consciences from works that lead to death (sin). This is the knowledge of the Messiah. The potential of death is swallowed up by life (1 Corinthians 14:54-55, Isaiah 25:7-8, Hoshea 13:14, Revelation 7:13-17, Revelation 21:1-4, Revelation 22:1-5).

"How blessed are those who washed their robes, so that they have the right to eat from the Tree of Life and go through the gates into the city" (Revelation 22:14). To wash their robes meant to have their consciences cleansed from works that lead to death. The robes are our conscience. You can't take old mindsets, wounds, values, or attitudes with you into the Torah. We can't go into the Torah from a human perspective, or we will just twist the Word. The Lord will spew this mindset out. We won't find life in the Torah but a famine.

He cleansed our conscience from works that lead to death, the desire to do evil. Now, we might approach our wedding vows once again in union with *Yeshua*. This is the Torah of the garden, and it will actually flow out of us as living waters. This is the gospel of the garden. The Torah outside the garden (spirit) is man's perspective of the Torah and becomes one connected to the old nature. This becomes the law of sin and death in our lives.

מ

REMARRIED

Who will free us from this body bound for death? What will it be like? The power of our union with the Messiah is the power over death. Think about death being swallowed up in life. Is that not what *Yeshua* did? Even though the *Yetzer Hara* was there with *Yeshua*, you never saw it. It was literally swallowed up by His life. Sin is swallowed up by righteousness when, instead of sinning, you find yourself doing righteous deeds. When we sin, the shame and guilt devastates our self-esteem, but when we do righteous deeds, it boosts our self-esteem.

> Thanks be to God [He will]!—Through *Yeshua* [this name of God is an attribute of God, called salvation, which manifests in the earth. This attribute swallows up death.] The Messiah, our Lord! To sum up: with my mind, I am a slave of God's Torah— But with my old nature, I am a slave of sin's "torah." Therefore, there is no longer any condemnation awaiting those who are in union with the Messiah *Yeshua*.
> Romans 7:24-8:1 (CJB)

When is there no condemnation waiting for us? On Yom Kippur, for those in union with *Yeshua*. In union with *Yeshua*, Yom Kippur becomes the great day of deliverance from the body bound for death.

Why? Because the Torah of the Spirit [God's Torah], which produces this life [resurrection life, life of the garden] in union with Messiah *Yeshua*, has set me free from the "torah" of sin and death [curse of the human perspective]. For what the Torah could not do by itself [produce life], because it lacked the power to make the old nature cooperate [cleanse our conscience form works that lead to death], God did by sending his son [becoming like you] as a human being with a nature like ours [*Yetzer Hara*] own sinful one [but without sin]. God did this in order to deal with sin, and in so doing he executed the punishment against sin in the human nature.

Romans 8:2-3 (CJB)

What does it mean to execute judgment against sin in the human nature? When you lay hands on someone to pray for them, you are executing judgment. It means to deliver them. *Yeshua* is not coming to judge us but to deliver us by executing judgment on our enemy, in this case, sin in the human nature. This enemy prevented us from seeing from God's perspective. We experienced the world through a veil of illusions. This inhibited us from seeing the "oneness of God."

This enemy at its root is the desire to be God, this desire in the human nature to add to or subtract form God's Torah. Freeing us from this enemy gives us access back to the garden, God's kingdom, as we will rule and reign with God. No longer will sin and death rule and reign in us. "So that the just requirement of the Torah might be fulfilled in us who do not run our lives according to what our old nature wants but according to what the spirit wants" (Romans 8:4).

Running our lives by what the old nature wants is working the soil by our own efforts. It is only by the Spirit that we are able to fulfill the Torah. It makes sense that if *Yeshua* fulfilled the Torah then those in union with (married to) Him will also fulfill it. What does it mean to fulfill the Torah? To teach the Torah and walk it out in the spirit it was intended. The ultimate fulfillment should manifest in love, a Torah that covers a multitude of sin, not one that exposes people.

> Don't owe anyone anything—except to love one another; for whoever loves his fellow human being has *fulfilled* Torah. For

the commandments, "Don't commit adultery," "Don't murder," "Don't steal," "Don't covet," and any others are summed up in this one rule: "Love your neighbor as yourself." Love does not do harm to a neighbor, therefore, love is the fullness of Torah.

Romans 13:8-10 (CJB)

Paul says the only debt we should owe anyone is to fulfill the Torah. This fullness should manifest as love. The question we can ask ourselves is this: Does our idea of fulfilling Torah look any different than *Yeshua*'s life? Do we view *Yeshua* teaching anything other than the Torah? If we answer yes, then we might have a distorted view of the Torah or *Yeshua*'s teachings.

Don't think that I have come to abolish [add to or subtract from] the Torah or the prophets. I have not come to abolish but to complete [or fulfill]. Yes, indeed! I tell you that until heaven and earth pass away, not so much as a *yud* [smallest Hebrew letter] or a stroke [a crown on top of a Hebrew letter] will pass from the Torah—not until everything that must happen has happened. *So whoever* disobeys [adds to or subtracts from] the least of these *Mitzvots* and teaches others to do so will be called least in the kingdom [loss of privileges or access to the kingdom, garden, Tree of Life] of heaven. But whoever obeys and teaches others will be great in the kingdom of heaven [have access to God's movement upon the earth].

Matthew 5:17-19 (CJB)

Outside the garden are those who choose not to fulfill the Torah. They are called least in the kingdom which is a loss of access. Those who approach God's Word from a human perspective, they twist the word into something it is not. "For those who identify with their old nature set their minds on the things [sin, sinful people] of the old nature, but those who identify with the Spirit set their minds on the things of the Spirit [Torah and spiritual people]" (Romans 8:5, CJB).

It is the Spirit of God that writes the Torah on our hearts and minds. The only place the Spirit leads us is into the realms of the Torah. The Spirit does not connect to manmade commandments or traditions. The Spirit empowers us to walk a Torah lifestyle; the Spirit connects to that which originated from the Spirit.

> For I will take you from among the nations [dust of the earth] gather you from all the countries and return you to your own soil [Torah]. Then I will sprinkle clean water on you [wash you with the Word, Ephesians 5:26] and you will be clean: I will cleanse you from all your uncleanness and from your idols [cleanse your conscience from works that lead to death, Hebrews 9:14]. I will give you a new heart [cleansed conscience] and put a new spirit inside you; I will take the stony heart [*Yetzer Hara*] out of your flesh and give you a heart of flesh [new nature, new earth]. I will put my Spirit [one spirit with Messiah, new heaven] inside of you and cause you to live by my laws, respect my rulings and obey them. [This is walking with God in the cool of the day].
>
> Ezekiel 36:24-28 (CJB)

The Spirit causes us to walk in God's Torah. It gives us the desire to pursue His commandments.

> Having one's mind controlled by the old nature [tree of knowledge] is death, but having one's mind controlled by the Spirit [tree of life] is life and Shalom. For the mind controlled by the old nature is hostile to God [It can't see the oneness of God and instead of being one with God, it wants to be God], because it does not submit itself to God's Torah—indeed it cannot [because it is cursed to eat the dust of the earth]. Thus those who identify with their old nature cannot please God.
>
> Romans 6:6-8 (CJB)

So the Lord knows how to rescue the godly from trials and how to hold the wicked until the Day of Judgment while continuing to punish them [bringing the curse of eating the forbidden fruit to its fullness], especially those who follow their old nature in lust for filth and who despise authority [won't submit to God's Torah].

2 Peter 2:9-10 (CJB)

Therefore, do not let sin rule in your mortal bodies [because the curse has been broken, now you are to overcome the seed of the Serpent], so that it makes you obey its desires, and do not offer any part of yourselves to sin as an instrument for wickedness [You are no longer joined to the old nature but to the Messiah]. On the contrary, offer yourselves to God as people alive from the dead [curse of eating fruit], and your various parts to God as instruments for righteousness. For sin will not have authority over you; because you are not under legalism [law of sin and death] but under grace [Torah by the Spirit].

Romans 6:12-14 (CJB)

But you, you don't identify with your old nature [human perspective] but with the Spirit [God's perspective]—provided the Spirit of God is living in you, for anyone who doesn't have the Spirit of the Messiah does not belong to him. However, if the Messiah is in you, then, on the one hand, the body is dead because of sin [eating the forbidden fruit]; but on the other hand, the Spirit is giving life [causing you to overcome the seed of the serpent] because God considered you righteous. And if the Spirit of the one who raised *Yeshua* from the dead [overcame the sinful nature] is living in you, then the one who raised the Messiah *Yeshua* from the dead will also give life to your mortal bodies [cause you to overcome or crush the head of the serpent] through His Spirit living in you.

Romans 8:9-11 (CJB)

The word *head* in Hebrew is *Rosh*. It can mean authority. The head of the serpent is the authority, power, or control of the serpent (human nature).

> So then, brothers, we don't owe a thing to our old nature [the second husband] that would require us to live according to the old nature [the *ketubah*, law of sin and death, for we are married to God now]. For if you live according to your old nature, you will certainly die; but if, by the Spirit you keep putting to death the practices of the body [crushing the head of the serpent], you will live.
>
> Romans 8:12-13 (CJB)

Let me explain this for a minute. When we are married to God, we have the Torah as our *ketubah* (marriage vows). This is the order that governs our married life together. The Torah is God's righteousness. When God drove Adam out of the garden and divorced the house of Israel, he freed her from her *ketubah*, the Torah of righteousness. She was freed from righteousness and became a slave of sin and death.

> For when you were slaves of sin [joined to the old nature, married to another], You were free in relationship to righteousness [freed from the Torah], but what benefit did you derive from the things of which you are now ashamed? The end result [of eating from the tree of knowledge] was death. However, now, freed from sin [old nature was put to death] and enslaved [married] to God, you do benefit—it consists in being made holy, set apart for God, and its end result [of eating of the tree of life] is eternal life.
>
> Romans 6:20-22 (CJB)

All who are led by God's Spirit are God's sons. For you did not receive a Spirit of slavery to bring us back again into fear; on the contrary, you received the Spirit, who *makes* us sons and by who's power we cry, "Abba!" [That is, "Dear father!"]. The Spirit himself bears witness with our Spirit that we are children of God [we originated from God]; and if we are children, then we are also heirs, heirs of God and joint-heirs with the Messiah—provided we are suffering with Him in order also to be glorified with Him.

Romans 8:14-17 (CJB)

We receive the Spirit, which makes us sons. This is the Spirit that causes us to manifest as sons of God. In order for this manifestation to occur, there must be a demand put on the potential of God within us. The suffering is the demand put on our potential as we begin to overcome the earthly nature and manifest the presence of God in the earth.

Yom Kippur mirrors the Passover. What was accomplished on Passover remained as potential; for example, *Yeshua* freed us from sin, yet it appears as though we are still bound to sin. Yom Kippur is the bringing of this potential, what *Yeshua* accomplished, to actualization or manifestation. Once we become one Spirit with God, the Spirit now causes us to overcome sin and manifest as sons.

Each year, when we come to Yom Kippur, we will overcome a new level. We will change from image to image and from glory to glory. In other words, the things we struggled with, the demand that was put on our potential, we will overcome. The next year, we will overcome a new level of lifestyle. The things we struggled with last year are no longer a struggle this year, as we have already overcome them.

> Next I heard a voice from heaven saying, "Write, 'How blessed are the dead who died united with the Lord [old nature was put to death with Messiah on the stake], from now on!' 'Yes', says the Spirit, 'now they may rest from their efforts [now they have entered into the Spirit life no longer working the soil by their

own efforts], for the things they have accomplished [overcome] follow along with them [into their future].'"

Revelation 14:13 (CJB)

"But the path of the righteous is like the light of dawn, shining ever brighter until full daylight" (Proverbs 4:18). It grows brighter and brighter as we overcome more and more of the darkness. We are overcomers, and we are in the process of overcoming the human perspective. The Spirit bears witness with our Spirit that we are one with God and we are His.

Also, we are suffering with Him as we go into the world, out into the field, and bring others to Him, as we look past the flesh by the Spirit of God and see the potential in others. As mentors, we help bring their potential out and manifest it. Help them serve the instruction God has placed in them to the universe.

Up to this point, we have had a lot of teaching. I would like to give a little instruction on how we can apply this to our lives. We have discussed that we cannot approach the Torah by the human perspective and produce life. The land, the Torah, the people, and the God of Israel are *echad*, one. If we can't approach the Torah from the human perspective, then we can't approach people from the human perspective and produce life.

If we approach our brother from the human perspective, all we will see is flesh. We will see the failures and faults of each other. We will find ourselves judging our brothers instead of delivering our brothers. This is not the fruit of the Torah, of love.

God's garden or vineyard is people. If we approach people of God by the Spirit, we will look past the flesh, the veil, and we will see the potential of God in our brother. We will see the Messiah. We will be able to eat the fruit of the tree of life that is planted in the heart of our brother. The fruit is the instruction of God contained in our brother for our future.

However, we are not to eat the fruit of carnal men. This is the tree of knowledge. This fruit is the instruction of man and man's wisdom. It will not produce life. You will be serving and obeying creation and not the Creator. People are likened unto trees. You need to be able to distinguish between the two trees.

> How blessed are those who reject the advice of the wicked [tree of knowledge], don't stand on the *way* of sinners or sit where scoffers sit! Their delight is in *Adonai*'s Torah; on His Torah they meditate day and night. They are like *trees* planted by streams—they bear their fruit in season, their leaves never wither, everything they do succeeds.
>
> Psalm 1:1-3

The men who meditate on God's Torah day and night are the trees God told Adam He could eat from, the fruit of righteous men. This is the instruction, the living Torah, for our future.

These men are also described in Revelation 22:1-4—the trees whose leaves are healing for the nations. They are the men whose instruction brings healing to the nations. This was a description of a Torah scroll, and these men are living Torah scrolls.

We must use discernment and not take instruction or advice from wicked men, for their fruit will abort the life of God in us. Carnal men can't see by the Spirit. All they see in the earth is judgment. It is by the Spirit that you see deliverance. It is by the Spirit that you see God's kingdom, His movement on the earth. Anyone seeing from the human perspective wants to flee or escape the earth rather than rule and reign in the earth. In the garden, heaven and earth work for us. It is paradise.

There are two trees: the tree of knowledge—the human perspective—and the tree of life—God's perspective. When Adam ate the fruit of his earthly nature, he lost dominion. Heaven and earth worked against him. He was working the land by his own efforts.

Now that the Messiah came at Passover and fully saved and redeemed us, why has it remained in potential form? Why have we not eaten the fruit of the tree of life?

The house of Israel has rejected the Torah for a season. They can't see the tree. If you don't know God's commandments (tree of life), how can you distinguish between His and man's commandments (tree of knowledge)? You can't. The house of Judah has not been able to see the Messiah. They have been approaching the Torah from the human perspective.

YHYH said that in the last days, when all these things have come upon us, both the blessing and the curses, He would reverse our exile. When this happens, it will be the last generation. It will be *Yeshua* who does this.

"All your children [last generation] will be taught [Torah] by *Adonai* [Spirit], your children will have great peace" (Isaiah 54:13). *Yeshua* quotes this same verse when He refers to the last days:

> No one can come to me unless the Father—the one who sent me—draws him [goes and gets him]. And I will raise him up [from the dust of the earth] on the last day [Yom Kippur, referencing the millennial kingdom]. It is written in the prophets, 'They will be taught by *Adonai*.'"
>
> John 6:44-45

Just as Adam was taught by *Adonai*, so will be the last generation. *Yeshua* never came to abolish the Torah but to expound it and bring it into its glory, teach it to us from His perspective, how it was intended to be from the beginning.

This is done when we study the Torah by the power of the Holy Spirit, also as we talk to Holy, spiritual men about the Torah. The Spirit causes (instructs) us to see the Torah from God's perspective and puts God's desires on the inside of us, written on our hearts.

We know that when Adam ate the fruit, the serpent was cursed to eat the dust of the earth. This alludes to the strong desire for sin and death. Now the desire for sin was written on our hearts.

> By God's grace, you, who were once slaves to sin, *obeyed from your heart* the patterns of teachings [related to generational curses] to which you were exposed; [Law of sin and death] and after you had been set free from sin, you became enslaved to righteousness [Torah written on your heart].
> Romans 6:17-18

After the Torah is written on our hearts, will the potential to miss the mark remain? This is an interesting question from a Christian aspect. The Christian mindset is to die and go to heaven an instant transition a sort of escape where the Hebrew mindset is the model of inheritance where God takes you from instruction (glory) to instruction (glory) to an inheritance. In other words, there is an instant transition, but then we bring the process of overcoming. We will overcome death from one revelation of life to the next. It is a process of healing and revelation. God loves process.

Heaven is a lifestyle. We inherit a lifestyle. You have to be taught how to inherit a lifestyle.

ב

HELL

As we have seen, by adding to YHVH's Word, Adam, in essence, was lifting Himself up above God's Word and above God. Whether Adam fully comprehended what he was doing or not, that is what he was doing.

Isaiah describes this fall of Adam falling from the heavens or heavenly realms down to earth. In fact, Isaiah uses the term *she'ol* which is the grave or pit. The word *she'ol* does not mean a place of punishment when you die, just simply the grave, where all people good or bad go when they die. It also alludes to the realm of death. Adam entered a spiritual grave. This spiritual grave would lead to an eventual physical grave as well.

Adam died spiritually, and it was as if he was buried in a grave called the earthly nature. We are going to take apart a scripture that most of us are familiar with. However, this might be a completely new way of looking at it: "How did you come to fall from the heavens, morning star, son of dawn (Lucifer)? How did you come to be cut to the ground, conqueror of nations?" (Isaiah 14:12).

The name *morning star* is translated as *Lucifer* in many translations. Lucifer is a reference to Venus, which is the morning star. This is traditionally taught to be Satan. I'm not disagreeing with that, as there are further references to this in the New Testament. Once again there is more to *HaSatan* than what is usually taught.

Adam was a son of God, *Yeshua* is the Son of God, and all of creation is waiting for the sons of God to manifest. Adam was created in the image of God. Adam fell from this image into the image of mortal man, *Yeshua* came in the exact image Adam was originally created in. *Yeshua* came to resurrect us from the image of death to the image of the son of God. *Yeshua's* image is our image and was Adam's original image.

Let's look at another name for the image of the Son of God. If it is a name for *Yeshua*, then it was a name for Adam and a name for us. Let's look at another name for *Yeshua*: "I, *Yeshua*, have sent my angel to give you this testimony for the Messianic communities. I am the root and offspring of David, the *bright Morning Star*" (Revelation 22:16).

Morning star is the name that Isaiah used that we see translated as *Lucifer*. Is *Yeshua* comparing Himself to Lucifer? Is *Yeshua* calling Himself Satan? Think about this. Some religious denominations draw from this that *Yeshua* and Satan are brothers, but who does *Yeshua* call his brothers? "For both *Yeshua*, who sets people apart from God, and the one being set apart have a common origin—this is why he is not ashamed to *call them brothers*" (Hebrews 2:11). Now *Yeshua* calls men his brothers.

This is explained in this next verse. "Because those whom he knew in advance, he also determined in advance would be conformed to the pattern of his son [bright Morning Star] so that he might be the firstborn among many brothers" (Romans 8:29).

Now we see *Yeshua* is conforming people into His image, the image of a son of God. Another name for this image is the *Morning Star*. Could it be that Adam was called the Morning Star before the fall? Could that be one of the things that Isaiah was alluding to? "How did you come to fall from the heavens, morning star [Adam], son of the dawn? How did you come to be cut to the ground, conqueror of nations?" (Isaiah 14:12).

Let's look at another verse. This one is found in the book of Job. It is in Hebrew poetry. Hebrew poetry will say the same thing twice but word it differently. For example: "When the morning stars sang together, and all the sons of God shouted for joy?" (Job 38:7).

Job alludes to the morning stars and the sons of God as the same thing. Abraham's descendants are likened unto the stars. Could it be that Adam was the morning star that fell and was brought down to *she'ol*, the dust of the earth? Now, *Yeshua* came to resurrect them from the dust of the earth and set them like stars once again in the heavenly realms.

> Many of those sleeping in the dust of the earth will awaken, some to everlasting life and some to everlasting shame and abhorrence. But these who can discern will shine like the brightness of heaven's dome, and those who turn many to righteousness like *stars forever* and ever.
>
> Daniel 12:2-3

They will be raised from the dust to the stars. Now let's go back to Isaiah and watch from stars to dust. Adam was taken from the dust of the earth. This is a type of mortal nations. He is clothed in immortality, or everlasting life, and then he falls back to the dust of the earth. This fall was rooted in pride, adding to and subtracting from the command of God: "You thought to yourself, 'I will scale the heavens, I will raise my throne above God's stars. I will sit on the Mount of Assembly far away in the north'" (Isaiah 14:12).

Is Isaiah describing Adam's thought process, or is he maybe describing the desires of the *Yetzer Hara*? It was from this serpent that the thought of adding to God's commandment flowed. Maybe when the serpent spoke to Adam it was more subtle. Maybe Adam simply thought, *Now that God has given me Eve, I want to protect her. I will build a fence around the commandment just to make sure she does not break it.*

You begin to see a connection between fear and pride. The fear of Eve breaking a commandment reveals distrust in God's Word being sufficient. Adam began to think he was wiser than God. His decision is to elevate himself above God and His commandment by making his own commandment.

This is where the thought gets even more interesting. When Adam was joined to God, Adam, Torah, and *Yeshua* were one. Adam had dominion over the earth, including his earthly nature. It was not that Adam did not have an earthly nature; after all, he was taken from the dust of the earth.

Adam was placed in the garden. The serpent did not stand a chance. Adam had dominion over the serpent. In Isaiah's words, "How did you come to fall from the heavens, morning star?" How did Adam fall? By himself, Adam would not have fallen. Maybe the serpent would have never gotten dominion. The same thing goes for Eve. Eve had dominion as well.

When Adam passed a manmade commandment to Eve as God's command, it left her vulnerable, exposed. Watch this dance take place for a moment between the serpent and the woman.

> He said to the woman, "Did God really say, 'You are not to eat from any tree in the garden?'" The woman answered the serpent, "We may eat from the fruit of the trees of the garden, but about the fruit of the tree in the middle of the garden God said, 'You are neither to eat form it *nor touch it*, or you will die.'"
>
> Genesis 3:1a-3

The woman answers the serpent exactly the way *Yeshua* did in the wilderness, He quoted scripture. She quotes what she thought was God's Word back to the serpent. Had it been God's Word, she would have had dominion over the serpent. Eve did exactly what she was supposed to do, only it was man's command instead of God's that she quoted. It was added to God's Word.

The Spirit of God does not empower us to walk out manmade commandments. The Spirit of God does not attach itself to manmade commandments. What we might be discovering is that it took two. It took two people in order for man to fall. The serpent might not have been able to get dominion over either one by themselves. Look what God says after the fall and they both ate: "To Adam, he said, 'Because you listened to what your wife said and ate from the tree about which *I gave you the order*, "You are not to eat from it"'" (Genesis 3:17a).

Notice God reiterates that He gave Adam the order. It does not say He gave Eve the order. So the answer to Isaiah's question, "How did you come to fall?" might be, "It took two." "I will rise past the tops of the clouds; I will make myself like the Most High" (Isaiah 14:14).

How is someone who is already in the image of God going to make himself like the Most High? By adding to God's commandment and trying to rule over people. We were not created to rule over people but the earth and the animals. In doing this, he broke the covenant. Now, instead of being one with God, he was severing the relationship. This was the fall of his purpose. Now, like God, Adam was making his own commandments.

Well, the results of this choice led to Adam falling from the heavenly image of immortality down to *she'ol* and the image of mortal man, from the realm of life to the realm of death: "Instead you are brought down to *she'ol*, to the uttermost depths of the pit" (Isaiah 14:15).

I have several things I would like to talk about here. We know Adam fell from the heavenly realms down to *she'ol*. We saw that the serpent was cursed to eat the dust of the earth, to crawl on its belly. This is as low down to the earth as one gets.

This is just something to think about. What if, before Adam ate the fruit, the human perspective was not cursed to eat the dust of the earth, it was not bound to sin and death? In other words, the human perspective did not have to be bound to sin. There is a tradition in Judaism that Adam was going to eventually eat from the tree of knowledge. He just did it before its time. It is taught that Adam was first to eat of the tree of life and then he would be able to eat from the tree of knowledge.

We can look at it this way: Adam ate from the human perspective before it had matured and been fully connected to the will of God. It is interesting to me that the serpent was not cursed until after the fall of man. In the same way, *HaSatan* is not initially the personification of evil but a servant of the Most High. I can't help but see the connection between Adam, the serpent, and *HaSatan*. "Instead you are brought down to *She'ol*, to the uttermost depths of the pit" (Isaiah 14:15).

This is the ultimate picture of exile. The morning star is being exiled from heaven and sent to the lowest parts of *She'ol*. Adam is being exiled from the garden out into darkness. We must take a look at a Hebrew concept here. The topic is exile often translated and interpreted as hell. This idea is an exile from what we were created to be.

The word *she'ol* in Hebrew is the place where all the dead go, the netherworld. Both good and bad people alike go there. *She'ol* was not connected to punishment when you die like the concept of hell is pictured today. This concept of punishment did not occur until long after the times of *Yeshua*.

People had a hard time with both good and bad people going to the same place, so they taught that this only happened until *Yeshua*'s ascension. Then the saints went to heaven and all the bad people stayed in Hades. Hades became a place of torment and torture forever. The Greek concept of Hades merged into the biblical world. Keep in mind hell is very real it is just different than what modern Christianity has taught. Hell was understood in ancient times as to go out into the unknown. This is where Adam went, out into the unknown; the garden was the known.

In the Hebrew world, the term *she'ol* can refer to a grave for those who are physically dead but also is used to elude to a spiritual grave. When someone died spiritually, they were sent into an exile, an exile from the presence of God. The Hebrew language describes these exiles in imagery that paints a picture to the heart and imagination, like lake of fire, darkness, and gnashing of teeth, etc.

The big problem that occurs is that in the Western Greek mindset, we have rearranged these descriptions to refer to a place where you go when you die. We were right, but it is where you go when you die spiritually. The real complication happens when you are born in exile, already spiritually dead. You were born in Egypt (world), that fiery furnace, and you never experienced the garden. It is hard for a carnal man—which we all were when we first came to *Yeshua*—to realize that your life prior to *Yeshua* and the Torah is the biblical definition of hell.

We see terms like *life* and *death*, and *eternal life* and *eternal punishment*. We are never really taught what they meant. We don't realize that these terms can refer to a physical life and death and then there are ones that refer to a spiritual (eternal) life and (eternal punishment) spiritual death. When Adam ate of the fruit, he died, but not physically right away. He died spiritually. He began to experience eternal punishment, which meant to be exiled from God's presence. We experience eternal life when we return to God's presence and we are spiritually alive.

Think about seminary today. Who taught the seminaries their information? We see a huge transition from the Roman Catholic era until mainstream evangelical Christian era of today. Most of the transition has occurred by men realizing there were errors in theology, and they began to correct them. You cannot look at church history and see evangelical theology taught from Jesus's day until today, not at all. My point is the *Ruach HaKodesh* (Holy Spirit) is bringing us back to the beginning. There might still be some skewed ideas that need to be adjusted. The only reason the Holy Spirit would be revealing this to us is to bless our lives.

There are many words, ideas, and concepts that the church would be blessed to learn from the house of Judah, and then they (Jews) would be blessed to discover the Messiah in the house of Israel. I would like you to meditate on this verse for a moment: "Then what advantage has the Jew? What is the value of being circumcised? Much in every way! In the first place, the Jews were entrusted with *the very words of God*" (Romans 3:1-2).

Do you realize that the very words Paul is speaking about are the Torah, the very word's God said will never change? These are the very words that historically the church has rejected or at the very least neglected. We took the New Testament out of its context, the Torah, and took the concepts we knew as the Gentile world and attached them to the words of the Bible.

If we could take the New Testament and drop it off into a Buddhist colony in Tibet and, years down the road, they sent missionaries to America to teach the gospel to us, it would be very different than the one we have today. It would have taken on a synchronized feel. It would have a Buddhist feel to it. People from America would say somebody needed to teach them how to read the New Testament. They would have had no choice but to interpret the Word through the lens of what they already knew. They did not do anything wrong; that is just what happened.

This is exactly what happened in the church world. We were separated from the Jewish people, the ones Paul said were the very keepers of God's Word, and we were forced to try to figure out what they meant. We have come a long way. We don't need to blame anybody, but we do need to be wise enough to dig back to a sure foundation.

Every one of us should come to a place where we can say, "I'm in a relationship with the God of Abraham, Isaac, and Jacob. I'm in a relationship with *Yeshua HaMachiach*, not a rapture theory. I'm not in a relationship with a theology." I find that when I discuss a concept that is new to people, some get angry and offended; in fact, I was one of them. The reason is because we are in more of a relationship with a concept than with the Messiah.

Listen, most of us confessed *Yeshua* long before we knew any theology. We are in a progressive revelation lifestyle now. God is taking this generation further than last generation. We have got to be able to talk with each other and realize we just might not know everything, especially between the church and the Jewish people.

The word *Hades* in Greek is the equivalent to the word *she'ol* in Hebrew. However, when you read the definitions, they shift. Hell became a place you go when you physically die, or if you are saved, you went to heaven. The gospel became a message to be summed up, that God created an earth, a heaven, and a hell. If you don't accept Jesus as your savior in the sixty to seventy years you are on the earth, with a darkened mind and spirit of stupor, you will burn in hell forever. Is that really the message from the beginning? Then *Yeshua* makes statements like, "You don't choose Me, I choose you."

Jewish people believe in hell, *she'ol*, etc., but not the way the church does. Remember, Paul says they are the very keepers of God's Word. Let's take a quick look at the origin of hell. Everything God created can be found in the seven days of creation. In Genesis, we see God creates heaven and earth, not hell. Somewhere in the beginning, we have to find the concept of hell or lake of fire, etc. Where is it found? Keep in mind that from the beginning, God created us for relationship and to demonstrate His love, not so much to give us a brief choice so He could punish us for all of eternity. It was about relationship. He only took us out (exile) of Himself to return (ingather) us to Himself. "The earth *was unformed* and *void, darkness* was on the face of the *deep*, and the Spirit of God hovered over the surface of the water" (Genesis 1:2).

The word *was* is the Hebrew word *hayah* #1961. It means, "to become, occur, come to pass, or be." In the T.W.O.T. 491, it means, "to be, become, exist, happen."

The word *hayah* can be translated as *was*, but that is not the full understanding of the word. In fact, most of the time, this word is translated as a process of becoming or became. Many scholars believe that the first verse of Genesis was a complete heaven (a-z) and a complete earth (a-z) and then in verse two, something happened and the earth became unformed and void.

Let's take a little time and look at the meanings and concepts of the words *unformed, void, darkness,* and *deep*. I will use Strong's and the T.W.O.T. for the definitions.

The word *void* is *bohuw*: "waste, ruin, empty, undistinguishable." This can be read that the earth became an undistinguishable empty ruin.

The word *without form* is *Tohu*: "to lie waste, a desolation, i.e. desert, a worthless thing, confusion, chaos, like a desert wasteland or a destroyed city, moral and spiritual emptiness or confusion, nothingness, *unreality*." This can be read that the earth became an undistinguishable ruin and it was laid to waste. It became a worthless thing full of chaos and confusion, a moral and spiritual emptiness.

Now let's look at Adam, who was without form and void when God took him from the dust of the earth. We see a picture of God not only taking him from the physical earth but on a deeper level of a moral and spiritual wasteland. This is exactly what God is doing again as He takes us from an unformed life with a spiritual void. This realm is of chaos and confusion. "For God is not the author of unruliness [confusion] but of peace" (1 Corinthians 14:33).

Now follow me as the Torah begins to take us deeper into this realm of destruction. It is amazing how many words and concepts find their origin right here in this second verse of Genesis.

The word *darkness* is *chosheck*: "the dark, misery, destruction, death, ignorance, sorrow, wickedness, as of the plague of darkness over Egypt, *judgment*, curse, evil and unbelief." We will begin to see the concepts connected with hell right here. The only thing we did not see right off the surface was fire. The concept of judgment is always associated with fire. We find the origin of death and curse here as well.

This entire realm of darkness is when the earth becomes unformed and void. The darkness is the absence of light, the light of Torah, the order of God. This is a clear picture of moral and spiritual chaos. The earth was empty of the breath of God. This was the place of misery, sorrow, and wickedness.

This darkness was also the plague that came upon Egypt. Egypt is a type of the world. This is the same darkness that is upon the world today. Before we came to the Messiah and His Torah, we were this very darkness. Genesis 1:2 was describing our unformed (Torahless) and void (of the Spirit) life before God took us from the dust of the earth. "For you used to be darkness; but now, united with the Lord, you are light" (Ephesians 5:8).

"But you are a chosen people, [chosen from the dust of the earth] the king's *cohanim*, a holy nation, a people for God to possess! Why? In order for you to declare the praises of the one who called you out of darkness into his wonderful light" (1 Peter 2:9). God only took us out (exile to darkness) of Himself in order to bring us back to Himself (the light) so we would declare His praises. This generation was born in the darkness and exile. They don't realize if they were in the nations, they were born in the biblical description of hell. *Yeshua* came to call them out of this darkness.

We keep shifting this to hell as a place you go when you die. Because of this, we have not been able to overcome the darkness we were born into. In fact, most don't even understand that it is possible. The church sees the only solution as a rapture or escape from the earth, but *Yeshua* is going to speak over the darkness of our life and say, "Let there be light."

> For it is God who once said, "Let light shine out of darkness (you)," who has made his light shine in our hearts, the light of the knowledge of God's glory shining in the face of the Messiah *Yeshua*. But we have this treasure in clay jars, so that it will be evident that such overwhelming power comes from God and not from us.
>
> 2 Corinthians 4:6-7

We have been exiled from the garden, fallen from the heavenly realms to the lower parts of *she'ol*. We became unformed and void, and our lives were full of darkness—a living hell. We are not waiting to die to go to hell; we were born in it. *Yeshua* is taking us from the nations, and he is bringing us into His Torah (forming us) and filling our void with His Spirit (breathing on us). It is happening right now. That is why you are reading this book.

This is what the church calls the rapture, but in Hebrew, it is called the ingathering. It is already happening. The church was interpreting the ingathering from a Western mindset instead of a Hebrew mindset.

Yeshua is forming us and breathing into us and placing us back into the garden. You can't compare what I'm writing about to anything you have ever seen because both houses of Israel have been in exile. Paul wrote about it, but we tried to relate it to what we knew and understood, and we missed part of it.

The word *deep* is *tehom*: "the abyss, the deep mass of water, to make an uproar, or to agitate greatly, also, tumult and vexed." It is related to panic, turmoil, severe disturbance, and discomfort. The word here refers to a sea, a mass of water. It is a picture of a sea of people. People are made up of mostly water. They are a body of moving water. This word *deep* or *abyss* is alluding to people as the water was not vexed, panicking, or in turmoil and discomfort; it is people who are. All through the Bible, the sea is alluding to people. "Then he said to me, 'The waters that you saw, where the whore is sitting, are peoples, crowds, nations and languages'" (Revelation 17:15).

This is another example of Hebrew imagery. There are many other examples as well. All these words that we have looked at begin to form a picture, one we usually call hell, a place of torment, pain and panic, great destruction, judgment (fire), sorrow, and misery. I'm going to give you a list of words found in the definition of these four words: *unformed*, *void*, *darkness*, and *deep*.

Ruin, a worthless thing, chaos, emptiness, confusion, unreality, misery, destruction, death, sorrow, wickedness, judgment, curse, ignorance, evil, unbelief, abyss, panic, turmoil, discomfort; all these words are related. This is the origin of hell, *HaSatan* and the realm of death.

All the concepts of judgment, punishment, curse, hell, etc., find their origin in the beginning in Genesis 1:2. We even find the lake of fire here. The word *darkness* means judgment, which is associated with fire in Hebrew. And, of course, *lake* originates from the word *deep*, a body of water. You find the lake of fire as describing darkness on the face of the deep. All of this is the root of *HaSatan*.

Is this a place we go to when we die? No. The source of all this pain, destruction, and torment is when our earth becomes unformed and void. When we are outside of Torah and separated from the Messiah, we are in hell, the dust of the earth, a spiritual grave, the realm of death. This is actually outside of the kingdom of God. "The earth [Adam] became unformed [Torahless] and void [Spiritless], and darkness [curse, death, and judgment] was on the surface [what is revealed] of the deep [people] and the Spirit of God hovered over the surface of the water [people]" (Genesis 1:2).

Notice the spirit of God was not in the sea. It hovered above the sea, the chaos. "Then *Adonai*, God, formed [Torah] a person [Adam] from the dust of the ground [unformed earth] and breathed into his nostrils [filling the void with] the breath of life [the light that shined out of darkness]" (Genesis 2:7).

The first creation, seven days of creation, God dealt with the physical order of creation, including our physical bodies. We see this order every day in creation. This is physical order. The physical order precedes the moral and spiritual order. "Note, however, that the body from the Spirit did not come first, but the ordinary [physical] human one; the one from the Spirit comes afterward" (1 Corinthians 15:46).

The spiritual does not precede the natural or physical order. Watch the pattern. In the first creation, God creates the heavens and the earth. Darkness is on the face of the deep (Genesis 1).

The second type of creation, Genesis 2: God forms Adam from the dust of the earth (new earth) and breathes the breath of life (new heaven) and places him in the garden; no more darkness.

Now let's look at a much bigger picture of this pattern:

> In the beginning God created the heavens and the earth. The earth was unformed [Torahless] and void [no breath of God], darkness [curse, lack, and decrease] was on the face of the deep [the nations] and the Spirit of God hovered over [not in] the surface of the water [people in chaos].
>
> Genesis 1:1-2

Now watch the second creation. Notice the differences. This is the moral and spiritual order that is Torah and Spirit:

> Then I saw a new heaven [Spirit-filled void] and a new earth [Torah-formed earth], for the old heaven and old earth [former life] passed away, and the sea [people in chaos and confusion] was no longer there. Also, I saw the holy city, the New Jerusalem [people who were formerly in the sea], coming down out of heaven from God, prepared [formed] like a bride beautifully dressed [in Torah's white linen garments] for her husband [*Yeshua*]. I heard a loud voice from the throne say, "See! God's *Sh'khina* [the Spirit that hovered over the sea] is with [in] mankind and he will live with [in] them. They will be his people, and He will wipe away every tear from their eyes [no more sorrow, darkness]. There will no longer be any death [darkness that was on the face of the deep, hell]; there will no longer be any mourning, crying, pain; because the old order [fleshy nature] has passed away."
>
> Revelation 21:1-4 (CJB)

This old order of pain, sorrows, etc., all find their origin in Genesis 1:2. Now God places them into the garden. Think about this for a moment. The Hebraic view of hell was not so much a place you go when you physically die but a place you are in when you are physically alive but spiritually dead. It was the six-thousand-year exile from the garden while Adam, Torah, and *Yeshua* were separate. When Adam ate the forbidden fruit, this order of oneness went into chaos. Curse, pain, sorrow, and death became a reality. Adam went out into darkness, which is what was described in Genesis 1:2. Adam was exiled. Notice God did not say, "The day you eat of the fruit you will go to hell when you physically die."

When Adam ate of the forbidden fruit, he became unformed and void. Darkness enveloped his life like a sea of chaos. Hell is when we are unformed and void. This is the biblical understanding. This darkness of exile is what *Yeshua* came to take us out of. He was a light to the nations (darkness). This is the light of the first day of creation: "Then God said, 'Let there be light'; and there was light" (Genesis 1:3).

How did the earth become unformed and void? God is not the author of chaos. Who was given free choice? Who could cause the earth to become a desert wasteland (*tohu* without form)? All of creation does what it was created to do. Only man was given a free choice. Let's get back to Isaiah: "Those who see you will stare at you, reflecting on what has become of you. 'Is this the *man* who shook the earth, who made kingdoms tremble, who made the world a desert, who destroyed its cities, who would not set his prisoners free [forgive people]?'" (Isaiah 14:16-17).

Once again, we see a connection with Satan and man. It seems that man was the author of confusion. He made his own choices, and it brought destruction on the world. I hope you found some thought here that sparks your interest for further study. I'm sure it has been a challenge for many. We just might be waking up from hell and about to experience something right here on earth that can't even be described. All efforts in a human language will fail to describe experiencing God. It will be like heaven on earth.

The focus of the Gospel from the beginning was the return of man to the garden of Eden. The focus of scripture was not where you go when you die. Think of the Bible as the book of decisions, not the book of destination when you die.

ס

NAKEDNESS

As I start off this chapter, I want to explain something about heaven and the heavenly realms. When I talk about Adam's fall, what did Adam lose or fall from? He lost dominion in the earth. He did not lose heaven in the sense of a place you go when you die. That was not the model. Was Adam ever going to die? When I talk about walking in the heavenly realms or falling from heaven, I'm alluding to the kingdom of heaven that was ruling on earth through Adam. Adam never lost heaven in the sense that we are taught in Christianity; he lost dominion that was given to him by heaven over the earth. Walking in the authority of heaven, he fell from that place of authority.

In the garden, Adam was clothed in righteousness. He walked in the heavenly realms or in the spirit life. Adam walked in the heavenly kingdom. He was clothed in the presence of God. In fact, the Torah states that Adam was naked and not ashamed. Adam was not hidden from the face of YHVH. The heavenly kingdom or court system never brings shame; only the earthly kingdom or court system does. This is pictured today in religion: "They were both naked, the man and his wife, and they were not ashamed" (Genesis 2:25).

After they ate of the fruit of the tree of knowledge, their eyes were opened and they realized they were naked. What does this mean? We will take a closer look at this, as it is a theme that runs through the whole Bible. Think about it. What would their eyes be open to that they were formerly not open to? Could it be the realm of death? Could it be they saw themselves no longer through the eyes of the heavenly kingdom? "Then the eyes of both of them were opened, and they realized that they were naked. So they sewed fig leaves together to make themselves loin clothes" (Genesis 3:7).

Let's start taking this apart. What exactly changed? What were their eyes opened to? They both became aware of their earthly nature or the ego. They became aware of self in a way they never had before and were married to the fleshy nature with its desires. As they became one with this nature, they could no longer separate themselves from it. In other words, they experienced the earthly nature as themselves.

As with all sin, they, for the first time, experienced guilt and shame. This bad choice filled their lives with shame. In the world of Judaism, their concept of hell is to experience shame. The shame we feel because of sin is like being on fire, as it destroys and consumes our lives, our image, and our potential. You can't see purpose through the lens of shame.

The idea of being naked is to no longer have a covering. Yom Kippur is the Day of Atonement. *Kippur* also means "cover or covering." Adam and Eve found themselves outside of God's covering. They stepped outside of Torah into the realm of whoredom. They experienced the shame and guilt as nakedness. They needed a Yom Kippur in their lives. Paul describes the covering that Adam once had and that we will have again:

> We know that when the tent [earthly nature] which houses us here one earth [the earthly realm] is torn down [overcome], we have a permanent building [Spiritual nature] from God [originated from God], a building not made by human hands, to house us in heaven.
>
> 2 Corinthians 5:1

This building (kingly garments) from God is the part of Adam that died or fell asleep when he sinned and fell from the heavens. It was a picture of royal garments, that of a king. Now Adam was bound to the earthly realm to live according to the limited human perspective. Some take this verse as talking about shedding our physical earthly bodies. I believe there is more to this verse than that. I don't want to miss what Paul is really getting at.

Let's continue through these verses from Paul's perspective as he explains them. He will explain that this earthly body or nature is naked because of its desire for sin, which exposes us, and the constant shame we experience. This is the body bound for *she'ol* or bound for death: "For in this tent, our earthly body [body bound for death] we groan with desire [birthing pains] to have around us the home from heaven [Spiritual body with its desires, royal garments] that will be ours" (2 Corinthians 5:2).

Paul describes this heavenly body as a covering that will be around us. While in our earthly body, we groan with desire. This phrase should take us back to Romans 7:8, where Paul wants to be freed from the body bound for death. Paul groans and eagerly waits to be made a son. That is, to have his whole body redeemed and set free, freed from the desire for sin and the fruit of shame: "With this around us we will not be found *naked*" (2 Corinthians 5:3).

Death, the earthly nature, is swallowed up by life, the heavenly nature. Then we are no longer naked, no longer hidden from the face of God. This is a reference back to the nakedness that Adam and Eve experienced. Again, we must take the gospel back to the beginning. I might sound repetitive, but for so long, we have turned the gospel into something that it is not. It is human nature to do so. We must see from God's perspective and clothe ourselves in His nature.

This nakedness is connected to the guilt and shame we experience because of sin. Adam and Eve needed a covering, but this covering would have to be connected to a cleansing, a cleansing of the guilt and shame. This is the theme of Yom Kippur. This cleansing, however, could not be accomplished by the blood of bulls and goats. This new body was a cleansed conscience. The nakedness was a defiled conscience. The human perspective is a defiled conscience. This needed to be cleansed so we would receive a new God conscience.

> But when the Messiah appeared as High Priest of the good things [you] that are happening already [notice this was already happening], then, through the greater more perfect tent [you, the heavenly temple or building from God]. Which is not manmade [that is not of this created world], he entered the Holiest place [our conscience] once and for all… then how much more the blood of the Messiah, who through the eternal spirit offered himself to God as a sacrifice [offering] without blemish, will purify our conscience [the Holiest place] from works that lead to death [body bound for death] so we can serve the living God [by the Spirit].
>
> Hebrews 9:11-14 (CJB)

Obviously, the conscience cleansing not only cleansed us from works that lead to death but also from the shame (nakedness) that resulted from these works. I mentioned earlier, in Revelation 22:14, that it stated we had washed our robes. These robes are a reference to our conscience, which was washed in the blood of the Messiah.

In Leviticus, the Torah teaches us that the life is in the blood. The blood of the Messiah is the life of the Messiah. The Messiah was giving us His lifestyle, so not only did the blood cleanse us but it clothed us in His life. His life swallows up our death.

Genesis 3:7 could be understood like this: "Their eyes were opened and they became aware (conscious) of their nakedness (guilt and shame) and they needed a covering (Kippur)." Let's continue with Paul's comments in Corinthians:

> Yes, while we are in this body [the one bound for death], we groan with the sense of being oppressed [sold as a slave to sin]: it is not so much that we want to take something off, but rather to

put something on over it [clothed in the righteous deeds of the saints, of course, Adam sewed fig leaves on]; so that what must die may be swallowed up by life.

2 Corinthians 5:4 (CJB)

Paul was not so much talking about shedding our physical bodies but about the earthly nature. We long to have our earthly nature (death) swallowed up by our spiritual nature (life). Remember, from the beginning, this was about overcoming not escaping. We would overcome the earthly nature and have dominion over it. This is what Paul was talking about in 1 Corinthians 15:

> And just as we have borne the image of the man of dust [death], so also we will bear the image of the man from heaven [life]... For this material which can decay must be clothed with imperishability, this which is mortal [earthly nature] must be clothed with immortality [spiritual nature]. When what decays [carnal man] puts on immortality [the Messiah], then this passage in the *Tanakh* will be fulfilled: "Death is swallowed up in victory."
>
> 1 Corinthians 15:49-54(CJB)

Let's take another look at Yom Kippur. This day is a day of cleansing, a covering and a joining (wedding).

> Let us rejoice and be glad! Let us give him glory! For the time [feast day] has come for the wedding [Yom Kippur] of the lamb, and His bride has prepared herself—fine linen, bright and clean has been given her to wear! [Fine linen means righteous deeds of God's people].
>
> Revelation 19:7-8

The bride is clothed in fine linen, the righteous deeds. This is a lifestyle. The whole Bible is about a lifestyle. This is the covering given to the bride. Keep in mind that the garden is a lifestyle, so heaven is a lifestyle as well. Why do you think everybody wants to go there? The bride is not just given Torah (the righteous deeds); she becomes a living Torah. This is the gospel of the garden. Bride, Torah, and Messiah are one. "Moreover, it is God who has prepared us for this very thing, and as a pledge he has *given us His Spirit*" (2 Corinthians 5:5).

"For we are of God's making, created in union with the Messiah Yeshua *for a life of good actions* already prepared by God for us to do" (Ephesians 2:10). This is the life of the garden, where God has given us His Spirit as a guarantee. This is the guarantee that we will overcome sin and death. His Spirit will cause us to walk in His commandments. God has given us dominion over the earth, but His Spirit takes dominion over or in us.

In essence, Adam was clothed with the garden, the secret place of the Most High. He was clothed with the *Sh'khina*, the clouds of glory. He was not just clothed with the Torah but the personified Torah, the Torah of the garden. Adam was clothed in the Messiah, the lifestyle of salvation.

> Because as many of you as were immersed into the Messiah have clothed yourselves with the Messiah, in Whom, there is neither Jew nor Gentile, neither slave nor freeman, neither male nor female, for in union with the Messiah *Yeshua*, you are all one.
>
> Galatians 3:27-28

Being clothed in the Messiah, Adam was one with God. He saw from God's perspective, and he understood and experienced the oneness of God. He could see how all things were connected. At this place, Adam could see the potential of God in all things. Adam was even able to name the animals, naming them by their potential, their activities, characteristics, and attributes.

Adam could see beyond the physical. He could see the spiritual energy (potential) in the animals and connect this to the corresponding Hebrew letters that represented each aspect of the spirit. These names then represented each animal's lifestyle. Adam could see the spiritual and the physical world as one; this is the kingdom of heaven on earth as one. There were no illusions that governed His life. He was clothed in godliness or the attributes of God.

The nakedness of Adam and Eve after eating the forbidden fruit was more than just a physical nakedness. They could no longer see the face or presence of God. They could only see the physical realm. They were previously naked and not ashamed. Now, they find themselves naked and ashamed. This shame is likened unto being on fire, like a lake of fire. This nakedness is also used to describe when someone appears in front of a superior being. As we will look at later, Adam and Eve hid themselves from God.

After eating the forbidden fruit, Adam and Eve felt guilt and shame. This was not because the fruit had some special power but because they were disobedient, breaking covenant with God. Their sin created an adversary (Satan), a veil. This veil prevented Adam and Eve from seeing God's oneness. The world became a place of illusions. They could no longer see the heavenly realms. Adam's consciousness fell down to the *she'ol*, the lower physical realms. Losing consciousness of the spiritual realm, we see Adam and Eve trying to clothe themselves with something physical: "Then the eyes of both of them were opened. So they sewed fig leaves together to make themselves loincloths" (Genesis 3:7).

Why did they choose fig leaves? Does the fig tree have any special significance? Well, let's take a look at the fig tree and what it can represent. The Torah is likened unto a fig tree. Unlike the other trees in Israel, which are harvested all at one time, the fig tree is harvested a little at a time, over time" (Proverbs 27:18).

Like a fig tree, we can harvest a little fruit from the Torah today and much more tomorrow. We simply cannot harvest all the fruit of Torah at one time, but some today and more tomorrow. Remember, a Torah scroll is made of dried, stretched sheep skins from their stomachs. They are called leaves, and when sewn together, these leaves become robes of righteousness or garments of righteousness or salvation.

Adam chose fig leaves to sew together, as it was a symbol of God's teachings and instructions. He tried to clothe himself in the salvation he once lived in. He was trying to clothe himself in the tree of life. It is interesting that the Torah records that they made loincloths because of what the belt represents. It is a part of the priestly garments: "Justice will be the belt around his waist, faithfulness the sash around his hips" (Isaiah 11:5).

"Stand therefore, having fastened on the belt of truth, and having put on the breastplate of righteousness" (Ephesians 6:14 ESV). Again, this alludes to the Torah, as it is God's truth and justice. The Torah is also God's standard of righteousness. The fig leaves sewn as loincloths definitely have some significance. Adam was trying to clothe himself in the tree of life.

In Psalm 1, David likens a righteous man to a tree. This is the same description we saw in Revelation 22. A righteous man is like a tree whose leaves never wither and who bears fruit in season. Israel is also likened unto a fig tree. You will see a continuous flow of this imagery all the way through the Bible: "When I found Israel; it was like finding grapes in the desert; when I saw your ancestors; it was like seeing a fig tree's first figs in its first season" (Hoshea 9:10a).

It is interesting as we continue to move forward in time we see *Yeshua* and He comes upon a fig tree. You can hardly help but think of when He came looking for Adam in the garden and there he was, dressed like a fig tree: "Spotting a fig tree [Adam] by the road, he went up to it but found nothing on it except leaves [the one's Adam sewed on]. So he said to it, 'May you never again bear fruit!' and immediately the fig tree dried up [became the dust of the earth]" (Matthew 21:19).

This fig tree represented Israel but also alluded back to Adam. In the time of *Yeshua*, Israel had the Torah, but in their hearts, they were still carnal or earthly natured. Remember Paul's words in Roman's 7: "The Torah is spiritual but I am carnal, sold as a slave to sin." Israel was outwardly following the letter of the law (fig leaves sewn on), but inwardly, they were full of dead men's bones. They were joined to the earthly nature, and therefore, they bore fruit for death or a false fruit (Romans 7:5). When Adam fell, he was no longer joined to the Spirit of God. No longer clothed with the Spirit of God and unable to produce the fruits of the Spirit, he realized his nakedness and tried to sew on fig leaves. In other words, he was trying to clothe himself in the Torah, but apart from the Spirit of God, and he could bear no fruit. He might look like a fig tree, but once *Yeshua* walked up to Adam, there was no fruit. A tree can only produce after its kind. Adam was no longer connected to the true vine and could not produce after God's kind.

> Beware of the false prophets! They come to you wearing sheep's clothing [fig leaves] but underneath they are hungry wolves [old nature]! You will recognize them by *their fruit*. Can people pick grapes form thorn bushes, or *figs from thistles*?
> Matthew 7:15-16

Notice that *Yeshua* says you will recognize them by their fruit, not by their leaves. *Yeshua* also alludes to the curse pronounced on the land, to produce thorns and thistles. The land, Israel, and Torah are synonymous terms. Adam might be clothed with fig leaves, which He sewed on by his own efforts, but He is producing thorns and thistles.

Unless we are connected to the true vine, *Yeshua*, we cannot produce any fruit. We are naked, fruitless. When we are not connected to *Yeshua*, we are hidden from His face. The white linen garments given to the bride are the righteous deeds (fruit) of the saints. These garments are only given at the wedding, only when we are in union with the Messiah.

When *Yeshua* came upon the fruitless fig tree, Israel was in the same status Adam was in after the fall. Here are Paul's words. Realize that he is describing the transition as we go from this status and are being joined back to the Spirit of God.

> But now we have been released from this aspect of the Torah, because we have died to that which had us in its clutches [old nature], so that we are serving in the new way provided by the Spirit and not in the old way of outwardly following the letter of the law [sewing on fig leaves].
>
> Romans 7:6

We see a repeat with Israel of what took place with Adam. Adam realized he was naked, he had no fruit, so he sewed on fig leaves so he would look like a fig tree; however, when God came upon Adam, there was no fruit. He was a counterfeit. Likewise, the same thing occurs when *Yeshua* visits Israel at the time of visitation. Like Adam, Israel is outwardly following the Torah, but they were not producing the fruit that the Torah offers, as this fruit can only be produced in union with the Messiah.

> I am the real [as opposed to the counterfeit] vine, and my father is the gardener. Every branch which is part of me but fails to bear fruit [found naked], he cuts off [divorces or exiles]; and every branch that does bear fruit, he prunes, so that is may bear more fruit. Right now, because of the word which I have spoken to you, you are pruned. Stay united with me, as I will with you—for just as the branch can't put forth fruit by itself apart from the vine, so you can't bear fruit apart from me.
>
> John 15:1-4 (CJB)

The fruit that the Torah offers can only happen in union with the Messiah. This is the fruit of life, eternal life: "Why? Because the Torah of the Spirit, which produces this life [fruit] in union with Messiah *Yeshua*, has set me free from the 'torah' of sin and death [thorns and thistles]" (Romans 8:2).

When *Yeshua* appeared to Israel, they were naked. They hid from His presence. Israel sewed fig leaves together to try to cover themselves. They were outwardly following the letter of the law, but they were producing a false fruit.

> For you keep saying, "I am rich, I have gotten rich [sewed on fig leaves], I don't need a thing!" You don't know that you are the one who is wretched pitiable, poor, blind and naked! My advice to you is to buy from me gold refined by fire, so that you may be dressed and not have to be ashamed of your nakedness [fruitlessness]; and eye salve to rub on your eyes, so that you may see [God's oneness and from his perspective].
>
> Revelation 3:17-18 (CJB)

It is not just Torah but the Torah of the garden that produces fruit. The garden alludes to the heart. This is the Torah written on the heart of flesh. The Torah must be connected to the Spirit of *Yeshua* in order to produce the fruit of the Spirit. Torah by itself produces a false fruit because it is connected to the earthly nature.

The Spirit of God will not connect to a lie. This is why Eve had no power over the serpent. We must understand that it is crucial that we speak the truth to each other. A lie will only connect to the flesh and will only produce after the flesh. We will eat the fruit of our lips. These are the trees we may eat from. Adam and Eve tried to cover their shame and nakedness from God with fig leaves. This only dealt with the physical realm and could not cover (atone, Yom Kippur) the spiritual realm. *Yeshua* became our Yom Kippur offering, to cover our nakedness and to clothe us in His life.

ע

TIME OF VISITATION

> They heard the voice of *Adonai*, God walking in the garden at the time of the evening breeze, so the man and his wife hid themselves from the presence of *Adonai*, God among the trees in the garden.
> Genesis 3:8 (CJB)

This is an interesting verse. There is a lot going on here. They hear God's voice and hide themselves from His presence. Notice that after Adam and Eve sinned, it was not God who hid from them, but they hid from God. This sets a precedence for sin from here on out. Sin causes us to hide from God. He does not hide from us. This hiding is the fruit of shame.

When Adam added to the command of God, he was severing the relationship. When Adam ate the fruit for the first time, he experienced himself as wicked, which means "to be broken to pieces or used for other than what he was created to do." Like a woman or wife with no covering, he was naked. The shame would now cause Adam to hide from the presence of God.

When we sin, we create an adversary (*HaSatan*). This adversary of guilt and shame prevents us from seeing God, his oneness and even His attributes. It causes us to hide from God instead of running to His mercy, grace, and salvation.

Notice in this verse that they heard the voice of God at a specific time: the time of visitation. Why would Adam hide from God at his time of visitation? It's as though he did not recognize it. Remember, Israel does not recognize their time of visitation either: "And shall lay you even with the ground, and your children within you, and they shall not leave in you one stone upon another; because you *knew not the time of your visitation*" (Luke 19:44, Restoration Scriptures).

They were laid even with the ground (dust of the earth) just as Adam fell from heaven to the lower parts of *she'ol* for not knowing the time of his visitation. Why did they not recognize their day of visitation? Because of pride. The first sign of pride is missing your appointments with God.

Pride is not just thinking you are better than someone else. It can flow from a much more deceptive river of thought, like fear and shame. Shame is also considered idolatry, likened unto idol worship because we will obey its voice. They hid from God. Their thoughts of guilt and shame once again rose up above the knowledge of God. Can you see the pride in this? They hid in the time of visitation. They hid from their true covering and clothed themselves in a counterfeit.

What is a time of visitation? Look at what happens to Job on his day of visitation: "You have granted me *chayim* [life] and favor, and your visitation has preserved my *ruach*" (Job 10:12, Restoration Scriptures).

God preserves us in his time of visitations. In many verses, this same word is translated as *punishment*. Well, for Adam, he hid from God's presence and found himself in exile. The day would almost seem as a day of punishment; however, it could have been a day of preservation.

I suggest we run to God with a repentant heart on a day of visitation or else it will become a punishment. Adam exiled himself from God's presence. God did not hide from Adam. A visitation is a time for deliverance. The feast days of God are called *moedim*. They are appointments in time to meet with God for deliverance. When we miss these, we are punishing ourselves. That is why the word *visitation* is related to punishment. Let's take a look at what God is delivering you from and what He is punishing: "God did this in order to deal with sin; and in so doing, he executed the punishment against sin in the human nature" (Romans 8:3b).

God is executing punishment against sin in the human nature, not people. He is coming to deliver you from sin and the curse upon the human perspective. However, if you are a carnal man who loves sin and can't distinguish between yourself and the carnal nature, this would be experienced as punishment against you. Or if you are so full of guilt and shame and all you can see is the illusion, you will hide from your deliverer. How many times, when we are in a lifestyle of sin, do we hide ourselves from rabbis, pastors, or even parents? We must realize that God judges sin but delivers people.

> So who will bring charge against God's chosen people? Certainly not God—he is the one who causes them to be considered righteous! Who punishes them? Certainly not the Messiah, *Yeshua*, who died and—more than that—has been raised, is at the right hand of God and is actually pleading on our behalf.
>
> Romans 8:33-34

Again, we need to ask ourselves how the gospel became a fear-filled message. When the gospel was approached from the human perspective, it was distorted and salvation began to revolve around not going to hell when you die. Many people were saved not out of a desire for relationship but a desire to not burn in hell forever, right?

From the beginning, God took us out (exiled) of Himself only to bring us back so that the two would become one. He wanted to demonstrate His love in the process. God wanted to lay down His life for His people. This was His doing, not theirs.

Paul gives an excellent description of this day of visitation. In this description are some clues as to why it might seem fearful for those whose lives are worldly.

For no one can lay any foundation other than the one already laid, which is *Yeshua* the Messiah. Some will use gold [salvation], silver [redemption] or precious stones [instruction] in building on this foundation [all pictures of eternal things]; while others will use wood, grass or straw [symbols of human nature and that which is temporary]. But each one's work will be shown for what it is; the day [of visitation] will disclose it, because it will be revealed by fire—the fire will test the quality of each one's work. If the work someone has built on the foundation survives, he will receive a reward, if it is burned up, he will have to bear the loss: he will escape with his life, but it will be like escaping through a fire.

1 Corinthians 3:11-15 (CJB)

Those whose work was from the earthly nature will be a loss. Those whose work was from a spiritual nature are the eternal works. Sewing on fig leaves were the works of the earthly nature. There was no fruit. The word *fruit* means "reward." There is no reward for the works of the earthly nature. In fact, this caused Adam to go into exile.

Because Adam was seeing from the human perspective, which was temporary and limited by the veil of guilt and fear, he sewed on fig leaves. This was a temporary fix or covering, not an eternal one. He perceived the day of visitation as one of punishment and fear instead of deliverance. This remains the same today in the world, especially in the house of Israel. In fact, in most cases, the church is unaware of the time of visitation, as they are unfamiliar with the feast days of God, called times of visitation. When they are taught about the feast days of God, they still hide themselves from His presence. The feast day of Yom Kippur is the day that we come face-to-face or presence to presence with God. In fact, when you see the term "face-to-face" in the Bible, it is a Hebrew idiom for Yom Kippur.

I want to show you a pattern. I'm going to focus this one around the fall feasts, also called the feasts of the ingathering, the picture painted in these feasts. Those who are prepared are gathered in and enter a year of blessing and favor. Those who are not prepared are sent back out into the furnace for another year of anguish, curse, etc. We are going to first look at Adam being prepared and placed in the garden. Next, we will see Adam unprepared, miss his visitation and go out into exile or anguish. There are three feasts in the fall feasts: Feast of Trumpets, Yom Kippur, and *Sukkot*. The church sees these as the pre-tribulation, mid-tribulation, and post-tribulation rapture.

> Then *Adonai*, God, formed a person from the dust of the ground [Feast of Trumpets] and breathed into his nostrils the breath of life, so that he became a living being [Yom Kippur]. *Adonai*, God, planted a garden toward the east, in Eden, and there he put the person whom he had formed [*Sukkot*].
> Genesis 2:7-8

This is the picture of a bride prepared, married, and brought into the bridal chamber. This is the pattern that most Christians interpret as going to heaven. This is also the pattern that the rapture flows from. This is the picture of God taking someone out of the realm of death and bringing them into the realm of life.

If we really believe that the end is found in the beginning and we believe that *Yeshua* is about to return for His bride, then we should be researching the Scriptures leading up to Adam being placed into the garden, the place the Messiah went to prepare for us.

Here is the picture: God takes Adam from the dust of the earth, a picture of those who are outside of Torah and separated from the Messiah, the nations. They are dead—not necessarily physically dead. They are in exile from the presence or face of God. On the

Feast of Trumpets, He wakes them up and prepares them; they are formed. This is the betrothal stage of a Hebrew wedding.

On Yom Kippur, they come face-to-face with YHVH and He breathes into them and they become one spirit with *Yeshua*. This is the wedding phase. Next, He places them into the garden, the place He has prepared for His bride. This is the celebration phase of the wedding, where they build a greater household.

This was a picture of leaving an earthly realm being resurrected and brought back into the heavenly realms. This was not about leaving the physical earth and being raptured to another world or place called heaven. The picture is right there in front of us.

Now, let's look at a pattern of an unprepared bride who misses her appointment and is sent out into the furnace. This is the pattern most Christians interpret as going to hell. However, this pattern is not referring to a place you go when you physically die but when you are physically alive but spiritually dead. It is an exile from God's face (presence). "They heard the voice of *Adonai*, God [Feast of Trumpets], walking in the garden at the time [feast day] of the evening breeze, so the man and his wife hid themselves from the presence of *Adonai* [Yom Kippur], God, among the trees in the garden" (Genesis 3:8).

Now, when Adam hears the *shofar* blast, the voice of God on the Feast of Trumpets, instead of preparing for Yom Kippur, he hides from God's presence. Now, instead of being placed in the garden, he is thrown out into the furnace of exile, hell, and God pronounces the curses. "Therefore *Adonai*, God, sent him out of the garden of Eden to cultivate the ground from which He was taken" (Genesis 3:23).

Instead of being planted in the garden on the Feast of *Sukkot*, he is driven out to cultivate the ground. This is to live by the earthly nature. Adam was going into the lake of fire where he would experience the judgment of living according to His earthly nature and its desire for sin.

This pattern occurs on a yearly cycle. Each year, we prepare for a blessed year of favor or we go into a year of anguish and misery. This is why Judaism does not believe in a hell that you go to forever for making mistakes in a very short temporary life. They believe it would be immoral for a moral God to punish you forever for something you did or didn't do in a temporary life. They believe the most would be a year in a cleansing fire.

Of course, each year, we have a choice to show up or to hide from God's presence. Let's look at some more pictures of this pattern.

Many times, those who are unaware of God's time of visitation, unaware of His feast days, will say things like this, "No man knows the day or the hour of His return." What they don't know because they have been disconnected from the Hebrew roots of their faith is that this is an idiom. No man knows the day or the hour is an idiom for the end of the betrothal phase of a wedding, and it is also an idiom for the Feast of Trumpets.

The Feast of Trumpets starts with the spotting of the new moon, and then they sound the trumpets. However, nobody knows the day or the hour of the new moon. To this day, it is scheduled for two days because we don't know when it will appear. The moon will come like a thief in the night. For someone in a Hebrew culture, no man knows the day or the hour was very specific. It marked a season and the beginning of the ten days of awe leading up to Yom Kippur. Let's examine Paul's words.

> But you have no need to have anything written to you, brothers, about the times and dates when this will happen; because you yourselves well know that the Day of the Lord will come like a thief in the night [when the new moon is spotted on the Feast of Trumpets]. When people are saying, "Everything is so peaceful and secure [sewed on fig leaves]," then destruction will suddenly come upon them, the way labor pains come upon a pregnant woman, and there is no way they will escape. But you, brothers,

are not in the dark [outside of Torah, exile], so that the Day [visitation] should take you by surprise like a thief; for you are all people who belong to the light [Torah], who belong to the day [*Yeshua*]. We don't belong to the night [old nature] or to darkness [chaos and exile]. So let's not sleep [spiritual death], like the rest are; on the contrary, let us stay alert and sober.

1 Thessalonians 5:1-6 (CJB)

Notice those awake will not be taken by surprise. They understand the time of visitation. In fact, they prepare and show up for it. It is their deliverance. *HaSatan* is a veil of fear that causes others to hide from this visitation. Let's look what Isaiah says about this day of visitation:

> On this mountain *Adonai*, Tzva'ot will make for all people a feast of rich food and superb wines, delicious, rich food and superb elegant wines [sounds like a wedding feast]. On this mountain he will destroy the veil [of fear and shame, human perspective] which covers the faces of all peoples, the veil [which prevents us from seeing God's presence] enshrouding all the nation. He will swallow up death forever [by clothing their nakedness with the fruit of righteousness]. *Adonai*, *Elohim* will wipe away the tears from every face, and He will remove from the earth the disgrace [shame of exile] his people suffered, for *Adonai* has spoken.

Isaiah 25:6-8 (CJB)

The veil is removed from the bride at the wedding. The bride comes face-to-face or presence to presence with the groom. Let's see Paul's words:

> What is more, their minds were made stone like [pride of human perspective]; for to this very day the same veil remains over them when they read the Old Covenant; it has not been unveiled [they

see it from a human perspective and turn it into something it is not. It becomes man's torah], because only by the Messiah is the veil taken away. Yes, till today, whenever Moshe is read, a veil lies over their hearts [this is the foreskin of the earthly nature with its desires to add to or subtract from]. "But," says the Torah, "Whenever someone turns to *Adonai*, the veil is taken away." Now *Adonai* in this text means the Spirit. And where the Spirit of *Adonai* is, there is freedom [from the law of sin and death, the earthly nature, the second husband, *HaSatan*]. So all of us, with faces unveiled, see as in a mirror the glory of the Lord [You see not only God's oneness but your oneness with him]; and we are being changed into his very image [we are overcoming the old nature by the spiritual nature, death is being swallowed up by life and victory] from one degree [level] of glory to the next, by *Adonai* the spirit [we are crushing the head of the serpent by the power of the Holy Spirit].

2 Corinthians 3:14-18(CJB)

So if indeed our Good News [the Gospel of his visitation] is veiled, it is veiled only to those in the process of being lost [Adam, where are you? Those swallowed up by the earthly nature]. They don't come to trust because the God of the *'olam Hazeh* [The human perspective that *Yeshua* rebuked in Peter, Mark 8:33] has blinded their minds, in order to prevent them from seeing the light shining from the Good News about the glory of the Messiah. *Yeshua* as Lord, with ourselves as slaves for you because of *Yeshua*.

2 Corinthians 4:3-5 (CJB)

Where are they going to see the glory of *Yeshua*? They will see it in themselves and other people. It will be as if seeing in a mirror. We keep looking up to the sky to see *Yeshua* when the whole time he has been hidden behind a veil of flesh, in your brother. He is in people.

Adam was blinded by the god of the *'olam Hazeh*, his limited human perspective. He feared the time of visitation and hid himself from God. The *'olam Hazeh* is the present age, the age of the flesh. The *'olam Habah* is the age to come or the world to come. This is the age of the spirit. On Yom Kippur, we move from the age of the flesh to the life of the spirit.

In the age of the flesh, we are slaves of sin and death. This is the age of exile, where we walk a road of destruction likened unto being consumed by fire. This is symbolized by bronze, which represents judgment. We are in the outer court, where we deal with the flesh, the serpent: "But the court outside the Temple, leave that out, don't measure it; because it has been given to the *Goyim* [nations], and they will trample over the holy city for *forty-two months*" (Revelation 11:2).

Forty-two months is three and a half years. Hebraicly, this is a reference to thirty-five hundred years from the time the Torah was given and the golden calf was made until today.

Notice the nations are given the outer court. The outer court is lit up by the sun, the moon, and the stars. The most holy place is lit up by the *Sh'khinah*, and the holy place is lit up by the menorah. Those in the outer court are still looking up to the sky, the sun, the moon, and the stars for *Yeshua*, but he is not there. He is in people. The outer court is likened unto a furnace, the place of judgment.

> For this reason, do not look up at the sky, *at the sun, moon, stars,* and everything in the sky, and be drawn away to worship and serve them; *Adonai* your God has allotted these to all the peoples under the entire sky. No, you *Adonai* has taken and brought out of *the smelting furnace,* out of *Egypt,* to be a people of inheritance for him, as you are today.
>
> Deuteronomy 4:19-20 (CJB)

Egypt is the Hebrew word *Mitzrayim*, and it means narrow straits, constriction, or a place of confinement. Egypt and the world are synonymous terms through the Bible. They are associated with a furnace.

The Gospel of the Garden

The enemy who sows them is the adversary [realm of death], the harvest is the end of the age [age of the flesh], and the harvesters are angels. Just as the weeds are collected and burned up in the fire, so will it be at the end of the age [fall feasts, Yom Kippur]. The son of man will send forth his angels, and they will collect out of his kingdom [the garden, His movement upon the earth] all things that cause people to sin [earthly nature, adversary] and all the people who are far from Torah [those who were not prepared and hid themselves from the time of visitation, Adam]; and they will throw them into the fiery furnace [cast out of Garden into exile, another year in an unproductive life or lake of fire or Egypt] where people will wail and grind their teeth. [This is the curse lack and decrease, remember God will wipe away the tears from this wailing [Revelation 7:12] of an unproductive or unfruitful life of pain and sorrow]. Then the righteous [those who were prepared and showed up for the time of visitation, were given white linen garments, the fruit of a productive life.] will shine forth like the sun [*Yeshua* is the son of righteousness, this alludes to the first day of creation's light] in the kingdom [garden] of the father. Whoever has ears let them hear.

Matthew 13:39-43 (CJB)

It is believed that on the Feast of Trumpets, the books are opened. Between the Feast of Trumpets and Yom Kippur, you are written in the books for blessing (life) or curse (death), and then there is the book of undecided during these ten days. On Yom Kippur, the books are closed. "So it will be at the close of the age the angels will go forth and separate the evil people from the righteous and throw them into the fiery furnace [Egypt or world, outside the garden], where they will wail and grind their teeth" (Matthew 13:49-50).

The righteous enter into the garden or the New Jerusalem while those who are wicked and unprepared are exiled outside.

How blessed are those who washed their robes [were prepared] so that they have the right to eat from the Tree of Life and go through the gates into the city! *Outside are the homosexuals, those involved with the occult and with drugs, the sexually immoral, murderers, idol worshippers and everyone who loves and practices falsehood.*

Revelation 22:14-15

In Hebrew thought, to be involved in this sinful lifestyle is likened unto being in a furnace of hell. If you were to look around your life and find yourself in this type of lifestyle, surrounded by relationships with people in this lifestyle, then you are experiencing an exile. This is the hell *Yeshua* came to save His people from.

Those righteous who were prepared by washing their robes are brought into the New Jerusalem. They washed their robes by repentance and showing up. They enjoy the evening breeze, which is a reference to the Spirit life, where they rule as kings over the earth and their earthly nature.

What do we think of when we here about the New Jerusalm? We sometimes are taught this is some huge city that will come to the earth from outer space. This city is actually people. All of its descriptions allude back to the high priest's garments. Of course, *Yeshua* is the High Priest, and we are his body. Naturally, the body will look like that of a High Priest, right?

We see the holy city (people) coming down out of heaven, adorned like a bride. You don't dress buildings up like a bride; you dress people who are called God's building up like a bride. Notice the city has no need for the sun, moon, and stars to light it. This is a reference that they are no longer in the outer court. The holy of holies is also a synonym for heaven. They came down out of heaven (holy of holies) dressed like a bride.

The New Jerusalem can also be understood as the renewed Jerusalem. This holy city is the same one we read about earlier that was being trampled underfoot by the nations. "But the court outside the temple, leave that out; don't measure it; because it has been given to the *Goyim*, and they will trample over the *holy city* for forty-two months" (Revelation 11:2).

We have to ask ourselves a question here. How in the world are the nations going to trample over the holy city? We will let *Yeshua* answer this question:

> You are the salt for the land. But if salt becomes tasteless, how can it be made salty again? It is no longer good for anything except being thrown out [exile] for *people to trample* on. You are light for the world. A town built on a hill [New Jerusalem] cannot be hidden.
>
> Matthew 5:13-14

The New Jerusalem is the people who have come in from exile, from the world. They are the world to come. They have entered into the spirit life. Outside are those who are still lost and swallowed up by the earthly nature or the image of death. Let's look at one more verse:

> On the contrary, you have come to Mount *Tziyon*, that is, the city of the living God [people], heavenly [spiritual] Jerusalem [people]; to myriads of angels in festive assembly [on Yom Kippur we are likened unto angels]; to a community of the firstborn whose names have been recorded [written in book during the fall feasts] in heaven; to a Judge [deliverer] who is God of everyone; to spirits of righteous people who have been brought to the goal [a wedding where they become one spirit with God]; to the mediator of a new covenant, *Yeshua*; and to the sprinkled blood that speaks better things than that of *Havel* [Abel].
>
> Hebrews 12:22-24 (CJB)

These are the ones who have the right to eat of the tree of life. I hope you are seeing the picture that is painted by our Hebrew God. The time of visitation is our deliverance and salvation. We are the ones who hide from it: "They heard the voice [*shofar* blast, trumpet] of *Adonai*, God, walking in the garden at the time of evening breeze [visitation], so the man and his wife hid themselves from the presence [face] of *Adonai*, God, among the trees in the garden" (Genesis 3:8).

Let's talk about the parable of the ten virgins. We will look closely at the details, and we will find great parallels to Adam here.

> The kingdom of heaven [garden] at that time will be like ten bridesmaids who took their lamps and went out to meet the groom. Five were foolish [no Torah] and five were sensible [had Torah]. The foolish ones took lamps [sewed on fig leaves] with them but no oil [fruit of the Spirit]; with their lamps [Torah]. Now the bridegroom was late so they all went to sleep. It was the middle of the night when the cry rang out [Feast of Trumpets], "The bridegroom is here! Go out to meet him!" The girls all woke up and *prepared* their lamps. The foolish ones said to the sensible ones, "Give us some of your oil [fruit], because our lamps are going out [we are naked]." "No," they replied, "There may not be enough for both you and us. Go to the oil dealers [hide among the trees] and buy some for yourselves." But as they were going off to buy [hide], the bridegroom came. Those who were ready went with him to a wedding feast, and the door was shut [Yom Kippur]. Later, the other bridesmaids came, "Sir! Sir!" they cried, "Let us in!" But he answered, "Indeed! I tell you, I don't know you!" So stay alert, because you know neither the day nor the hour [Feast of Trumpets].
>
> Matthew 25:1-13 (CJB)

At the time of visitation, Adam was like a foolish bride. He had sewn on the fig leaves but had no oil. He had no fruit. In the time of visitation, Adam went and hid himself amongst the oil dealers, the trees of the garden. Genesis records that Adam "heard the voice of God." This is likened unto the *shofar* blast of the Feast of Trumpets.

Shortly after this event, the Torah records Adam being sent out of the garden into the fiery furnace; the door was shut. The curses are announced. These are the curses of the wailing and the grinding of teeth. They will be handed down from one generation to the next.

It was guilt and shame that caused Adam to hide from God's face. He was unable to repent (turn around and come face-to-face with God). One of the greatest battles we face is not letting guilt and shame cause us to hide from God's presence. This is why shame is likened unto idolatry. Adam obeyed the voice of shame and hid himself from God. Adam became married to the voice of shame (*HaSatan*).

> Don't you know that if you present yourselves to someone as obedient slaves [voice of shame], then, of the one whom you are obeying, you are slaves—whether of sin [human nature], which leads to death [Spiritual death and eventually an early physical death], or of obedience [Spiritual nature], which leads to being made righteous [a wedding where the bride is given white linen garments, righteous deeds].
>
> Romans 6:16 (CJB)

פ

WHERE ARE YOU?

Adonai, God, called the man, "Where are you?"
Genesis 3:9 (CJB)

There are many levels of thought found in this verse. We know that God knew where Adam was. So why the question "where are you?" Was it for God's sake or actually for Adam's? It is as though God is asking Adam if he realizes where he is . Think about this. Adam has fallen from the lofty heavenly realm, where he had dominion as a king over the earth, into the lower part of *she'ol*, where the earth was ruling over him. Now Adam is actually hiding himself from God's presence. It was not God hiding from Adam.

We know that God is everywhere and always with us. Nothing actually exists outside of His presence. We are seeing that when Adam sinned, he created an adversary (*HaSatan*). This is a veil that prevented him from seeing God's presence. Adam was hidden in his earthly nature. The human perspective, the god of *'olam Hazeh* (age of the flesh) blinded him from seeing God's presence. Adam, where are you? He is lost in the earthly nature.

We may experience it as though God is hiding His face from us. In fact, you will find places in the Torah where it says God hid His face from them. In reality, it is that the human perspective is unable to see spiritual reality. It is bound to the fragment illusions of its limited worldview. It crawls through the dust of the earth.

I find it interesting that Paul says when this veil that came upon Adam is removed we will see the glory, manifest presence of God, in us: "So all of us, with faces unveiled, see as in a mirror the glory of the Lord; and we are being changed into his very image, from one degree of glory to the next, by *Adonai*, the Spirit" (2 Corinthians 3:18).

We will see the glory of God in us. Where did we think we would see it? Let me share this with you. The word *garden* is related to the word *heart*. When it says that Adam heard the voice of God walking in the garden, it alludes to the voice of God in Adam's heart. After all, Adam, *Yeshua*, and Torah were *echad*. How many times have we ignored or hid from the voice of God in our heart (garden)?

The last place the human perspective wants to look for God is in himself or other people. It wants to look up to the sun, moon, and stars for God. This is where the nations are found, those still in the smelting furnace, looking for God. Paul reveals we will be discovering the glory of God in us.

Before Adam ate the forbidden fruit, he was clothed in the presence of God. He could see past the flesh (veil) and see the light of God in himself and everything else. Adam became lost in the earthly nature when he ate of the fruit. The voice of shame and guilt seemed to swallow up the voice of God. It might have seemed as though God was the one hiding, but that is not reality.

From a human perspective, it might be hard to swallow, but as we continue to study, we will find that the last days are about the revealing of the Messiah. Many are looking to the sky because they are not familiar with the Hebrew language, imagery, or idioms. The real revealing will be the Messiah coming in the flesh. We keep looking for the Messiah to come in bodily form, yet His body is here. We just have not been able to see past the flesh because, for a season, our minds have been veiled.

The idea of being hidden and revealed is a theme that runs through the Bible. In the New Testament, we see it as lost and found. Has God really lost any of His people? Of course not. He knows where they are. God knew exactly where Adam was. It was Adam who was lost to his true identity. Hidden, lost, or concealed, it seems to be a running theme. If there is one thing we learn from the Scriptures, it is that the world is a place full of illusions.

The Torah records the story of Joseph. Joseph is lost or hidden in Egypt (world). He is only hidden to later be revealed and to bring about a great deliverance. Joseph's brothers come before him because of a great famine. All they saw was an Egyptian (human being). They were unable to see the potential of God in Joseph. It had been veiled behind Egyptian garments (fleshly nature). It was not until Joseph stripped off the Egyptian garments (old nature) that they recognized Him. They recognized their salvation (*Yeshua*). Could it be that the Messiah is hidden in the hearts of men who look like Egyptians today?

The Torah records the story of Joseph's sons. They will continue in the pattern of their father. *Efrayim* is the youngest son of Joseph and the grandson of Jacob. In Genesis 48, we see that Jacob adopts *Efrayim* from the youngest grandson status up to the place of firstborn son. Later, *Efrayim* will become the head of the house of Israel and his descendants will number the sands of the seashore.

Yaakov blesses and prophesies over *Efrayim*. He says that his descendants will fill up the foreign nations.

> But his father refused and said, "I know that, my son, I know it. He [*Ma'nasheh*] too will become a people, and he too will be great; nevertheless his younger brother [*Efrayim*] will be greater than he, and his descendants will grow into many nations."
>
> Genesis 48:19

The Hebrew reads that he will fill up the foreign nations. The only way this could happen is if, for a season, *Efrayim*'s descendants become lost. They would have to become foreign themselves in order to mix with the foreign nations. Remember, the Israelites were not to mix with the other nations. The Hebrew says they will become the fullness of the foreign nations. Of course, this happens as *Efrayim* becomes the head of the house of Israel. They are swallowed up by the Assyrians; like Adam, they are lost and exiled.

> Yes, *Adonai* came to despise all the descendants of Israel. He caused them trouble and handed them over to plunderers, until finally he threw them out of his sight [likened to Adam being driven out of the Garden, away from the face of God]. He tore Israel [*Efrayim*, ten tribes] away from the House of David [Judah]. They made *Yarov'am* the son of *N'vat* king; and *Yarov'am* drew Israel away from following *Adonai* and made them commit a great sin. The people of Israel followed the example of all the sins that *Yarov'am* had committed and did not turn away from them, until *Adonai* removed Israel out of his sight, as he had said he would through all his servants the prophets. Thus Israel [house of Israel] was carried away captive from their own land to Ashur, and it remains so to this day.
>
> 2 Kings 17:20-23 (CJB)

This is by far the largest portion of the Israelites who became lost or hidden amongst the nations (trees). These became known as the lost ten tribes. The Jews pray three times a day that these exiles will return home. Where are they? (Where are you, Adam?) They have hidden themselves among the nations and become lost to their true identity. *Yeshua* said he was sent only for these lost sheep of the house of Israel: "He said, 'I was only sent to the lost sheep of the house of Israel'" (Matthew 15:24).

So where are these people that *Yeshua* came for, the ones who, like Adam, have become hidden? We know the Jews pray three times a day for the return of these exiles. However, the Christian world is all but completely unaware of their existence. Amazingly, the new covenant is only made with two people groups: "For God does find fault with people when he says, 'See! The days are coming,' says *Adonai*, 'when I will establish over the *house of Israel* and over the *House of Y'hudah* a new covenant'" (Hebrews 8:8).

Believe me, God knows where these lost sheep of the house of Israel are. Like Adam, they might be lost to their true identity, but God knows who they are. The only reason something is concealed or hidden is that it might be revealed. When Paul was taking the gospel to the nations, he taught them that if they belonged to the Messiah, then they were the seed of Abraham: "Also if you belong to the Messiah, you are seed of Abraham and heirs according to the promise" (Galatians 3:29).

When *Yaakov* was about to prophesy and bless Joseph's children, he saw into the future. He saw that they would become lost to their identity and that like their father, Joseph, they would look like Egyptians (Gentiles). First, he tells Joseph that his sons will become *Yaakov's* sons: "Now your two sons, who were born to you in the land of Egypt before I came to you in Egypt, are mine; *Efrayim* and *M'nasheh* will be as much mine as *Re'uven* and *Shim'on* are" (Genesis 48:5).

After telling this to Joseph, read what happens in this next verse as *Yaakov* looks into the future of these sons: "Then Israel noticed *Yosef's* sons and asked, '*Whose are these?*'" (Genesis 48:8).

Ya'akov already knew who the boys were and who they belonged to. The Torah is revealing something a little deeper here. He was seeing that they would become a foreign people who would be hidden amongst the trees of the nations. Isaiah also sees these sons in a time when they will return to their identity and home once again (Isaiah 60:8).

These are the same lost sheep *Yeshua* came for. He came to ingather them back to their true identity and back to the land. The church sees this as the rapture where they are caught up into the clouds. In Hebrew mindset, this is the ingathering of the exiles. We will see these same lost sons of Joseph appear in the book of Revelation.

> One of the elders asked me, "These people dressed in white robes— *who are they*, and where are they from?" "Sir," I answered "you

know!" Then he told me, "These are the people who have come out of the Great Persecution [exile]. They have washed their robes [stripped off their Egyptian garments] with the blood of the lamb."

Revelation 7:13-14

When these sons strip off the Egyptian garments, do you know what is revealed? The Messiah—he was hidden in them. They are the revelation of the Messiah, the manifestation of the sons of God.

Adam was a son of God. When he ate of the forbidden fruit, he lost or became lost to the image of the son of God. He was now concealed in the image of a mortal man, an Egyptian (Gentile). The human perspective blinded him to who he was, and Adam hid himself from the presence of God, his true identity. He was lost. The church continues to call themselves Gentiles (Egyptians) to this day. Could it be they are the very sons of Joseph who were lost in the nations (Romans 8:19)?

Where are they? Like Adam, they are hidden or lost. God knows exactly where they are. He never loses His people. They are hidden amongst the nations. When these sons of God manifest, they will be the revelation of the Messiah. This is the gospel from the beginning.

God created Adam to rule (as) Him over the earth. Adam, *Yeshua*, and Torah were one, *echad*. God manifested Himself in and through Adam. Adam was the kingdom of heaven, the temple of God. As it was in the beginning, so it will be in the end. We must understand the gospel of the Messiah from the beginning.

Adam hid from God because for the first time in Adam's life, He experienced himself as wicked or evil. For the first time, Adam did something he was not created to do. He viewed himself through the eyes of the earthly court system and saw himself as naked. He was experiencing an exile from his purpose. Adam was created to bear good fruit for God.

> God blessed them: God said to them, *"Be fruitful*, multiply, fill the earth and subdue it."
>
> Genesis 1:28 (CJB)

> This is how my Father is glorified—in your *bearing much fruit*; this is how you will prove to be my *talmidim* [disciples].
>
> John 15:8 (CJB)

> For we are of God's making, created in union with the Messiah *Yeshua* for a *life of good actions* already prepared by God for us to do.
>
> Ephesians 2:10 (CJB)

When Adam ate the forbidden fruit, which was not food for Him, he realized he had done something he was not created to do. He was no longer clothed in his purpose. Like the foolish virgins, Adam was afraid because he had no fruit or oil. Adam saw himself as wicked or evil.

Fear did not come from a lack of God's presence. Adam was hiding from God's presence. Fears came from a lack of direction and loss of purpose. Adam could no longer see his purpose. He became lost. His image had become shattered and fragmented to such a degree that there was no purpose or destiny to be perceived by his limited human perspective.

> My advice to you is to buy from me gold refined by fire, so that you may be rich; and white clothing [purpose and direction, the righteous deeds of the saints which we were created to do], so that you may be dressed [in purpose] and not have to be ashamed of your nakedness [fruitlessness or purposelessness]; and eye salve [so you can see from God's perspective] to rub your eyes, so you may see [the glory of God in you].
>
> Revelation 3:18 (CJB)

צ

THE SPIRIT OF UNFORGIVENESS

And he said, "Who told thee that thou *wast* naked?"

Genesis 3:11a (KJV)

Who did tell Adam he was naked? Adam was listening to the *Yetzer Harah*, the voice of guilt and shame. This voice was on the inside of Adam. This is a religious spirit full of accusation: (Genesis 3:11b KJV).

We are going to look at Adam's response to this question. By his response, we will see just how lost Adam has become. He really had no idea where he was. The *Yetzer Harah* had taken such a grip that he was unable to repent. Instead, Adam becomes the manifestation of the accuser (*HaSatan*). It certainly was not God who accused Adam (Romans 8:33).

Adam's human nature was the accuser. This nature accused others and themselves. This was a tragic event for Adam and Eve. God always forgives. It is man who does not forgive. God is revealing in stages what was taking place. It was not God who was accusing Adam or banishing Adam from His presence. God didn't tell Adam that He was naked. Adam was accusing himself and hiding himself from the presence of God. Adam might have perceived it differently, but this is the reality. Adam was punishing himself.

God realized that the only way he would be able to bring Adam back would be to rescue him from the grip that guilt and shame had taken on him. He would have to cleanse Adam's conscience. The real truth is that for six thousand years, man has been running from the garden and God's presence. God has been in pursuit of us. He will have to free us from the body bound for death and cleanse our conscience from works that lead to death in order to have a relationship with us.

The *Yetzer Harah* is sometimes called the inner pharaoh. This inner pharaoh is the spirit of unforgiveness. Adam could not forgive himself. The inner pharaoh would not let Adam go worship God. We begin to see who was punishing Adam: "Who punishes them? Certainly not the Messiah *Yeshua*. Who died and—more than that—has been raised, is at the right hand of God and is actually pleading on our behalf" (Romans 8:34).

The fall of man has been about the guilt and shame that took a hold of Adam. This caused him to hide from God's presence. Instead of repenting and returning, this inner pharaoh held Adam captive, causing him to eat the dust of the earth. Adam began to punish himself with thoughts and feelings of worthlessness and purposelessness. Adam was blinded to his potential and the ability to see God's oneness in creation or his oneness with God.

Our whole reality became fake, false, and incomplete. God was never punishing us. God is in pursuit of us to free us from ourselves. This limited reality has caused us to view the gospel almost backward, as though somehow we are trying to appease an angry God.

It was Adam who accused himself, saw himself as naked, and hid himself from God's presence, not the other way around. Adam was seeing from the perspective of the *Yetzer Hara*; he was joined to this perspective. As I mentioned earlier, Adam had the human perspective, but he also saw from God's perspective. These two perspectives were to be married, called heaven on the earth. When Adam fell and the curse to eat the dust of the earth was effected, it was as though Adam was cursed to experience life through the human perspective alone. He became lost in this realm.

It is not that we are trying to escape the human perspective entirely but to marry it to God's perspective. There is a story in the Bible that beautifully demonstrates this. It is Jacob's ladder, the ladder bridged between heaven and earth. It spanned between the human perspective and God's perspective. In the story, the angels are ascending and descending. In other words, there is a relationship and messages are flowing back and forth between the two perspectives. *Yeshua* is a picture of this ladder, where the human and divine are married. This is our image. "And he saith unto him, Verily, verily, I say unto you, Hereafter ye shall see heaven open, and the angels of God ascending and descending upon the Son of man" (John 1:51 KJV).

Because of the fall, this union was broken. Adam was limited, and the inner pharaoh dominated him. It would not let him go. He could not forgive himself. After *Yeshua*'s resurrection, He appeared to his disciples and breathed on them. He says: "Having said this, he breathed on them and said, *'Receive the Ruach HaKodesh! If you forgive someone's sins, their sins are forgiven; If you hold them, they are held'*" (John 20:22).

Yeshua correlates this *Ruach HaKodesh* with forgiveness. The issue being dealt with is the ability to forgive. It was about man's ability to forgive, not God's. Man was the one who held the sin. This creates an adversary when we hold sin.

The *Ruach Hukodesh* is the spirit of forgiveness, being able to see from the heavenly court system. *Yeshua* was empowering them to be able to forgive not only others but also themselves. The real illusion flowed from the spirit of unforgiveness. Instead of rivers of living waters, all that began to flow from this spirit was bitterness, accusation, and unforgiveness. What held Adam captive and punished him was unforgiveness, the spirit of pharaoh.

I want to explore this for a bit. Let's back up a verse here: "Then said Jesus to them again, 'Peace *be* unto you: as *my* Father hath sent me, even so send I you'" (John 20:21 KJV).

Yeshua is the spirit of forgiveness. He always forgives, as Paul says. *Yeshua* does not bring charges against us or punish us. We do this ourselves. Since the fall, the spirit of pharaoh has blinded us and caused us to hide from God's presence. This is an inability to make *Teshuvah* (repentance). Adam could not turn around and face God. Adam held himself captive with fear, bitterness, and unforgiveness.

Now the Messiah is commissioning us, just as the Father has sent him. So now He is sending us. *Yeshua* is sending us as a type of messiah and a king. Think about that. In another place Yeshua goes even further and says that all the works that he does we will do and even greater works we will do. "Verily, verily, I say unto you, He that believeth on me, the works that I do shall he do also; and greater *works* than these shall he do; because I go unto my Father" (John 14:12 KJV).

Yeshua is going to the Father. Adam was running and hiding from the Father. When *Yeshua* breathed on His disciples, it was as if He was hovering over the dark sea of bitterness and unforgiveness and said, "Let there be light, Forgiveness!" *Yeshua* said we will do all these works. These works are the works of Torah, the works of forgiveness and *teshuvah*, to return to the Father. *Yeshua's* return to the father was a picture of man finally returning from exile.

The true Torah is the Torah of forgiveness and can only be done in union with the Messiah, the Sprit of forgiveness. When the Torah is approached by the human perspective, the inner pharaoh turns it into a torah of condemnation, the earthly court system. We won't let God's people go. All we will see are their flaws and shortcomings. This is why *Yeshua* gave them the Holy Spirit, the heavenly court system.

The greater works that we will do that *Yeshua* never did is to forgive ourselves. *Yeshua* never sinned and never had to forgive himself. When we return to the father, we will have forgiven ourselves. Until we are able to forgive ourselves, we will be unable to forgive others. Watch what takes place with Adam. Keep in mind that forgiveness is related to a covering. Yom Kippur is about a covering. "The man said, 'The woman whom you gave to be with me, she gave me fruit of the tree, and I ate'" (Genesis 3:12 ESV).

There is a lot being revealed here, but before we get started, I want to mention something: God does not let Adam blame his wife. He reminds Adam that He gave him the command not to eat of the tree.

> And to Adam he said,
> "Because you have listened to the voice of your wife
> and have eaten of the tree
> of which I commanded you,
> 'You shall not eat of it,'
> cursed is the ground because of you;
> in pain you shall eat of it all the days of your life;
>
> Genesis 3:17 (ESV)

When Adam accused his wife, the Torah reveals that Adam was not a covering for his wife. He was operating in the earthly court system. This reveals that Adam was already being overcome with bitterness and accusation. The fruit looked sweet but turned bitter in Adam's stomach.

> So I went to the angel and told him to give me the little scroll. And he said to me, "Take and eat it; it will make your stomach bitter, but in your mouth it will be sweet as honey." And I took the little scroll from the hand of the angel and ate it. It was sweet as honey in my mouth, but when I had eaten it my stomach was made bitter. And I was told, "You must again prophesy about many peoples and nations and languages and kings."
>
> Revelation 10:9-11 (ESV)

When Adam began to speak, the river that flowed from his belly was full of bitterness. He began to accuse his wife. The spirit of unforgiveness was manifesting before God. Adam had not forgiven himself; therefore, he could not forgive Eve. This reveals that not only could Adam not see his oneness with God but he no longer saw himself as one with Eve. Adam failed to realize that when he accused Eve he was accusing himself.

We will read that, as a curse, the woman's desire will be for her husband, that she would run after her husband. A husband represents a covering (Genesis 3:16b).

Even desire for her husband is a desire for a covering. The reason she desires a covering from Adam is that he has become her accuser. The curse was simply describing what had already taken place. Adam did not realize it, but he was passing judgment upon himself, as he was one with Eve and was to be her covering. "Therefore thou art inexcusable, O man, whosoever thou art [Adam] that judgest: for wherein thou judgest another [Eve], thou condemnest thyself; for thou that judgest doest the same things" (Romans 2:1 KJV).

Today, we often fail to realize as a part of the body of Messiah we are all *one*. We must not accuse or judge each other, for we are judging ourselves. It is obvious today that the body of Messiah is still seeing heavily from the human perspective, as we are so fragmented and divided that we are operating in an earthly court system instead of the heavenly one.

Think about this. Adam is standing before God, accusing the bride. Do you understand who the accuser of the brethren is? It's men! *Yeshua* stands before the father, pleading on behalf of the bride. The question is: which model do we follow? *Yeshua* said, "As the Father sends me so I send you." Are we like Adam, the adversary, accusing each other before God, or like *Yeshua*?

Adam was not only accusing Eve but also accused God. He referred to Eve as the woman God gave him. Adam was isolating himself from Eve and now from God. Adam was quickly exiling himself.

> Brothers, stop speaking against each other! Whoever speaks against a brother or judges a brother is speaking against Torah and judging Torah. And if you judge Torah, you are not a doer of what Torah says, but a judge. There is but one Giver of Torah; he is also the Judge, with the power to deliver and to destroy. Who do you think you are, judging your fellow human beings?
>
> James 4:11-12 (CJB)

So we see from this verse that Adam was also judging the Torah. God has the power to deliver and to destroy. God will cause our brothers to stand. A judge connected to the spirit is actually a savior. A judge connected to the earthly nature tends to be a condemner.

> Therefore there is no longer any condemnation awaiting those who are in union with the Messiah [on Yom Kippur, Romans 2:16]. Why because the Torah of the spirit, which produces this life in union with the Messiah [spirit] *Yeshua* has set me free from the torah of sin and death [unforgiveness and condemnation].
>
> Romans 8:1-2

A spirit-filled person is truly recognizable by their fruit. This is the fruit of the spirit. They are able to forgive, and this is the spirit of forgiveness. They truly are a tree of life.

There is an interesting parable, if you can call it that, recorded in the book of Job. It records the sons of God coming to serve God and the adversary comes along with them. The book of Job is written similarly to the book of Revelation at times: "It happened one day that the sons of God came to serve *Adonai*, and among them came the Adversary [Hebrew: Satan]" (Job 1:6).

As the sons of God (Holy men) came to serve God, one of them came in a spirit of unforgiveness. One approached with accusation in their heart. In this particular dialogue, the adversary has something against Job, and God seems to be bringing it out. Adam came forth as the adversary against himself and his bride. Look at what *Yeshua* says. He might even be alluding back to this verse in Job:

> Therefore if thou [sons of God] bring thy gift to the altar [come to serve God], and there rememberest that thy brother hath ought against thee [an accuser]; Leave there thy gift before the altar, and go thy way; first be reconciled to thy brother, and then come and offer thy gift.
> Matthew 5:23-24 (KJV)

Adam tried to cover himself in Torah by sewing on the fig leaves, but without the spirit of forgiveness, there was no fruit. Instead, he began to accuse his bride. He used the Torah as a weapon. In a sense, he even began to use it against God, just as *HaSatan* tried to use the word against *Yeshua* in the wilderness. The Torah, by the spirit, manifests as *love which covers a multitude of sin*. Adam was not lying, but he used the truth as a weapon. This is not the Spirit it was intended to be used in.

Remember the story of the woman caught in adultery? The men (earthly court system) brought her before *Yeshua* to accuse her. *Yeshua* (heavenly court system) used the same Torah not to accuse but to deliver the woman. This is such a beautiful example of the Torah from the garden. When we think about it, the whole exile from the garden is rooted in unforgiveness. Adam could have simply covered his wife, even took responsibility, as he was her teacher.

The Torah by the flesh manifests as a multitude of accusations. The human perspective will try to divide, not join together. It turns the Torah of forgiveness into a weapon of destruction. Adam was clothed in offense rather than love and forgiveness.

As believers in the Messiah, our faith should originate in forgiveness. This was Messiah's message. The Torah we receive from the Messiah should flow from forgiveness.

"*Adonai*, God, said to the woman, 'What is this you have done?' The woman answered. 'The serpent tricked me, so I ate'" (Genesis 3:13 KJV)—this is a fairly accurate statement. Eve was deceived by the human perspective. The serpent tricked her when she saw that the fruit looked desirable for making one wise. It was the desire for wisdom. However, this did not occur until after she tried to use a manmade commandment against the serpent: "This worship of me is useless, because they teach manmade rules as if they were doctrine" (Matthew 15:9, Isaiah 29:13).

In essence, they are worshipping man and obeying his rules. Because of putting their trust in man, we end up seeing Adam isolating himself from Eve and God. We see this isolation occur in his accusations. It was those manmade laws that left Eve powerless and exposed her to the enemy.

> Here is what *Adonai* says, "A curse on the person who trusts in humans, who relies on merely human strength. Whose heart turns away from *Adonai*. [We see the curses that come as a result of trusting in man.] He will be like a *tramarisk* [tree] in the *Aravah* [desert, outside of garden]—when relief comes, it is unaffected; for it lives in a sun-baked desert [as opposed to the cool of the garden], in salty uninhabited land."
>
> Jeremiah 17:5-6 (CJB)

Notice Jeremiah's description of this man. He is like an isolated tree in an uninhabited, salty, unproductive, hot desert wasteland. This alludes back to the darkness in Genesis 1:2. Adam, because of eating the fruit of the earthly nature, began to isolate himself from

God, the garden, and even Eve. Adam and Eve stayed married, but something had changed that day. Let's look further at Jeremiah.

> Blessed is the man who trusts in *Adonai*; *Adonai* will be his security [garden is the place of protection]. He will be like a tree planted near water; it spreads out its roots by the river; it does not notice when heat comes; and its foliage is luxuriant; it is not anxious in a year of drought but keeps on yielding fruit.
>
> Jeremiah 17:7-8

It is as though God said to Adam, "Don't eat of the tree of knowledge because if you do you will no longer be able to see me. I won't be hiding from you; you will hide from me. You will become disconnected from reality and be so full of guilt and shame you will begin to isolate yourself from all that is good. You will wander in a dry, fruitless place; and, ultimately, you will die. Adam, it won't be me who accuses you or punishes you. You will become your own accuser, and you will run from me your salvation. Your life, your self-esteem, and your image will become so shattered that it will be as if you are in a smelting furnace where the pain and agony of the curse seems as though it will never end."

Now hidden in the Torah are many truths about what took place with Adam and Eve. As God began to pronounce the curses, it is not that God is cursing them but actually announcing what was already occurring. The curses were just the description of what was already happening in Genesis 3:7-13. He was naming the activities that were taking place.

ק

GOSPEL OF THE GARDEN

What is the gospel of the garden? Let's take a deeper look at the Messiah's mission from the garden and our mission from the Messiah. Now that we understand just what Adam needed saved from, let's look deeper: "And I will put enmity between thee and the woman, and between thy seed and her seed; it shall bruise thy head, and thou shalt bruise his heel" (Genesis 3:15 KJV).

The seed of the serpent is rooted in unforgiveness, and the seed of the woman is rooted in forgiveness. There is animosity between the two. One is a picture of the heavenly court system the other is the earthly court system. The enmity is between God's perspective and man's perspective. We just explored this in previous chapters. Today, we often, in almost all religious circles, see things backward. Our theologies tend to believe that God hides His presence from us and that He punishes us. Most salvation messages are centered on escaping God's punishment when we die. Our theologies reveal that, in most cases, we see ourselves as naked.

God has always seen our potential. He knew us before the foundation of the world. He only took us out of Himself in order to bring us back to Himself. He is the one that causes us to be considered righteous. He sees you as though you have fruit even when you don't because He sees what He created you for from the beginning to the end.

At the fall, it became evident that God was going to have to rescue mankind. The only way God could take us out of Himself is if we experienced an exile from Him. This would be experienced as a body bound for death. We would have to be rescued from this body. We have been our own accusers, not God. Somehow, God would have to cleanse our consciences from the curse that was placed on the old nature. Because of it, the Torah will be twisted and distorted by a defiled conscience. "Such teachings come from the hypocrisy of liars *whose consciences have been burned* as if with a red-hot branding iron" (1 Timothy 4:2).

We often imagine salvation as *Yeshua* coming to save us from going to hell when we die because we were bad people who sinned. Sin is just the fruit of the old nature. In order to be freed from the fruit of sin, we needed to be freed from the old nature (hell).

The Messiah came to cleanse our conscience so we could see God's presence. So we could see the glory of God in us. He came to strip the power of death, shame, and guilt from us, to bring us back in a relationship as one with Him and to restore our dominion in the earth. "How much more shall the blood of Christ, who through the eternal Spirit offered himself without blemish unto God, *cleanse your conscience* from dead works to serve the living God?" (Hebrews 9:14 ASV).

This is the theme of Yom Kippur and one of the names of God, where we come face-to-face with God. Can you imagine if Adam would have been able to come face-to-face instead of hiding from the face of God on this day? Now, because of the work of the Messiah, we are able to come face-to-face with God. We no longer have to hide from Him on Yom Kippur, the day of covering, where we enter the holy of holies. "Let us draw near with a true heart in fulness of faith, having our hearts sprinkled from an evil conscience [old nature]: and having our body washed with pure water" (Hebrews 10:22 ASV).

The blood is the voice and life of *Yeshua*. Now sprinkled on our hearts, He has given us His desires and perspective. Can you imagine the fruit that will come from this? "Holding the mystery of the faith in a *pure conscience*." (2 Timothy 3:9 ASV).

This mystery was a formerly hidden truth that when the Messiah came, like Adam, Israel was sewing on fig leaves. They were trying to cover themselves with the Torah, but because of their seared consciences, there was not fruit of forgiveness. Like Adam, the house of Judah was accusing Eve, the house of Israel, of idolatry, referring to them as Gentiles.

They drove walls of division between them and the nations instead of being a light (covering) to the nations. They were, to a degree, using the Torah as a weapon to accuse and divide from the nations. This is still alive today in most religions (earthly court systems) today. We find reasons to separate from each other. This is not the Spirit of the Torah.

The hidden truth was that the Messiah, *Yeshua*, came as YHVH and man to deal with both husbands, to cleanse our consciences so that we could serve Him by the spirit. Only then would we be able to produce the fruit and life offered by the Torah, the fruit of a relationship with the Spirit of forgiveness.

If our consciences are not cleansed by the blood of the Messiah on Yom Kippur, then we are approaching God, people, and Torah from a human perspective. We are like a wolf in sheep's clothing, a fig tree with no fruit.

Adam could no longer see his purpose or his potential. It became veiled. It was hidden from him. When the Messiah cleanses your conscience, you will see your purpose. In fact, you will get the revelation that you are one with the Messiah. We have been looking to the sky for Him in a second coming. However, from the beginning, the second coming would be the revelation of the Messiah in you. You become one spirit with the Messiah. The reality of this almost seems like blaspheming to the carnal man, but this is the power of the execution stake.

The manifestation of the sons of God is the revelation of the Messiah. It has been about relationship. The two became one from the beginning. God's movement upon the earth will not be apart from His people; it is His people. When you meet a true Israelite, the seed, you have met the God of Abraham, Isaac, and *Ya'akov*.

There were many prophesies that *Yeshua* fulfilled in His first coming. There were, however, many that he did not fulfill. In the church, we had taught that *Yeshua* would fulfill these prophesies about the Messiah in His second coming. This is not what *Yeshua* or Paul taught. Let's take a look at who will fulfill these. This is incredible. "Then said Jesus to them again, Peace *be* unto you: as *my* Father hath sent me, even so send I you" (John 20:21 KJV).

Yeshua was sent to be salvation to the ends of the earth. He did not come to condemn people but to forgive and release people. It is as though *Yeshua* holds a key to unlock forgiveness in people, to be able to forgive themselves and others. Now he sends us as the Messiah (body of Messiah) to bring salvation to the ends of the earth. We, the body of Messiah, fulfill the prophecies of the Messiah. The ones we saw connected to His second coming. He is one with us. Isaiah 49 reveals the mission of the Messiah. I want to look at one verse in particular: "He says: 'It is too light a thing that you should be my servant to raise up the tribes of Jacob and to bring back the preserved of Israel; I will make *you as a light for the nations, that my salvation may reach to the end of the earth*'" (Isaiah 49:6 ESV).

Now we will see Paul and Barnabas use this verse about themselves.

> And speaking boldly, Paul and Barnabas said, 'To you it was necessary that first the word of God be spoken, and seeing ye do thrust it away, and do not judge yourselves worthy [Adam] of the life age-during [eternal life], lo, we do turn to the nations; for so hath the Lord commanded us [the Messiah]: "*I have set thee for a light of nations--for thy being for salvation [deliverance] unto the end of the earth.*"
>
> Acts 13:46-47 (YLT)

These are powerful words here that should not be glossed over but meditated upon. They quote a verse about the Messiah and use it to refer to themselves. They understood they were one with the Messiah. His mission was now their mission. In fact, the Messiah came to restore our mission (purpose) to us. They truly saw the light of the Messiah contained in themselves. Paul even tells people to follow him as he follows the Messiah. This is a formerly hidden truth.

> Just as you yourselves were disobedient to God before but have received mercy (through the Messiah) now because of Israel's [house of Judah] disobedience; so also Israel has been disobedient now, so that by your *showing them the same mercy* that God has shown you, they too may receive God's mercy.
>
> Romans 11:30-31

The house of Israel received God's mercy through the Messiah who was from the house of Judah. Now the house of Judah would receive this same mercy from the house of Israel, where the Messiah is dwelling. We missed this verse in the church for some years. We were supposed to be the manifestation of the Messiah to the Jewish people. For a season, we were quite the opposite.

The Messiah does not accuse. He does not bring condemnation or punishment. His people who manifest His light should not either.

> *Yeshua* repeated, "Just as the father has sent me, I myself am also sending you." Having said this, he breathed on them [the breath that went into Adam's nostrils] and said to them, "Receive the *Ruach HaKadesh* [the Spirit of God, His nature, His potential]! If you forgive someone's sins, their sin is forgiven; if you hold them they are held."
>
> John 20:21-23

If we forgive, it is the tree of life. If we hold on to the sin, it is the tree of death. We begin to choose and decide what is good and what is evil.

Right after God breathed into Adam's nostrils, He placed him in the garden and warned him, "You may eat of all the trees including the tree of life, forgiveness, but don't eat of the tree of knowledge, unforgiveness, because if you do you will surely die. You won't be able to forgive yourself or anyone else. It will become a spirit of pharaoh, who 'won't let my people go.'"

Adam, in a sense, blasphemed the Holy Spirit, hid himself from God. He could not forgive himself or anyone else for that matter. Unforgiveness equals a life outside of the garden.

Blaspheming the Holy Spirit is rooted in unforgiveness. The reason it is unforgiveable is because it is unforgiveness. Until we are able to forgive ourselves and others, we will hide from the Holy Spirit, the Spirit of forgiveness.

When *Yeshua* cleanses our consciences and heals our fragmented view of ourselves and the world, we will begin to really get the revelation of the Messiah in us. We will begin to see His life in us. We will move past what has held us in its clutches, and we will begin to overcome sin. We will experience it as though we are the ones doing it, crushing the head of the serpent, but it is the Messiah in us who is doing it through us.

When we look at our lives and they begin to look like the life of the Messiah, the rivers of living waters begin to flow. We are able to pardon and forgive each other, as we realize we are all one, one body. When I forgive my brother, I am releasing myself. This is a key of life. It unlocks death and Hades, and we walk out. The Spirit of God is in us, and we will find ourselves fulfilling the Torah. This is the Torah of love, the Torah of the garden: "So that the just requirement of the Torah might be fulfilled in us who don't run our lives according to what the old nature wants but according to what the Spirit wants" (Romans 8:4).

The Torah of the garden is not a weapon to divide but the Torah of love. It is the Torah of forgiveness, where we cover a multitude of sins. God always forgives. Now, He gives us the Spirit so we can forgive each other and ourselves: "Don't owe anyone anything—except to love one another; for whoever loves [not accuses] his fellow human beings has fulfilled Torah" (Romans 13:8).

You know when the Torah has touched the Spirit of God, *Yeshua*, because it pardons and forgives, just as *Yeshua* pardoned the woman caught in adultery. *Yeshua* used the Torah to pardon. *HaSatan* (carnal men) will use the Torah as a weapon to accuse.

When God put Adam in the garden, he planted him there. We are the trees and the vines of His garden. Adam was a choice vine, a son of God. Adam was fully man (dust of the earth) and fully God (the Spirit God breathed into him). This is amazing, as God created Adam in His image. Adam was the express image of the invisible God in the earth. I'm amazed every time I think about this.

When Adam ate the forbidden fruit, it was to this image, his true image, that Adam became lost to. Adam was lost to his purpose and destiny. He lost his identity. When *Yeshua* came to the earth, it was to restore this image back to Adam, the image of God, to return us to our true image: "Therefore, since the children share a common physical nature as human beings, *he became like them* and shared that same human nature; so that by his death he might render ineffective the one who had power over death [that is, the Adversary]" (Hebrews 2:14).

YHVH became like us. This is what is meant in John 3:16 when *Yeshua* is called His only begotten son. Israel is called God's son. Adam was a son of God. *Yeshua* is YHVH, who became like us, like Israel, His son: "For I am a father to Israel, and *Efrayim* is my *firstborn son*" (Jeremiah 31:8-(9)b).

YHVH became like us in order to free us and restore us back to the image of a son of God. All of creation is eagerly waiting for the manifestation of the sons of God.

> The creation waits eagerly for the sons of God to be revealed... Because those whom he knew in advance he also determined in advance would be conformed to the pattern [image] of his son so that he might be the *firstborn among many brothers*.
>
> Romans 8:19, 29

"In order to prevent them from seeing the light shining from the Good News about the Messiah, *is who the image of God*" (2 Corinthians 4:5). We sometimes fail to realize that YHVH became like us. This attribute of God is *Yeshua*. He came in the image Adam originally was created in: the image of God. "He is the *visible image of the invisible God*. He is supreme over all creation" (Colossians 1:15).

This is the same description that Adam was created in, the image of God, and had dominion over all the earth (creation). When Adam fell from this image, it was to the image of mortal man, the dust of the earth. "Just as we have borne the *image of the man of dust*, so also we will *bear the image of the man from heaven*" (1 Corinthians 15:49).

Yeshua is restoring the image of the heavenly man to us. We will walk, talk, look, and even eat like Him. Take a look at what Paul says. "Try to imitate me, even as I myself try to imitate the Messiah" (1 Corinthians 11:1).

"For a man indeed should not have his head veiled, because he is the *image and glory of God*, and the woman is the glory of man" (1 Corinthians 11:7). Is this hard for a carnal man to grasp? Absolutely. This can only be received by the Spirit of God. He never called Adam naked. He always saw us as sons of God. He foreknew us before the fall and is restoring us back to our former state, the image of the son of God. That image is *Yeshua*, salvation. He is not trying to send people to hell when they die but to restore the image of heaven back to them. Hell is the spirit of unforgiveness.

Your true image is the image of salvation, the image of *Yeshua*. On Yom Kippur, the bride is given white linen garments called the garments of salvation. We don't need to sew on fig leaves (self-righteousness). YHVH will clothe you in His salvation. This is your destiny, your purpose, and your identity from the beginning.

ר

KASHRU, KOSHER

> Then God said, "Here! Throughout the whole earth I am giving you as food every seed-bearing plant and every tree with seed-bearing fruit."
>
> Genesis 1:29 (CJB)

Here, we see God gives man every seed-bearing plant and tree for food. Many find a connection here that the tree of knowledge had no seed. It could not reproduce life. We did find a connection with its fruit causing miscarriage, abortion, and childlessness. We found this in the word *wise* (*sakal*). Eve saw that its fruit was desirable for making one wise.

So if God has already given Adam every seed-bearing plant and tree, why does the Torah go on to tell us a second time what Adam is to eat? "*Adonai*, God, gave the person this order: 'You may freely eat from every tree in the garden except the tree of the knowledge of good and evil. You are not to eat from it, because on the day that you eat from it, it will become certain that you will die'" (Genesis 2:16-17).

The Torah is revealing that there is more to this than physical food. Then the question could be asked: was the tree of knowledge a physical tree? It absolutely could have been and most likely was. The physical realm is a mirror of the spiritual realm. Often, the physical becomes a point of contact for the spiritual.

We don't serve the physical, the creation. We serve the spiritual, the Creator. God give us the physical, what we can see, to teach us about the unseen realm.

> Because what is known about God is plain to them, since God has made it plain to them. Forever since the creation of the universe his invisible qualities—both his eternal power and divine nature—have been clearly seen, because they can be understood from what he has made. Therefore, they have no excuse.
>
> Romans 1:19-20

If it was a physical fruit, the next question might be asked: Did the fruit of the tree of knowledge have some special power? When Adam ate this fruit, was there some special power in the fruit that changed Adam? No. It was not the physical fruit. The fruit was just the point of contact, the opportunity to access the realm behind it, in this case, the realm of death. It was disobeying the commandment that caused the defilement.

When we *mikveh* (immersion in water), there is no special power in the water. The water becomes a point of contact (obeying the commandment) to change our status from death to life. This is a key that gives access to the kingdom. We don't worship the water as if it has some special power. We worship the Creator and obey his commandment. It was obedience that brought the change of status from the realm of death to the realm of life. Eating the forbidden fruit was the point of contact, the opportunity to disobey; it was a key giving access to the kingdom of darkness.

There is no special power in the physical realm, not in the physical fruit or in the water. It is obedience that brings the blessing and disobedience that brings the curse. Paganism looks for special powers in the physical, like some kind of holy water with power or some special formulas, etc. This inevitably leads to worshiping the creation and not the Creator.

Let's examine this a little closer. If someone eats non-kosher food, it is not the food itself that defiles them. It is disobedience that defiles the person. Granted, when we eat something non-kosher, we are eating something God never called food. This can absolutely cause physical ailments, but it is not what defiles us spiritually. Let's look at an excellent parable with *Yeshua*: "Then some, *P'rushim* and Torah-teachers from *Yerushalayim* came to *Yeshua* and asked him, 'Why is it that your *talmidim* break the traditions of the elders? They don't do *n'tilat—yadayim* [hand washings] before they eat!'" (Matthew 15:1-2).

The traditions of the elders were manmade commandments. These are also called fences. As I mentioned earlier, the rabbis drew the authority to build these fence from Genesis. They believe Adam was building fences around the Torah commands when He told Eve not to touch the tree. "He answered, 'Indeed, why do you break the commands of God by your traditions?'" (Matthew 15:3).

Yeshua might be alluding to the command not to add to or subtract from God's commandments. He is also going to give them an example. Notice He transitions away from physical food or washing of the hands.

> For God said, "Honor your father and mother," and "Anyone who curses his father or mother must be put to death." But you say, "If anyone says to his father or mother, 'I have promised to give to God what I might have used to help you,' then he is rid of his duty to honor his father or mother." Thus by your tradition you make null and void [abolish] the word [Torah] of God.
>
> Matthew 15:4-6 (CJB)

Yeshua was not necessarily against the hand washing before eating. After all, this is a good practice. The topic was actually traditions. *Yeshua* was addressing the traditions that made the Torah null or void. *Yeshua* was for the Torah and spoke up about traditions that abolished the Torah. *Yeshua* came to fulfill (cause to stand up, to teach, and walk out the Torah accurately) the Torah. "You hypocrites! *Yesha'yahu* [Isaiah] was right when he prophesied about you, 'These people honor me with their lips, but their hearts are far away from me. Their worship of me is useless, because they teach manmade rules as if they were doctrines'" (Matthew 15:7-9).

As we saw with Eve, manmade rules are useless against the Satan. This form of worship only brings pain and sorrow. It is not just Judaism that teaches manmade commandments as doctrine; the whole church system is set around manmade commandments, the number one being that the Torah is done away with, abolished, old or useless. The thought that we don't need God's Torah, we can live by our own ways, all originate in obeying man. "Then he called the crowd to him and said, 'Listen and understand this! What makes a person unclean is not what goes into his mouth; rather, what comes out of his mouth that is what makes him unclean!'" (Matthew 15:10-11).

What could possibly come out of their mouth that would render them unclean? It was not the physical food but their own laws, traditions, and evil desires that came out of their mouths, the desire to make their own commandments that led to disobedience that defiled them.

> The *talmidim* came to him and said, "Do you know that the *p'rushim* were offended by what you said?" He replied, "Every plant that my Father in heaven has not planted will be pulled up by the roots. Let them be. They are blind guides. When a blind man guides another blind man, both will fall into a pit." *Kefa* said to him, "Explain the parable to us." So he said, "Don't you understand even now? Don't you see that anything that enters the mouth goes into the stomach and passes out into the latrine? But what comes out of your mouth is actually coming from your heart, and that is what makes a person unclean. For out of the heart comes forth wicked thoughts, murder, adultery and other kinds of sexual immorality, theft, lies, slanders... These are what really make a person unclean, but eating without doing *n'tilat-yadayim* [hand washing] does not make a person unclean."
>
> Matthew 15:12-20 (CJB)

Yeshua even had to explain this to His disciples, as Judaism, in His day, had become blind. They were looking to control the outside of the body, the physical, like Adam, who sewed on the fig leaves. *Yeshua* was directing it back to the heart, inside, where the real fruit comes from.

When the Pharisees asked *Yeshua* why his disciples don't do a ceremonial hand washing before they eat, a manmade commandment, *Yeshua* saw this as an opportunity to fulfill the Torah, an opportunity to teach the Torah from God's perspective, heavenly court system. The rabbis were seeing from man's perspective, the earthly court system. He began to explain where defilement really came from. This points to where Adam's defilement came from. For *Yeshua*, this parable had nothing to do with declaring everything clean to eat. This was not an opportunity to declare pork clean at all.

The human perspective, an uncircumcised heart, wants to add to and subtract from God's Word. It desires to control the outside, which is an attempt to camouflage what is on the inside.

Yeshua was bringing Torah back to its proper place. This is called fulfilling the Torah. One of the first commandments in the Torah is to be fruitful and multiply. Next, God tells Adam to distinguish between what fruit was food for him and that which is not food for Him.

The physical, what we can see, teaches us about the spiritual, what we can't see. Paul touches on this when he says, "First comes the physical and then the spiritual. However, the spiritual does not precede the physical." This is why there was most likely a physical fruit in the garden to teach about a spiritual fruit.

Likewise, Paul says that if we can't obey an authority we can see, how are we going to obey an authority that we can't see? This is a biblical principle we should all strive to fully grasp.

The laws of kosher teach us to distinguish what is food for us physically. As we learn to identify what is food physically and we honor God by walking in His Torah, He will then expound it by the Spirit and teach us to distinguish what is food for us spiritually. When we obey what is already revealed, then God reveals more. Keep in mind God does not take us past the last instruction that we failed to obey.

For the Jewish people, they know if you are not eating a kosher diet physically, it is a sign that you are not able to distinguish a kosher spiritual diet. The house of Israel has tried to move past the physical and skip right to the spiritual. However, God's revelation *always* builds upon what He has already revealed. Here are a couple of scriptures about the house of Israel, who is scattered to the nations: "*Adonai* said, 'This is how the people of Israel will eat their food—unclean—in the nations where I am driving them'" (Ezekiel 4:13).

Under biblical law, if you can't distinguish what is food for you physically, then how are you going to distinguish what is food spiritually? Even in the garden, Adam was to distinguish between clean and unclean or between kosher and non-kosher. *Yeshua* is taking us back to the garden, the place He has prepared for Adam and us. The bride will need to be prepared to distinguish between clean and unclean once again, yes, even in the garden. Isn't this amazing? Our end was found in the beginning. "Therefore *Adonai* says, 'Go out from their midst, separate yourselves; don't even touch what is unclean. Then I myself will receive you. In fact, I will be your father, and you will be my sons and daughters,' says *Adonai Tzva'ot*" (2 Corinthians 6:17-18).

When we don't touch what is unclean, then we are acceptable (kosher). The priests of Israel are to teach the people the difference between what is clean and what is unclean. Paul was fulfilling his priestly duties by teaching this to the nations so that they would be acceptable, kosher before God. "To be a servant of the Messiah *Yeshua* for the Gentiles [house of Israel], with the priestly duty of presenting the Good News of God, so that the Gentiles maybe an acceptable [kosher] offering, made holy by the *Ruach HaKodesh*" (Romans 15:16).

Ultimately learning to distinguish between what is clean and unclean will teach us to distinguish between God's commandments and man's commandments. If we choose man's commands over God's commands, we will find ourselves in an unclean status where we are unable to produce life. Today, in both houses of Israel, we need to learn to distinguish between what are God's commands and traditions and what are man's commands and traditions.

The laws of kosher will give us insight into people. People are likened unto animals. Who is a kosher animal, and who is not? This teaches us whose words are food for us and those whose words are not. If their confession (chew their cud) matches their conduct (split hoof), then they are food for us. We can eat the fruit of their lips and live. If we don't know God's commandments (Torah), then how will we recognize their fruit? After all, *Yeshua* said, "You will recognize them by their fruit." He said, "Adam, distinguish or you will surely die the day you eat of it."

If we can't distinguish between God's commandments and man's commandments, then we can't distinguish between the tree of life and the tree of knowledge. Isaiah spoke of a people like this in his famous chapter on the vineyard: "Woe to those who call evil good and good evil. Who change darkness into light and light into darkness, which change bitter into sweet and sweet into bitter!" (Isaiah 5:20).

ש

FEAR

Why did Adam add to God's commandment? Did he doubt God's Word, or was he second-guessing God? Obviously, when we add to or subtract from something, we are saying that it is not sufficient. We are doubting, not trusting.

Where does doubt originate? It originates in pride and fear. Did Adam fear that Eve would eat of the forbidden fruit if he did not build an extra fence around the commandment? Did Adam fear that God's Word was not sufficient to protect Eve, or did he think he was wiser than God?

Fear is a false representation of our future. In essence, fear is an illusion, something that does not exist. We can meditate on that for a minute. Fear is related to the human perspective. *HaSatan* is really an illusion. This is having the Spirit of fear. It is when we move on fear that we give life to this unreality. If Adam built a fence out of fear, it was this very fence that brought his greatest fear upon himself. When we move on fear, we give life to something that did not exist. Powerful.

Fear is something false appearing real. This is the opposite of faith. Faith is the truth appearing real. Faith is really moving on the truth as it appears real. We have a tendency to move on what appears real to us. When we are operating from the human perspective (realm of death), we move on illusions, things that are not real. Keep in mind that God is the ultimate reality.

We don't enter into a relationship with God based on fear. If we do, we end up in a fake or false relationship with God. This is the difference between knowing about God and knowing God. God had to make Himself known to Israel because although they knew about God while in Egypt, it had been a long time since they knew Him.

It is a pagan (not real) idea that we are trying to appease an angry God for fear of going to Hades when we die. This approach comes out of Greek mythology. The Greek myths were adopted by the Romans as truth. Unfortunately, these ideas have bled their way into Christianity. Our approach to the gospel has been skewed. The gospel has been approached in fear. Many are saved out of fear of dying and going to hell. This is a false representation of your future, and it has prevented us from getting the maximum potential that the gospel really offers.

The gospel from the beginning is about a loving God who wants to take you out of the hell of being exiled from the garden, to free you from the human perspective with its desires and the shame and pain that goes with it. He wants to bring His bride back to the garden, the place of protection and pleasure.

The garden is the realm that God prepared for Adam to reach his full potential. The garden is still the place where we will reach our full potential.

When Adam ate of the forbidden fruit, guilt and shame grew over his heart and mind like a foreskin. For the first time, Adam experienced himself as wicked. This spirit of pharaoh (fear) would not let Adam go worship God. Instead of running to his salvation at the time of visitation, Adam hid himself. "They heard the voice of *Adonai*, God, walking in the garden at the time of the evening breeze, so the man and his wife hid themselves from the presence of *Adonai*, God, among the trees of the garden" (Genesis 3:8).

The spirit of pharaoh is the spirit of fear and unforgiveness. Adam could not eat of the tree of life (forgiveness). It would take a miracle for Adam to ever be free from the torment of this spirit of unforgiveness, for Adam to be able to forgive himself. Adam's whole reality would now be experienced through this veil of unforgiveness. It is this consciousness that *Yeshua* came to cleanse us from.

Eve saw this forbidden fruit as desirable for making one wise. This was something false appearing real. God, in His kindness, has given us his Torah to teach us the difference between what is real and what is not. What is real is what is eternal. What is not real is what is in the process of perishing.

The Torah teaches us what truth is. The Spirit of the Lord expounds upon this truth to teach us what truth is in the unseen realm by expounding on the Torah. What is eternal is what is unseen (2 Corinthians 4:18). The Torah refers to a carnal or pagan man as a non-existing thing (not a people). Those who are in the flesh are an illusion, something false appearing real. A wolf in sheep's clothing. You can see where the urge to not have fellowship with someone from the nations comes from. The Jews of Peter's days saw the Gentiles as something false appearing real. They were not a people or a non-existent thing.

> This accords with the Tanakh, where it says, "I have appointed you to be a father to many nations." *Avraham* is our father in God's sight because he trusted God [the truth appeared real] as the one who gives life to the dead and calls non-existent things [carnal people] into existence [spiritual men].
> Romans 4:17

The physical mirrors the spiritual, and the physical can teach us about the spiritual. It is the spiritual that is eternal and real. A carnal man cannot see or perceive the spiritual. When we see from the human perspective, we serve the creation. We inevitably see the illusion as the truth.

The more disconnected we become from our identity, our oneness with God, the more aware of ourselves (fleshly nature) we become. In the beginning, Adam was married to God and to the will of God. He saw from God's perspective; in fact, he was created in God's image. Adam experienced God's will as his own will.

After Adam ate of the forbidden fruit, the first question God asked Adam was, "Where are you (*Ayekah*)?" This was not a question of Adam's location. This question, "Where are you?" contains profound psychological meaning. Before eating from the tree of knowledge, Adam knew exactly who and where he was. He was one with life, one with the music and rhythm of reality. He was not necessarily aware of how he was feeling, as he was not joined to the ego or human perspective.

I want to take a minute and share a concept from Judaism:

High and Low

God desires a dwelling place in the lower realms. With these words our sages describe the divine in creation. What are the lower realms? It is common to refer to the Spiritual as higher than the material, and to the physical universe as the lowest of God's creation. But are these designations truly justified? After all, God not only created all spiritual and physical entities but also the very concepts of spirituality and physically. He transcends both realms equally and, at the same time is equally present in both, for his all-embracing truth knows no limits or categorization. So why should the spiritual be deemed loftier than the physical?

To understand why the physical is indeed lower than the spiritual, we must first examine the meaning of the term *olam*, the Hebrew word for world. Olam means "concealment." A world is a framework or context within which things exist; and in order for anything to exist, a concealment must first take place.

The reason for this is that the basic (and only) law of existence is that "there is none else besides Him" (Deuteronomy 4:35). That is the only true existence and that nothing exists outside of His all-prevailing reality. In order for anything else to possess even the slightest semblance of somethingness or selfhood, this truth must be veiled and obscured. Hence God's creation of worlds—concealments within which things may exist distinct and apart (at least in their own conception) from the all nullifying reality of God.

God created both higher spiritual creations and lower physical ones. The difference between them lies not in their essential closeness to or separateness from God, but in the degree of the concealment their worlds provide. A lesser concealment may allow for things to exist, but these existences will be conscious of their Creator and utterly subservient to Him, acknowledging their total dependence upon Him. In this there are many gradations and degrees (image to image or glory to glory as the apostle Paul said)—the greater the concealment in any given world, the more of a self the creations of that world will possess (by worlds this does not mean planets).

In this sense, the physical world is the lowest world of all. So great is the physical worlds concealment of godliness, that the selfhood of its inhabitants is absolute: by nature, the physical object or creature strives only for its own preservation and advancement, regarding its own as the axis around which all else revolves. The world of the physical not only dims its divine source but obscures entirely, even allowing for creations that deny their own origin and essence.

Week in Review, BH Vol. 6, Noach 5764

When Adam ate the forbidden fruit, in a sense, he fell asleep or became disconnected from the higher spiritual realm (heaven) and became lost in the lower physical world. Adam was lost in the world of the ego or self. Adam became a slave of creation, serving the illusion. It is not that man needs to escape the planet earth but wake up the spiritual world in Him. Here is what Paul says: "All who are led by God's spirit are God's sons. For you did not receive a spirit of slavery to bring you back to fear; on the contrary, you received the Spirit, who makes us sons and by whose power we cry out, 'Abba! [That is dear father]'" (Romans 8:14-15).

When we see from God's perspective or we are led by the spirit, we are now seeing or experiencing true reality. You have overcome the world (illusion of concealment). The truth appears as real and is no longer veiled. *HaSatan*, the *Yetzer Hara* or human perspective can all be understood as the veil that blinds us to the reality of God and our oneness with Him.

> You used to be dead [to the upper spiritual world] because of your sins [veils] and acts of disobedience [denying your origin]. You walked in the ways [illusions], of the *'olam hazeh* [present world or lower world] and obeyed the ruler of the power of the air, who is still at work in the disobedient. Indeed, we all once lived this way—we followed the passions of our old nature [the ego, human perspective] and obeyed the wishes of our old nature [the Satan] and our own thoughts…
> Ephesians 2:1-3a (CJB)

The god of the present age is man, flesh, his ego with its desires and passions. The earthly nature is revealed to be the father of lies. The earthly nature causes us to deny our origin. This is to hide from God's face. This nature is the father of lies. "They have been ransomed from among humanity [dust of the earth, lower realm] as first fruits for God and the lamb; on their lips *no lie* was found— they are without defect" (Revelation 14:4b-5).

These are the ones who have overcome the old nature (the world). They are able to see the physical world in union with the spiritual and no longer see it as separate. These are the trees we may eat from. You will know them by their fruit. It is the ego that pictures God as far off and distant. It sees itself as separate from God. How do you see God?

One of the first commandments of the Torah flows from the laws of *Kashru* (kosher). Does God care what we eat? Ask Adam and Eve. They will tell you God absolutely cares what you eat, and then they would remind you that God never changes. He is the same yesterday, today, and forever. They would warn you just as the author of the book of Revelation does, you can lose your share in the tree of life.

If you add to or subtract from God's Torah, the tree of life, you will eat the fruit of your lips. What world are you operating in? Do you see God as far off, or have you truly woken up to the reality that you are one with Him? Do you see the glory of the Messiah in yourself or others? Does this reality still remain obscured or veiled?

When we talk about Torah or the laws of kosher, it is often difficult for those from the nations. They have been taught that when they are saved, they are no longer carnal but spiritual. Many simply don't realize that they are just as carnal as they were two minutes before they prayed. They are just beginning the process of spiritual awakening. It is a process of overcoming the world (veil) or old nature. Just the struggle alone to accept God's Torah can reveal just how alive the old nature is in us. "For the mind controlled by the old nature is hostile to God, because it does not submit itself to God's Torah—indeed, it cannot. Thus, those who identify with their old nature cannot please God" (Romans 8:7-8).

Here is the problem: the old nature sees the Torah as something that tries to control us. We don't want to be told how we are to live. Submitting to God's Torah seems like bondage to the carnal mind. However, to the spiritual mind, God's Torah is freedom from the bondage of serving the creation or human perspective with its evil desires.

Here is the reality. The Torah is better understood as what you were created to do, your purpose. Rather than seeing it as a set of rules, dos and don't dos, we should approach the Torah as a manual to teach us what we are created to do. It reveals your potential and how to reach your potential. When we adapt to God's Torah, we begin to operate in what we were created to do, and this is how we cling to God.

Loving *Adonai* your God, paying attention to what he says and clinging to him—for that is the purpose of your life! On this depends the length of time you will live in the land *Adonai* swore he would give to your ancestors *Avraham*, Isaac and *Ya'akov*.

Deuteronomy 30:20

How do we love God? We obey Him. In the church, we have not clearly known what to obey. It has been abstract. Our God is not abstract or vague: "For loving God means obeying his commands, moreover his commands are not burdensome" (1 John 5:3).

ת

ALEF-TAV

In all truth, as we examine the gospel from the beginning, we realize that when man ate the forbidden fruit, he lost the ability to love God. Man became a lover of himself. God's wrath or anger can be understood as God turning a man over to himself, to love himself. A carnal man is a man who worships himself.

When Adam ate the fruit, he lost the ability to fulfill his purpose, which is to love and cling to God, to bear good fruit for God. Adam fell from the heavenly realms down to the lowest world, where he became a god unto himself. Adam was doomed to eat the dust of the earth, to serve the desires of the *HaSatan*.

Yeshua saved man from himself so that, once again, he could fulfill his purpose. Man would be able love God because God loved him first. Once again, God's desires would be man's desires, as he is resurrected back up to the lofty spiritual reality that he had fallen from.

When Adam ate the fruit, he saw himself as naked. The Morning Star had fallen from the heavens down to the earth or lowest realm called *she'ol*. Adam's nakedness was he had no fruit, the fruit of the presence of God. The Torah takes us into another story that demonstrates this for us.

The story is the story of *Noach*. Amazingly, there are many parallels between *Noach* and Adam. *Noach* and his sons pass through the veil of one world to a new world via an ark. Let's look at one of the first things the Torah records after the flood: "*Noach*, a farmer [cultivator of a garden], was the first to plant a vineyard. He drank so much of the wine that he got drunk and lay uncovered [naked] in his tent" (Genesis 9:20-21).

Ani Yosef

Does this sound a little familiar? We are seeing a repeat. Adam was taken from the dust of the earth, and *Noach* is taken from a generation that was likened unto the dust of the earth. Adam was to cultivate a garden, and *Noach* is a farmer. Adam is planted in the vineyard (garden), eats of the forbidden fruit, profanes the vineyard, and finds himself naked; and Noach plants a vineyard, gets dunk on the wine, profanes the vineyard, and finds himself naked. What takes place next is quite a revelation: "Ham, the father of the *kena'an*, saw his father shamefully exposed [nakedness], went out and told his two brothers" (Genesis 9:22).

Ham exposes his father's nakedness. This is a picture of the earthly court system, the same one Adam fell into after the fall. The key words in the verse are: *he saw his father's nakedness*. Adam saw his nakedness, and God asked, "Who told you that you were naked?" Now Ham saw his father's nakedness. Ham is obviously seeing from the same perspective as Adam was after he ate of the forbidden fruit. The Torah is revealing a mindset here, one that is connected to be cursed.

Ham went out and told his two brothers. Ham had become the accuser. Ham is one third of *Noach's* descendants and can be likened unto a type of the third part of the stars (angels) that had fallen. He is a picture of the third part of the rivers that turned bitter. Ham and his descendants have fallen and will be exiled just as Adam was and is a picture of Lucifer and the fallen angels. Ham and his descendants are a picture of the fruit of Noach's flesh (Revelation 8:10-12, 12:9; Isaiah 14:12-15).

Noach's fruit (of the Spirit, his spiritual descendants) covered his nakedness: "*Shem* and *Yefet* [*Noach's* fruit] took a cloak, put it over both their shoulders, and walking backward; went in and covered their naked father. Their faces were turned away, so that they did not see their father lying there shamefully exposed" (Genesis 9:23). This is a picture of the heavenly court system. This is the Torah of love that covers a multitude of sins. In fact, they form a picture of a Torah scroll as the each brother (*Yefet*, house of Israel, and *Shem*, house of Judah) represent one of the poles (*etz chim*) of the Torah. The cloak they draped over their shoulders represented the lamb skins. The words of the Torah are written called garments of righteousness. *Noach's* fruit of the Spirit clothed him in garments of righteousness.

The fruit of *Noach's* earthly nature (Ham, sin) exposed his nakedness and accused him. Again, we are seeing a mindset. *Shem* and *Yefet* represent a heavenly kingdom mindset; they are a covering for their father. Noach pronounces a blessing over them and this mindset. However, he pronounces a curse over Ham and his mindset. The curse is connected with being a slave and is related to the law of sin and death: "When Noach awoke from his wine, he knew what his youngest son had done to him. He said, 'Cursed be *Kena'an*; he will be a servant of servants to his brothers'" (Genesis 9:24-25).

Cursed to be a servant of servants is to say that *Kena'an* will serve the creation and not the Creator. When it is associated with his brothers, it is to say that this human perspective (Ham) will be a servant of the godly perspective (*Shem*, Torah, and *Yefet*, Spirit). *Shem* and *Yefet* will crush the head (perspective) of the *Kena'an*. *Kena'an's* curse is likened unto that of the serpent to eat the dust of the earth. Later, Israel (seed of the woman) is commanded to wipe out (crush the head) the *Kena'anites* (serpent). "Then he said, 'Blessed be the *Adonai*, the God of Shem; *Kena'an* will be their servant. May God enlarge *Yefet*; he will live in the tents of *Shem*, but *Kena'an* will be their servants'" (Genesis 9:26-27).

Yefet can be understood as the Greeks or the nations. *Shem* is the Semitic people. This blessing states that *Yefet* will dwell in the tent, teaching and instructions, of *Shem* but that *Yefet* will be the larger people. Today, this is seen as the church (*Yefet*) is returning to the tens of *Shem*, the Torah.

Adonai—Tzava'ot says, "When that time comes ten men [lost ten tribes who were scattered into the nations, *Yefet*] will take hold—speaking all the languages of the nations—will grab hold of the cloak of a Jew and say, "We want to go with you, because we have heard that God is with you."

Zechariah 8:23

The church today knows who the Messiah is, and now is the time that they are grabbing hold of His cloak or *tallit*, which is His tent. They are returning to the tents of *Shem*.

Notice that of the three sons or three rivers that flowed from *Noach*, one was cursed to be a river of bitterness. Why? Because of the blazing torch that fell from the sky because of Adam's fall. Adam's fallen mindset had fallen on the river of Ham's descendants (Revelation 8:10-11).

Hebrew is an evasive language. The language loves to use synonyms to say things without having to say it. People are likened unto stars in the Torah (Daniel 12:1-3). One third of *Noach's* descendants (stars) had become dark, as it is only men who turn others to righteousness that are called stars.

Ham had become an angel (messenger) of death (accusation). He was thrown down (cursed) to the earth (lower realm where he would serve creation rather than creation serving him). His desire would be to accuse the brethren. This mindset is called the inner pharaoh (Revelation 11:7-9).

I hope this is giving you a little insight and that it causes you to look into the deeper revelation of God's Word, that it will cause you to take a second look at God's Word and how we see each other and how we see ourselves.

When we say things like we will never be like *Yeshua*, it is just like seeing yourself as naked. *Yeshua* is your original image, and if we don't see that image, we will continue to hide from God's presence and His Torah. Do you realize you were not created to sin? The question should be: how are we going to continue in wickedness? We were not created to be wicked. We are returning to our original design.

God is calling His people out from among the trees. Where are you? Are you still lost to your identity? Can you find yourself in the Torah, called the lamb's book of life? Are you walking in what you were created to do, the Torah led of the *Ruach HaKodes* (Holy Spirit)?

Adam was not able to love God after he ate of the forbidden fruit. He could not obey God, as his evil desires began to drive out of the garden and away from God.

By God's grace, He has given you the ability to love Him and obey His commands, your original design. *Yeshua* has given you the ability to reach your full potential, to return to what you were created to do. He has prepared the place: the garden. This realm has become accessible now. Adam knew this realm, and it is your destiny to know it as well.

The gospel from the beginning is about a God who loves and pursues his people. He is taking us back to our beginning. There is a river that flows out of Eden. Eden means a place of pleasure. This alludes to intimacy with the Messiah. A husband cultivates the intimacy he has with his wife, as it is a river of life for both of them.

Now the Messiah, *Yeshua,* is cultivating intimacy with his bride, and rivers of living waters are beginning to flow from this intimacy.